The personnel managers

International Library of Sociology

Founded by Karl Mannheim

Editor: John Rex, University of Warwick

Arbor Scientiae
Arbor Vitae

A catalogue of the books available in the **International Library of Sociology** and other series of Social Science books published by Routledge & Kegan Paul will be found at the end of this volume.

The personnel managers

A study in the sociology of work and employment

Tony J. Watson
School of Human Sciences
Trent Polytechnic

Routledge & Kegan Paul
London, Henley and Boston

First published in 1977
by Routledge & Kegan Paul Ltd
39 Store Street,
London WC1E 7DD,
Broadway House,
Newtown Road,
Henley-on-Thames,
Oxon RG9 1EN and
9 Park Street,
Boston, Mass. 02108, USA
Set in Monotype Times by
Kelly and Wright, Bradford-on-Avon, Wiltshire
and printed in Great Britain by
Lowe & Brydone Ltd
© Tony J. Watson 1977

British Library Cataloguing in Publication Data

Watson, Tony J.
The personnel managers.—(International library of sociology)

1. Personnel management
I. Title II. Series
301.5'5   HF5549   77 30278

ISBN 0 7100 8743 8

To Jack and Phyllis Watson

Contents

Preface

This study is a sociological one. It is concerned, not just with describing, but with theorising and with generalising about both the world of the personnel manager and a number of wider issues. I am aware that many of those in employing organisations like the ones which I have studied are not too interested in theoretical pursuits as such. Nevertheless, it is one of my major concerns that studies like this can be read and found of value both by students of sociology and by those who are more directly involved in those areas which the sociologist studies. I would simply express the hope that those who come to this book with the primary purpose of finding an analysis of the personnel occupation, its nature, problems and prospects, will recognise that, in addition to providing such an analysis in this study, I have attempted to do a number of other things. I am very concerned with the refinement of the analytical equipment which sociologists can bring to bear on issues relating to work and employment generally and I have therefore attempted to make theoretical and methodological generalisations which go beyond the issues which provide the occasion for this specific investigation. But I have not only made use of the personnel occupation as a vehicle for discussing procedural aspects of sociology. I have also tried, in my analysis of personnel workers, to throw light on a range of more substantive issues. In the course of the study I have tried to say something of a general nature about occupational choice and career patterns, orientations to work, professionalisation processes, managerial ideologies and social science utilisation, power relations within organisations and the more widely significant 'managerialism' debate.

How well I succeed in any of these purposes will, of course, be judged by my readers. However, I would like to express my gratitude to all of those who have influenced, encouraged, and assisted me as teachers, students, colleagues, friends, interviewees and informants. I must acknowledge my friends at Trent Polytechnic and at the University of Nottingham, where this study was submitted for the award of a doctorate, and I must express my gratitude to all of those in industry, commerce, and public administration who gave me so much of their time and discussed themselves and their work so freely. It was, to a large extent, the pleasure which I derived from these contacts which helped me to talk to the number of people that I did, both in the personnel field and in employing organisations generally. I hope that what follows does justice to all of those who helped me and, in particular, to Diane Watson who has given me so much support in every way.

Introduction

Industrial relations officers, training managers, job evaluation experts, remuneration managers, manpower planners, personnel managers, employee relations directors and the rest are all people whose work is of increasing significance in the modern world of work. They can be seen as making up an occupational group which is of potentially key importance in modern industrial capitalist society. The work of all of the personnel specialists, regardless of their particular sub-specialism or organisational level, is *managerial* work – work which involves them in the selection, deployment and control of people as 'human resources' in the increasingly large and complex organisations of modern working life. It therefore becomes highly relevant to an overall understanding of work and its organisation in contemporary society to analyse this developing occupation, its members, their practices, ideologies and 'professional' aspirations. Whether or not the individual personnel specialist is seen as particularly significant in terms of his or her own power to initiate events, we have to recognise that he or she works in a milieu in which the power relations of a capitalist industrial society operate in a particularly direct way. I suggest that analysis of the occupation can yield insights into problems and trends in work at societal, organisational and individual levels.

The personnel management occupation is sufficiently interesting in its own right, then, to warrant serious sociological attention. Sociological study of the occupation to date has been sparse, incomplete and unsatisfactory. Ritzer and Trice's American study (1969) is limited by its theoretical perspective, the restricted range of issues tackled and its research methodology, whilst Timperley and Osbaldeston's analysis of the Institute of Personnel Management (1975) is sadly inadequate if not in error (see Watson 1976b). What neither of these studies does is to examine the *societal* role of the

occupation and its members' activities. The present study is intended
to be more complete in that it will focus on each of the levels of
analysis relevant to such a sociological study, moving from the
experience of individual personnel specialists through their place in
the employing organisation, to the contribution of their work
towards the integration of the society in which they live and
work.

However, the case which can be argued for the sociological
analysis of the personnel management occupation does not provide
the complete rationale or justification for the present study. Sociology
is not here simply the tool which is being used in the analysis of an
area of social life, it is also, in part, the subject of the work. The
intention is to analyse the personnel occupation whilst, at the same
time, using the occupation as a vehicle to contribute to something of
a reorientation in the sociology of work. My own practical and
research experience in work organisations, as well as my experience
in teaching sociology to students with both primarily academic and
primarily practical interests, has indicated the futility of a continua-
tion of the splitting of sociological study of work into relatively
discrete areas such as occupations, organisations, industrial relations,
industrialisation and so on. The direction in which I wish to see the
sociology of work move is to counter this tendency by taking its
problems, concepts and level of theoretical sophistication from the
main stream of sociology – the sociology created by the classical
writers who operated at the levels of understanding the nature,
structure and dynamics of the type of society which came about in
the wake of the industrial and other revolutions. The study of work,
its performance, institutions and organisation, is the study of a
central fact of life in society. And to develop a sociology of work
which can do justice to this fact is to involve oneself in tackling the
major theoretical problems of sociology itself: the problem of
the relationship between theory and research, the problem of the
analyst's value position, the action-versus-system dilemma, the
conflict-versus-consensus question and the issues surrounding
the tendency towards both stability and change.

To attempt to deal with theoretical and methodological issues of
this nature within one study which is also, and primarily, intended to
throw light on a substantive area of social life is indeed ambitious.
But I have in this work been willing to take the risks involved in
over-ambitiousness since I believe that it is only through taking such
risks and rejecting the over-developed task specialisation and almost
parochial theoretical exclusiveness of much contemporary work
that sociology will avoid losing its way – the way established by its
founding fathers and classical writers. As I see it, the way ahead for
sociology is to continue its development of a sophisticated body of

theory – the sophistication of this theory as well as its variety of emphases matching the complexity and variety of social life itself – but with this theory development taking place within a context of pursuing empirical investigation. *Sociology is a theoretical pursuit*, but the point of theory, as of sociology, is as a means towards an improved *understanding of the world* as its members experience it and as it makes itself available to investigation.

One of the costs that is incurred by the sociologist who attempts to do work of the nature advocated here is that he will tend, I feel, to be forced by the need to *contain* such a range of issues to design and execute his study as a personal rather than as a team-based piece of research. To achieve the kind of synthesis required the researcher has to pay the price of being able to do only the empirical investigation with which one person can cope. Only then can the final account of that research do justice to the essential subjectivity of any researcher's interpretations and the limitations of his methods. My carrying out of this research as a one-man effort, and the consequent limitations of time and resources available, has meant that the study is to an extent limited by its concentration on the personnel specialists and the personnel writers themselves at the expense of collecting the comparative data which would have been yielded by formally interviewing non-personnel managers and trade union representatives – both of which I would have *liked* to have done. The individual doing a one-man project is restricted by the amount of investigation that he can carry out on his own. However, I feel that the advantage gained by such an approach is considerable: it allows the reservations, assumptions and polemical tendencies of the researcher to be brought out and made visible to the reader of the final research report. This is something I have tried to do throughout the writing of the following account. I do not believe in the possibility of a neutral or 'value-free' sociology, but I do believe in the duty of the researcher to achieve some element of 'objectivity' through revealing as much as possible of himself and of the limitations of his research methods to his reader. To this end I have taken up the theme of *reflexivity* in my approach to writing sociology. This will be explained in the first chapter, as will the underlying 'critical' intent of the proposed type of sociology of work and employment being attempted. My analysis is intended to be a radical one – radical in that it attempts to go to the roots of the phenomena under investigation both through an initial historical study of employment under industrial capitalism, and the relationship of personnel management to this, as well as through a constant interest in going beyond the surface of phenomena to the underlying patterns or 'structures'. What I wish to see, and to contribute towards the development of here, are studies of work, employment, industrial or organisational life which have this type of critical function whilst still retaining a respect for and a closeness to the problems experienced by those whose lives are lived outside the insulated world of academic institutions.

1 The sociological framework

The academic discipline of sociology and the practical activity of personnel management can both be seen as having developed as responses to major historical changes. These are changes associated with the processes of industrialisation and modernisation. But sociology and personnel management are not only *responses* to societal changes: each is itself now a part of that world which has come into being with the growth of large-scale industrial capitalist organisation in the West. The two phenomena are very different in nature but each can be understood in part as an attempt to come to terms with the human problems associated with a particular social order. Nisbet (1970) has shown how nineteenth-century sociology involved theoretical efforts to reconsolidate a European order which was being dislocated by forces emanating from the French and Industrial Revolutions. The problems with which the classical sociologists dealt are to be seen 'in the almost inevitable contexts of the changes wrought on European society by the forces of division of labor, industrial capital, and the new roles of businessman and worker' (*ibid.*, p. 24). The contexts in which sociology grew are those which presented practical problems to the men building the new order, the order to which the sociologists can be seen as partly in reaction. The moral concerns and the interests behind the activities of those practical men are quite distinct from those of the sociological thinkers but to a significant extent the development of personnel management was a way of engaging with some of the same set of problems.

This study is not simply a sociological examination of the attitudes and practices of those engaged in the activities covered by the heading 'personnel management'. It is, rather, an attempt to study these activities and the experiences of those carrying them out in the context of a particular type of society. The aim is, then, to add to the

1

understanding of both the occupational activity of personnel management and the industrial capitalist society of which it is a part. But, in this study, the discipline of sociology is not simply the instrument through which these two aims are to be fulfilled. A third aim of the study is to contribute to the discipline of sociology itself by paying close attention to the problems and potentialities of the discipline, with particular reference to the study of the world of work and employment. The three major foci and their relationships can be represented diagrammatically as in Figure 1.1.

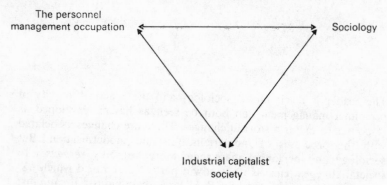

FIGURE 1.1

The concern behind this chapter is the nature of sociology itself and the more specific aim is to construct the sociological apparatus which will be used throughout the study. The theoretical and methodological discussions which follow are not to be seen simply as some sort of preamble; the desk-work which precedes the real research. These deliberations are an integral part of the researcher's experience, both as an empirical observer and as a reader of books. To clarify what is seen as an essentially dialectical relationship between research and theories, on the one hand, and the researcher and his theories and generalisations on the other, I shall introduce at this point the notion of reflexivity.

Reflexive sociology

The idea of a 'reflexive sociology' was introduced in Gouldner's widely discussed analysis of a coming crisis in Western sociology (1971). A reflexive sociology is proposed as a way of dealing with the fact that sociologists' theories are 'not the product of "immaculate" theoretical conception' and are 'not only the product of a technical tradition, of logic or of evidence, but of *their whole social existence*' (Gouldner, 1975, p. 148). Gouldner's new sociology appears to be dependent upon the willingness of sociologists to build new com- munities and institutions which will 'provide the social basis for the natural emergence of various new theories' (*ibid.*, p. 95). The interest in reflexivity in this study is one with far more modest intent than Gouldner's, and I would argue that it may not be appropriate for all sociologists to go about 'creating theoretical collectivities for rational discourse by social theorists' (*ibid.*, p. 78), particularly if one way of advancing knowledge of social life is believed, as it is here, to be through the researcher's involvement in the everyday lives of non-sociologists. A more useful discussion of a possible reflexive sociology is that of Dawe (1973). His version utilises and makes explicit the relevant experience of the sociologist but takes us beyond the level of the *personal* experience with its inherent danger of individualistic subjectivism and navel-gazing[1] by stressing the requirement for the experience which is drawn upon to be *representa- tive experience*. This is valuable in that it takes account of Wright Mills's notion of the sociological imagination with its analytical distinction between the individual and the social structural (Wright Mills, 1970) and recognises that the sociologist is himself linked into the same social structure as are those whom he is studying and those for whom he writes:

> The representative experience goes beyond the particular, localised, albeit intersubjective experience. It articulates the connection between the latter and the major currents of social and political concern, between the personal trouble and the public issue. Quite simply, to have any impact on social, political or any other form of public thought and action, the particular must stand for the general (Dawe, 1973, p. 35).

This conception of reflexivity is taken up in this study to enable the reader to make better sense of my theorising activity and to enable him more easily to evaluate both my own reporting and interpretations by revealing to him something of my *self*, the nature of my involvement in my research settings and, most importantly, the value positions and the structure of sentiments which are behind the accounts which make up this volume. If the reader of a socio- logical study can see something of the way that the sociologist generally fits into and interprets the world which they both, to varying extents, are bound to know, then he can more effectively decide which of the findings to assimilate into his own understanding of the world and which to reject. The assumption is being made here that sociology cannot be value-free. It must therefore be incumbent upon the writer to reveal to his audience his value position for two reasons. First, one's values cannot be stated briefly in a few intro- ductory comments or summarised in an appendix, and second, they

3

Values

are a part of one's *self* and *experience*, so the sociologist's value stance must be brought from the background into the foreground. This is particularly important in a study like this, where the author has closely involved himself with the activities of those whom he is studying.

To meet the requirements of a reflexive approach and to give my readers the requisite insight into the background and the value basis of the study, I shall do several things. One of these is to indicate the experiential background to both the theorising process and the various forms of involvement in the milieu under examination. Another is to reveal, in the course of developing the theoretical scheme which provides the framework for the study, what Gouldner calls the theorist's *background assumptions* (1971, p. 29). In revealing the 'world hypotheses' and 'domain assumptions' which make up the assumptions on which the more specific 'postulations' are based and by providing some biographical context to indicate the 'sentiments' to which these assumptions relate, I hope to assist the reader in his evaluation of the work. I shall deal first with the experiential background but must, before I do this, take note of some important observations which have been made about the relationship between the theorist and his theories.

So

Blum has argued that theorising is a 'self-transforming operation, where what one operates on is one's knowledge of the society as part of one's history, biography, and form of life' (Blum, 1971, p. 313). Without accepting the full implications of Blum's overall position[2] the insights here are taken to be valuable and indicative of the need to relate, or to enable the reader to relate, the theorist's and the audience's experience of the world under review. As Blum argues

> As a user of language and a follower of rules, the theorist is simultaneously addressing self and community, for the self is essentially public and the community is part of his self (part of his history, his biography, his corpus of knowledge) (*ibid.*, 1971, p. 308).

Although the detailed work which makes up the bulk of this study was done from a relatively conventional position in an academic institution, a large part of the underlying theorising work was done whilst I was employed in industry. Many of the orienting questions and 'hypotheses' about the personnel occupation as well as a large quantity of informal 'data' originated during this period of my biography. This fact, combined with the inevitable suspicions which are aroused by any sociologist's close involvement in his research milieu, make it incumbent upon one, it is felt, to give some detail of this experiential base. Although I believe that Glaser and Strauss (1967) underestimate the extent to which any researcher, explicitly

4

or otherwise, brings prior theoretical orientations to his research work, I do accept many of their criticisms of 'logically deduced theory' and wish to see the generation of theory 'grounded' in the process of research. I go further than Glaser and Strauss, however, and argue that as one's researches and one's theorising are parts of one's *self* then one must locate them in their biographical context.

The experiential background

Like many other sociologists I found my way onto a first degree in sociology by way of a working-class upbringing and a grammar school. The study of sociology gave an opportunity to formalise a fascination with making theories about the social world which went back to my early childhood when I first became aware of class differences and differences between English and Scottish cultural patterns. As an undergraduate I became highly attached to sociology and was attracted to it as a way of life. The area of industrial sociology was particularly engaging given a powerful drive on my part to learn about the factory life experienced by my father. It was this particular concern, combined with a reluctance to continue life on a grant, that turned my attention towards industrial employment. My suspicion that the literature of industrial sociology did not always effectively engage with the realities of industrial life and rarely 'got inside' industrial organisations, and particularly 'inside' management, added to the resolve. The choice of work in the industrial relations sphere is especially important here because, as will become apparent later in the study, I am here revealing myself as following a pattern shared with some of my respondents – to put it crudely at this stage, what might be seen as other than 'managerial' sympathies among those in industrial relations work, at least in the early stages of the career, is not untypical. I attempted to retain my academic identity by registering for a part-time research degree at a local university, something which would systematise my learning about the industrial world and provide me with a passport back to academic life at a later stage.

During the three years spent in the engineering industry I became involved in most of the aspects of personnel management, but specialised in industrial relations. My involvement in this work, together with a recognition of the very quickly growing importance of the personnel function within management and some experience of the would-be professional body (the Institute of Personnel Management), sowed the seeds of interest in what has become the present study. The research work which I did at the time, however, was on sociological aspects of organisational change (Watson, 1972). But the greatest advantage of this particular setting for doing sociology

5

was, I believe, a more general one. It enabled me to ground all my thoughts about sociological theory and methods, the 'relevance' of sociology, the utility of existing studies and so on, in a setting of 'active social relationships'.[3] I found the industrial setting of value as a sort of laboratory in which to investigate issues of major interest in sociological theory. As I have put it elsewhere,

> In complex industrial organisations we can see with more clarity than in many other settings what has been called the 'dialectical interplay between human striving and social constraint' (Rex, 1974, p. 4) as individuals and groups articulate and play out conflicts of interest; structures and strategies are devised in processes whereby power is wielded and resisted, and life chances of participants (and indirectly their families) are both reflected and created (Watson, 1976a, p. 1).[4]

It was in thinking about sociology on a day-to-day basis whilst being intimately involved in the ongoing practical issues of organisational life that I developed the theoretical scheme which is to be set out shortly and which is to provide the framework of this study. The theoretical scheme as it now stands has been developed and reformulated throughout my subsequent few years as a full-time academic, in the light of further reading and, more particularly, through its use in teaching sociology to a range of students.

I now wish to set out the considerations and criteria upon which the theoretical scheme is based. I must, however, point out that these criteria are at the same time partly conclusions of the same theoretical process. It is difficult to do justice to the dialectical relationship between research and theory; the process of writing down an account of one's theorising does tend to suggest an apparent but unreal process of development.

The subdivisions in the sociological study of work

One of the criteria behind the devising of the theoretical framework for this study is that it should facilitate the breaking down of the divisions which exist between the sociological study of the various aspects of what men and women experience in their involvement in work. The artificiality of these divisions became a matter of considerable concern to me as I reviewed the relevant sociological literature with a view to bringing its perspectives to bear on my earlier research work in the industrial plant in which I was employed. One was clearly involved in a formal *organisation* which had one 'sociology'; one was a member of an *occupation* which had another quite distinct 'sociology'; one was dealing with industrial relations issues which were covered by yet another section of the literature . . . and

6

so on. And a large proportion of the material contained in these subsections seemed to be dealing with issues far removed from the concerns of the classical writers in the sociological tradition, writers whom I felt had raised issues about the place of work in society which were still of crucial importance.

Rose has commented that 'special sociologies are largely artificial creations, which result partly from careerism among academics, partly from tidy-mindedness amongst teaching administrators and partly from a sloppy kind of commonsense thinking' (Rose, 1975, p. 14). But the concern here is not with reintegrating these special sociologies simply for the sake of integration, or to create an even tidier structure. Both the splitting-off of the sociological study of work from the main stream of sociology as well as the subsequent subdividing of this study are seen as highly unfortunate. In as far as work is central to the lives of a large proportion of members of society, the study of work should retain a position at the centre of the study of society. And, since people tend in their experience of work to become involved in organisational, occupational, professional, industrial relations and motivational issues, it seems reasonable to look at these issues sociologically with the expectation of there being interconnections between them. It might be argued in response to this that sociologists, like any other academics, must specialise in order to come to terms with the vastness of reality. But this does not justify the developing of separate analytical frameworks for these areas which, by their very nature, tend to preclude the seeking of interconnections between different elements of people's work behaviour and experience. Whereas one recognises and sees value in a multiplicity of perspectives within the general discipline of sociology, one is bound to question a situation where this diversity not only leads to the dividing of what might be indivisible in experiential terms but also causes divisions where, according to the very rationale of sociological thinking, one expects to be seeking connections and interrelationships.

This tendency to develop different types of perspective with varying underlying assumptions for different aspects of the work experience can be illustrated by looking at three of the subdivisions: organisations, occupations and industrial relations.

Organisational sociology has been dominated by a perspective which emphasises notions of system, structure and goal and which is in sharp contrast to the perspectives of Max Weber, the sociologist whose writing is often taken as a starting point for this subdiscipline,[5] and who, unlike the majority of writers in this field, was operating at the level of issues of societal and historical change. Ironically they also diverge from the ideas of the man whom they take as their founder in that they rarely pay attention to the motives and interests

7

of participants. Both Burns (1969) and Albrow (1968) have discussed the tendency in this field to treat organisations in terms of the conceptions of those who control them, a tendency which, as Albrow describes it, 'is not only misguided in its empirical analysis of organisations but [is] taking sides in a struggle for power' (Albrow, 1968, p. 163). Much of organisational sociology can be seen as *partial* both in the sense that it is, in sociological terms, 'incomplete' and in the sense that it contains an inherent bias (Watson, 1972, p. 10).

Occupations can be seen as another way, in addition to the bureaucratic, in which work experience is structured. Yet traditionally the sociological study of occupations operates with an entirely separate perspective, most typically the symbolic interactionist approach of the Chicago sociologists who pioneered this area, providing a set of concepts like career, ideology, identity and socialisation[6] which are quite distinct from the conceptual apparatus usually brought to bear on bureaucratic aspects of work structuring.[7] The study of professions has tended to develop as a subdivision of this subdivision and here we can see a frequent partiality not dissimilar to that occurring in the organisational field, with a tendency to view professions in terms of the professional's own conception of the problems to be considered (Johnson, 1972).

The study of industrial relations has developed within perspectives quite separate from the above two, following either a pragmatic, empirical approach or, more recently with the work of people like Lockwood (1958), Banks (1970), Fox (1974), Goldthorpe (1969), Hyman and Brough (1975), beginning to follow up some of the large-scale societal concerns of the major thinkers who created European sociology. It is towards this latter approach, albeit still involving a multiplicity of theoretical perspectives, that I shall be arguing shortly that the various sociologies concerned with aspects of work should move.

The tendency towards the partiality of a large proportion of the literature of the sociological study of work can be seen as resulting from a number of factors. A very significant factor is the place of the social sciences in general in what Weber saw as the increasing rationalisation of the modern world. Rose points to the value to those concerned with such goals as profit and growth of knowledge about workers' behaviour and motivations:

> Such knowledge, the analogue of natural science, would be the
> basis for practical improvements. Social technology could
> complement mechanical technology, with beneficial effects on
> productivity. In other words, the study of man at work may be
> seen as part of the general rationalisation of exploitation
> ('exploitation' here carries no necessary pejorative overtone)
> (Rose, 1975, p. 16).

Baritz (1965) used the phrase 'the servants of power' to characterise work which, interestingly in the present context, can as readily be taught in academic institutions under the headings of either industrial sociology or personnel management.

Another very important factor, not unrelated to the above, is the notorious problem of access to do research in work organisations. All work organisations are power structures and it is rare for the powerful to allow, even less to invite, scientific scrutiny of the ways in which they operate. For this reason much of the work in the sociology of industry has been done either by, for, or under the approval of managers. Thus the perspectives used, if they are not clearly oriented to managerial concerns, are at least such that they will not conflict with those of managers. The models used tend to exclude variables which would need to be present to allow any radical analysis of the work situation or its context. The concept of power is noticeably absent from the literature in this area.

To locate my comments here in the experiential context I would point out the irony of the fact that the personal research which I did whilst employed in industry was free of this type of restriction because I was myself part of the management. In addition to my being able *covertly* to study 'power behaviour' there was the advantage of my note-taking and observing being seen as normal and legitimate for an industrial relations officer (inveterate busybodies and minute writers!) who was doing some university work which would enhance his academic qualification thus producing, perhaps, a 'better employee'. And this point is particularly apposite in view of the fact that I was able to observe the plant personnel manager steer away a group of university social scientists who had been brought in to help with managerial problems on an 'action research' basis,[8] from what were described as 'politically sensitive' areas of the plant. It is interesting how few sociologists have adopted the strategy of participant observation in industry in a form which has produced analyses other than managerially oriented ones.

These problems of 'partiality' and the factors which lead to them all tend to divert sociological investigation away from the concerns of the founders of modern sociology regarding the place of work in society. As Rex said, in his review of British sociology, we should work 'to produce an industrial sociology which draws on the tradition of Weber and Marx as well as of Mayo' (1973, p. 85). This, with the breaking down of the barriers necessary for it, is a major criterion for this study.

A critical perspective

The above criterion and the arguments which lead to it imply another essential requirement which will inform the theoretical scheme and its ensuing application. This is the requirement to construct a framework which is based on those concepts which are necessary for any sociologically radical analysis of social life. A theory or model of industrial or working life which excludes considerations of power, conflict, social class and the like, inevitably lacks the kind of radical potential which I argue any sociological analysis should have.

This is in no way a call for sociology to be destructive. As Burns has said,

> The practice of sociology is criticism: to criticise or to raise questions about claims and assumptions concerning the value or meaning of conduct and achievement. It is the business of sociologists to conduct a critical debate in this sense with the public about its equipment of social institutions. This purpose is as important in the social study of industry as in any other field (1962).

A critical role for sociology is one which is quite separate from one of propaganda and political advocacy, and whilst it is recognised that '. . . we should be prepared to describe structures of social relations without assuming that they must be preserved or that they must be changed' (Rex, 1974, p. 9), it is most important to recognise the relevance of such analysis for demystification and change.[9] As Child argues,

> Social science can assist the process of change through its scrutiny of the conventional wisdom, ideology and prejudice which still pervade many aspects of our social life. By identifying social conventions for what they are, the social scientist helps to create an awareness of the possibilities for alternative modes of action and organisation which may provide benefits not previously achieved (Child, 1973, p. 234).

The practicalities of concept use

Another facet of the theorising work in which I am engaged here is a willingness to indulge in what might be seen as a kind of conceptual promiscuity. This interest in utilising concepts from a range of sources goes back to my experience in industrial employment when, in the process of analysing complex problems in discussion with both employee representatives and managers, I found myself drawing on the ideas and research findings of a disparate selection of writers in the social sciences.[10] In referring to the practicalities of concept use I am borrowing and adapting a notion from the ethnomethodologists (Zimmerman, 1971) to describe an approach in which, given one's *purpose*, say, that of, explaining or aiding the understanding of certain phenomena, one makes use of whatever concepts come to hand to achieve that end. An example here, and one that has an important relevance in what is to follow, is the way that one might choose to use the concept of *function* in what is intended as a 'radical' analysis. This is despite the fact that this is a central concept in what has been criticised as a particularly conservative approach in sociology.[11] Nisbet (1970) refers to the conservatism of concept, but I would dispute such a notion, claiming that a concept is merely a device and that any ideological implications can only come from the way it is used and, particularly, from the background assumptions of the model or scheme of which it is a part.[12][13]

Throughout this study, then, I will be drawing on various sociological traditions. However, I would emphasise that I am not attempting what Ekeh has called a 'uniformitarian synthesis', one 'intended to achieve uniformity and thus silence controversy' and which 'ignore[s] underlying philosophical assumptions of the authors of the differing perspectives, especially with regard to the differences in their conceptions of the relationship between society and the individual . . .' (1974, p. 17). These latter assumptions are precisely those which Gouldner calls 'domain assumptions', and one of the ways in which I shall be following my requirement to be reflexive will be clearly to indicate my own set of assumptions, thus enabling a type of synthesis to occur. Here I follow Ekeh:

> My own personal preference is synthesis in favour of combining the strengths of various perspectives in order to *enhance the level of explanation of a phenomenon*. This is different from what I call uniformitarian synthesis in that the original perspectives are not thereby abolished . . . (Ekeh, 1974, p. 18, my emphasis).

As will become fairly clear shortly, the particular approach taken in this study is an essentially Weberian one. But within this framework it will be apparent that emphasis may be greater at times on notions which derive from traditions which are distinct from, came before, or developed subsequent to Weber's own work. There is, for example, an important Marxian element, an element from 'functionalism' and some influence from the more phenomenological approaches in recent sociology.

Actor rationality and dynamic orientations

The recent trend in the sociology of work and organisations to adopt a social action frame of reference is seen as a healthy one.[14] The interest in the motives of actors and the way situations are defined within work organisations is a necessary corrective to the more traditional tendencies in large parts of the literature either to see

11

work behaviour as determined by technological or by environmental constraints. But my adoption here of a position based on methodological individualism and my assumption of actor rationality also have an experiential and a value relevance. My involvement in a wide range of employment and industrial relations issues in industry indicated the necessity for understanding or examining the rationales, motives and interests of actors and a rejection of what one saw as a common managerial assumption (one by no means foreign to industrial sociology[15]) that some actors are more rational than others.

There are, nevertheless, dangers in using the social action framework. One of these, which I will deal with in more detail below, is the tendency to play down the importance of what are traditionally viewed as the 'structural' factors in social life. Another is the danger which has become apparent in the influential and important work of Goldthorpe, Lockwood *et al.* (1968) where a tendency arises for 'orientations to work' to appear to become more 'fixed' than is justifiable. Daniel (1973) has indicated this type of danger and Beynon and Blackburn have shown that, whereas with other approaches there has been a frequent problem of overemphasising the influence of the work situation, 'it would seem that recent attempts at an "action approach" in British industrial sociology have come dangerously near to being stuck the other side of the factory gates' (1972, p. 156). To avoid the problem one has to ensure that one's theoretical scheme can cope with the tendency for orientations to be dynamic and adaptable to changing contexts. In the same way that Daniel suggests that the instrumental worker of one context may become the intrinsically oriented worker of another, my industrial experience showed me the extent to which the 'moderate' shop steward, for instance, may become the 'militant' very quickly as situations and perceived interests change. Such a realisation is particularly important in the case of the personnel specialists whose orientations, as I shall show in a later chapter, tend to be particularly responsive to contextual, organisational, factors. The overemphasis on prior orientations of the Goldthorpe and Lockwood model could, if that model were adopted here, seriously reduce the analytical potential of the investigation.

The structural level

The immediate question which is raised by the above argument is one of whether, as Poulantzas suggests, a 'problematic of social actors' reduces the radical potential of an analysis by underplaying the structural constraints imposed by 'objective relations' (1972). This issue is a serious one, given the criterion earlier put forward for the development of a *critical* approach. If one is going to provide an analysis which can meet this type of argument one has to face that question of, as Mills put it, 'what holds a social structure together' (1970, p. 54). Sociology is concerned with the regularities underlying social life and these regularities include the inequalities and unfreedoms into which sociological analysis can give insight and hence potentially can inform action. In looking at any society, then, one has to consider the particular nature of its 'mode of integration' (*ibid.*, p. 54) and such an analysis is endangered by too atomistic a theoretical perspective. On the other hand, there is an equal danger of reifying structures and giving them a status which equally undermines radical potential by disguising the extent to which, in the final analysis, power, dominance, exploitation, are always the power, dominance or whatever of men over men.

Weber carefully avoided the dangers of reification, warning against *falschen Begriffsrealismus* (false conceptual realism) and avoiding the term 'structure'.[16] Nevertheless, he recognised the necessity of some kind of 'functional analysis of the relation of "parts" to a "whole" ' (1968, p. 15), despite its dangers. As he said in his discussion of the organicism of Schäffle,

> For purposes of sociological analysis two things can be said. First, this functional frame of reference is convenient for purposes of practical illustration and for provisional orientation. In these respects it is not only useful but indispensable. But at the same time if its cognitive value is overestimated and its concept illegitimately 'reified' it can be highly dangerous. Second, in certain circumstances this is the only way of determining just what processes of social action it is important to understand in order to explain a given phenomenon. But this is only the beginning of sociological analysis as here understood (1968, p. 15).

This, according to Outhwaite, coincides with Habermas's view that functionalism can be best understood as

> a possible mode of *interpretation* which grasps relations which, although not present in the minds of social agents, can be described, if only metaphorically, in teleological terms and hence understood as 'meaningful' (Outhwaite, 1975, p. 88).

This suggests that, as Outhwaite says, 'Social science cannot do without general concepts which are not reducible in any simple way to the conceptions of individual agents' (*ibid.*, p. 54). Such conceptions as structure and function are indispensable to a critical sociology and, as Outhwaite implies in the conclusions of his book, one may have to be less particular than Weber in one's conceptual terminology. The important thing here is the avoidance of reification

13

and the recognition that such concepts are only analytical devices. They have to be removed from the paradigm of the discredited structural-functionalism with its 'conservative' world view and domain assumptions. As Mennell argues,

> Historical and action analysis is not an alternative to systematic analysis, but is most fruitful precisely when combined with it. It is exactly because the consequences of people's activities often do not coincide with what they intended that it is essential to make a systematic analysis of the causal links within social organisation (1974, p. 165).

The theoretical scheme to which I am gradually moving has, then, to combine a concern with meanings, individual motives and so on, with recognition of the need to use structural concepts in analysis. Central to the scheme will be the notion of *interest* and the above two elements of sociological analysis will be recognised through the consideration of both *subjective* and *objective* interests.

Subjective and objective interests

In the process of working as an industrial relations officer and at the same time developing my own theoretical ideas in sociology, I found myself trying to make some kind of systematic sense of the way different individuals and groups defined conflict situations in different ways. In seeking to relate 'meanings' to some sort of existential base I found myself drawn to the work of Schutz and the sociologists influenced by him. Schutz's insights are valuable in that he relates the individual's definitions of situations, and hence his conduct, to his interests, and these in turn are related to his biography and his membership of groups. These include both those in which he finds himself and those which he chooses (*existential* and *voluntary* groups) (Schutz, 1964, p. 242). The importance of these insights will become apparent in my scheme. However, there is a problem in confining the notion of interest to a subjective sense.

Lukes has shown how conceiving of interests merely as subjective phenomena – whereby interests are defined in terms of the individual's wants or preferences – precludes the possibility of a radical analysis (1974). It has this effect because it fails to relate people's interests to 'what they would want and prefer, were they able to make the choice' (Lukes, 1974, p. 34). Stolzman has indicated the tendency of action sociologies to confine themselves to this type of conception of interests (1975). It is clear then that if I am to meet my criterion of radical potential I have to avoid the problem into which I might be led by the influence of phenomenological theories. One has got to pay attention to the issue of the relationship between interests as felt wants and objective interests. Objective interests are to be recognised in situations where the individual has, as Balbus puts it, an 'interest in something' in that he 'has a stake in it or is "affected" by it', this being regardless of whether or not the individual is aware of that interest (1975, p. 152). And it is at this point that one has to turn to Marxian analysis in order to find the link between subjective and objective interests. This link is to be found in the notion of the conversion of the objective to the subjective through a process of the development of consciousness. My intention is to extrapolate from Marxian class analysis the concern with the growth of the subjective recognition of interests and apply it to all situations of group formation and consequent action.

The formation and interaction of social groups at all levels, from the micro to the macro, are to be understood, I suggest, in terms of processes whereby objective and subjective interests are discovered, articulated and even created. I agree with Stolzman's argument that it is

> seldom enough for theorising to simply counterpose the objective and subjective dimensions of men's interests: *the real task is to explore the dialectical interplay between them in concrete situations* (1975, p. 113, my emphasis).

The theoretical scheme – basic assumptions

I have made great play throughout all that I have said so far of the importance of making explicit the theorist's *background assumptions*, these including both 'world hypotheses' and 'domain assumptions'. The revealing of these assumptions is a requirement of the reflexive approach as I have conceived it and is taken to be an important way of coping with the 'value problem' inherent in all sociological study. These notions are related to the distinction which Dahrendorf makes, following Konig, between a 'theory of society' and sociological theories (Dahrendorf, 1968, p. vi). By displaying the para-theoretical assumptions and general orientations which compose the 'theory of society', one can indicate the value orientations which lie behind the more specific sociological theories which are developed out of it. And this gives the reader a 'basis for making judgements of [the] value' of the more substantive generalisations (*ibid.*, p. vii).

The most general set of assumptions followed here coincide with the philosophical underpinning of Weber's sociology and particularly his very important conception of the *ethical irrationality of the world*. This conception is divided into two parts by Freund (1972, pp. 25–32). The first is what he calls *axiological irrationality* in which the diversity of reality leads to a fundamental antagonism of values. In Dronberger's words, 'the plurality of interests, ideals and postulates leads those who subscribe to them into perpetual conflict. . . . Power and

15

struggle then remain, in Weber's view, the tragedy of man's fate' (1971, pp. 362–3). Weber's image of life is 'a struggle of man against man' (Mommsen, 1974, p. 29). The second aspect of the ethical irrationality of the world is the *paradox of consequences* whereby we recognise the antinomy between means and ends and the inevitable tendency for there to be unforeseeable consequences of human actions.[17]

These assumptions are at the core of the theoretical scheme which now follows and will be present throughout this study, most noticeably in the next chapter where the scheme is applied at the level of modern capitalist industrial society. I shall now describe the scheme at the level of social life in general.

The theoretical scheme

The starting point is a world in which there are scarce resources, material and otherwise. The interests of all individuals with regard to what is available are not generally compatible. A tendency thus arises for individuals to be located in coalitions of interest with others as they recognise the existence of common interests *vis-à-vis* other coalitions against which they might compete.[18] These coalitions of interest are *social groups* in the widest sense used in sociology. Every individual belongs to a range of these groups and there are groups within groups and groups cross-cutting each other in terms of membership. An individual can be associated with almost any number of social groups, ranging from a social class, status or occupational group to a golf club or a darts team. Within the complex of social relations in any society there are always many logically possible 'objective interests' – that is potential *advantages* with regard to whatever is valued and scarce in that society.[19] Hence, there always exists a range of quasi-groups.[20] Central to the formation of actual social groups out of this range of potential groups are *ideas*. It requires particular individuals to express ideas which articulate and define latent objective interests, thereby creating consciousness of these, their conversion to subjective interests, and the mobilisation of the social group. Any statement which any group makes which acts to further the interests of that group (whether by articulating interests to increase group identity, an internal function, or to legitimate group interests with reference to other groups, an external function) is conceptualised as an aspect of *group ideology*.

The notion of *group ideology* is central to the theoretical scheme being developed. It is in the concept of ideology that Marxian and Weberian insights can be brought together in sociology.[21] The concept is being used here in a manner which is much wider than is generally the case in sociology (and in recognition of this I will retain the wording 'group ideology'). Within this theoretical scheme no statement is inherently ideological – it becomes ideological through the use to which it is being put. One speaks ideologically when one talks so as to legitimate, defend, or further the interest of any group to which one belongs. Very often one or more individuals within any group will tend to concentrate on speaking ideologically and these people I will conceptualise as *spokesmen*, implying far more in this than simply the idea of a 'mouthpiece'.[22] These spokesmen are key actors in processes of social change and I am here accepting the Weberian assumption of the importance of both ideas and of the role of individuals in social change. My theorising here is very much influenced by that of Bendix who writes:

> The attitudes of individuals do not become the public opinion of a group merely by the process of addition. Instead, public opinion is formed through a constant process of formulation and reformulation by which spokesmen identified with a social group seek to articulate what they sense to be its shared understandings. . . . I call these articulations *ideologies* in the specific sense of ideas considered in the context of group action (1963, p. xii).

We have, then, a scheme in which individuals form themselves and are formed into groups which compete for scarce resources. But some stability or structuring will occur. This will result from the tendency of some groups to do better than others in the competition and thus attempt to stabilise their advantage through the mobilisation of *power*, whether in the form of coercion, manipulation or authority (i.e. legitimate power).[23] Hence we get the basis of a *political structure* and those structures of inequality conventionally termed by sociologists *stratification*.

The basis of the theoretical scheme which underlies this study has now been set out and its assumptions made explicit. This general scheme will apply throughout the work but extensions of it will appear later at two levels, first, in chapter 2 at the level of capitalist industrial society and, second, in chapters 3 and 4, where it will be developed at the level of the individual and the group in the (employing) organisation. To clarify the way in which the overall scheme is intended to help break down the barriers between the divisions in the sociological study of work, it may be helpful to the reader to look ahead briefly at this point to the descriptions of the scheme at these levels in chapters 2, 3 and 4.

Methods and procedures

The research methods employed in this study have, I hope, been anything but unsophisticated. Nevertheless, I have not attempted to

17

use particular research *techniques* in any refined way. Nor have I worked in terms of any particular philosopher-of-science's well worked-out model of scientific method. I have, rather, followed Mills's precept to 'seek to develop and to use the sociological imagination' and to avoid 'the fetishism of method and technique' (1970, p. 246).

I do not see any essential dividing line between the sociologist and the layman in terms of the way that they look at the world. Both are concerned with making sense of what goes on around them and both approach the world with sets of preconceptions, typifications, values, and indeed theories. Although the sociologist's descriptions and generalisations are not *essentially* different from those of the non-sociologist there are, none the less, important differences. Put simply, these relate to the extent to which the sociologist approaches his analyses systematically and with rigour and the extent to which he presents his 'findings' to his audience (whom it is his task to serve) in such a way that they can judge his arguments and consider his evidence. And this brings us back to the point of the reflexivity which has been stressed throughout this chapter. The sociologist is a part of the scene which he is describing and about which he is generalising. If his audience is going to be capable of evaluating what he has to say then they have to know as much as possible about the way he has played that part and the assumptions on which he has made his interpretations of what he has observed and experienced. Both the sociologist and the layman start their considerations of any given social phenomena with a 'theoretical' position but it is, I argue, the duty of the sociologist to make as explicit as possible the theories and models with which he operates. And since every sociologist will tend, to a greater or a lesser extent, to have been educated in one or more literature-transmitted traditions, then these too have to be brought forward and discussed. Throughout this chapter I have attempted to reveal something of myself and to reveal the theoretical traditions of which I feel a part. This reflexivity, which admittedly can only ever be partial, will continue throughout the study.

Behind what I have said above it is possible to recognise the influence of recent writings of phenomenologically oriented sociologists. My intention is to avoid labouring the discussion of methods by locating in that literature the issues which have been raised implicitly in what I have said above.[24] I do, however, have to say something about one concept which is central to my reporting and which I have borrowed from the ethnomethodologists. This is the notion of *accounts*.[25] I use this term to refer to the statements which are made both by the writers of documents which I examine and to refer to the statements made to me in the course of my interviews with personnel specialists. This is because I do not see these statements as fixed 'attitudes' or 'beliefs' – both concepts which imply more concreteness than I am willing to recognise – but rather as utterances which need to be situated in the context in which they are being made and which, especially, have to be seen in terms of the *interests* of those making them.[26] All talk can be seen as part of the process whereby realities are being constructed, altered or consolidated. And this brings me back to my own theoretical scheme, which would suggest the prevalence of what we might call 'talking ideologically' in that, in their speech, people are frequently talking so as to legitimate, justify, rationalise or defend their interests – interests frequently shared with others. One is always interested to locate what is being said in terms of underlying interests but one is naturally not often in a position to do this. One does, I trust, in these cases sufficiently suspend judgment on such issues in using the notion of accounts.

Having displayed an agreement with certain aspects of the pheno-menological critique of conventional sociological research, I may be puzzling those who have noted from what I have said earlier that I am nevertheless willing to use 'second order constructs' like struc-ture and function and even objective interests.[27] My response to any such puzzlement is to argue that I take that critique as an important warning to sociologists to be far more modest in their scientific pretensions and not as an indication that we should reject any approach remotely susceptible to labelling as 'positivistic' (a much misused label – see Bechhofer, 1974, p. 71). The use of constructs which might be seen as a conceptual imposition on 'member' reality is justified as one of the ways in which the sociologist makes his analyses more systematic and hence different from those of the non-sociologist. Nevertheless to show the seriousness with which I take these recent critiques, I am happy to indicate the status of this written study by labelling it itself as an *account*, or if you like, a series of accounts: one sociologist's account of the personnel occupation and its place in 'society'.

The material on which these accounts are based is derived from various sources; from participant observation in a personnel depart-ment; from documents and 'academic' personnel management literature; from informal discussions with people operating in personnel management; and from one hundred more-structured interviews with specialists in the personnel field. The sample here is not a random one in a strict statistical sense, which means that *direct* inferences from the sample to the wider population cannot be drawn in a quantitative way. However, the sample is constructed (and its size is important here) to enable us to make some reasonable infer-ences of a qualitative nature. And the size is sufficient to enable us to make meaningful comparisons within the sample. Details of the sample and the interviews are given in the appendices and the way they are used will be made clear as I go along.

Something does need to be said here, however, on the way that I have played my 'part' in my involvement with those whom I have studied. In my sallies forth into the personnel world from my academic base I have not attempted to present myself as some neutral 'value-free' scientist, but rather, to quote the words I frequently used, as 'a sociologist who used to work in industry' who 'was very much involved in the problems of personnel management' and who now thinks that it is time a book was written 'not about how the job should be done but about the people doing the job'. If this opening is seen as biasing the responses then I would comment that *any* (or no) preamble would bias whatever accounts are then given, in some way or other. All the sociologist can do, I feel, is to reveal as much as possible in his research reports the ways he might have introduced such biases. Throughout my involvement with my respondents and in my sociological reflections on my experiences I have followed Douglas' advice in 'adopting alternating stances while maintaining one's ultimate identity as a sociologist' (Douglas, 1970a, p. 199). One has to 'alternate between "surrender" to member experience' and 'returning to reflect upon that experience in order to communicate it to sociologists' (*ibid.*, p. 199), as well as, I hope in this case, to non-sociologists, even though the interpretations are very much from a sociologist's point of view.[28]

2 Industrialisation, rationalisation and the emergence of the personnel occupation

The personnel management occupation can be seen as more than simply an occupation. It can be seen, 'like medicine or law' as 'an important *social institution* which, in the Toynbeean sense, represents one form of our society's "response" to the "challenge" of industrialisation' (Miller and Coghill, 1964, p. 32). To see personnel management in this light is to adopt a functionalist mode of analysis – which is what will be done in this chapter, accepting the argument outlined earlier that functionalism is methodologically appropriate as a device for provisional orientation and that it should not lead to any reification of the notion of society or system (pp. 13–14). The aim of this chapter, consequently, is to examine the nature of the 'mode of integration' (Mills, 1970, p. 54) of industrial capitalist society and to locate certain fundamental strains and contradictions which underlie it, concentrating on problems relating to the issue of the utilisation of human beings as human resources. This will enable a sociological interpretation to be made of the emergence of the forerunners of the present personnel management occupation and to establish the nature of the problems in which, throughout this study, the occupation will be shown to be involved.

The theoretical scheme set out earlier is one in which social life is seen in terms of the conflict and competition which occurs throughout history between social groups. These groups are formed around common interests and the formation and activities of groups are closely involved with processes whereby ideas are developed and expressed. Advantages over valued resources are sought and, once achieved, attempts are made to regularise, legitimate and maintain the pattern of advantage, in the face of potential and real conflicting efforts to alter such structures. This very general scheme can now be applied at the level of what will be termed industrial capitalist society.

Before I apply the scheme to this particular societal form, however,

21

it is necessary to state one important caveat. This is to point out that, although I am in this chapter dealing with processes which occurred historically, I am not attempting to write history. The mode of thinking is nomothetic rather than idiographic. My concern is with analysing general processes basic to a 'type' of society rather than with noting the place of unique occurrences in any chronological sequence. My ultimate concern is with the regularities and the tensions underlying the society in which I and the personnel specialists whom I have studied are living. To do this an account must be given of the dynamics of such a society and of the particular activities of some of the historical actors who contributed to these dynamics. Thus, in referring to, say, 'entrepreneurs' or to 'scientific management' one may cite, in the same instance, cases which, viewed from the historian's point of view, should be shown to be decades if not, in some cases, even centuries apart. The contribution to sociology of history might be, I suggest, that it provides a way in which causal and functional analysis can be combined. It can give some indication of where an institution 'came from' and, hence, what it contributes to a particular social order. The social order or society does not have to be reified in the process of such an analysis. On the contrary, it is more likely to enable one to see the human agencies behind the 'order': the creation by people of social structures in the form of both intended and unintended consequences of action.

The growth of capitalist industrial society is seen as the consequence of the emergence of new social groups and particularly of entrepreneurs and their utilisation and development of various rational calculatively based techniques in the social, technological, political and economic spheres of society. These groups gained ascendancy in their competition with established dominant groups, and in the British case (the only one with which we can, of course, be concerned when looking at the origins of industrial capitalism) these groups formed new coalitions of interest with members of the previously dominant groups. Central to the establishment of the dominance of the groups which emerged with the industrial revolution is the establishing of the idea of a work-based social order in which labour is a commodity which is bought and sold on the market against capital. To facilitate both the acceptance of and the operation of such an economic order, other political and cultural institutions of society were revised and reconstructed in terms of the interests of these eventually hegemonic groups.

The growth of industrial capitalism

The general scheme can now be applied to the development of the industrial capitalist order in Britain and the role played by members of certain social groups on the one hand and 'ideas' on the other. In emphasising social groups and the place of particular ideas in these processes of major social change, one has to be careful not to imply that there were not a *range* of complex factors which are very relevant to an understanding of what occurred. Weber, in his *General Economic History* (1927), does full justice to these complexities, with his more famous analysis of the influence of Protestantism taking its place among analyses of pre-capitalist developments, changes in colonial policy, in trade, in citizenship and the state, in technology, and so on. These are important background factors to the processes on which I will concentrate here.

At the centre of the processes contributing to the development of industrial capitalist society are that group of men, the entrepreneurs. The earliest English use of the word 'entrepreneur' appears to be in 1885 when, in a textbook on political economy by F. A. Walker, it is argued that

> the control and direction of capital and labour are so difficult that 'a distinct class is called into being, in all industrially advanced communities, to undertake that function. This class is known as the employing class, or, to adopt a word from the French, the *entrepreneur* class' (Gough, 1969, p. 9).

It is interesting that this author did not, in 1885, apparently see it as necessary to differentiate between entrepreneurs and managers. If one regards the entrepreneur as an intermediary, Gough points out, this suggests the salaried official, the modern 'personnel manager', rather than the genuine entrepreneur. The archetypal entrepreneur is something more than this: he is 'not only the man of initiative but the man who "runs his own show" ' (*ibid.*, p. 17). What this leaves to be clarified is the extent to which there is anything historically 'new' about the entrepreneurs of the early stages of industrialism and the extent to which they are, in any sense, a distinctive group or even 'class'. Pollard looks at the objectives and methods of undertakings which involved large-scale organisation of resources to build pyramids and road schemes, or applied large quantities of capital to profit making, or applied innovation to manufacture, and so on, prior to this era. But:

> the innovation, and the difficulty, lay in this: that the men who began to operate the large new industrial units in the British economy from the middle of the eighteenth century onwards had to combine these different objectives and methods into one. Like the generals of old, they had to control numerous men, but without powers of compulsion: indeed, the absence of legal enforcement of unfree work was not only one of the marked

characteristics of the new capitalism, but one of its most seminal ideas. . . . Again, unlike the builders of pyramids, they had not only to show absolute results in terms of certain products of their efforts, but to relate them to costs, and sell them competitively. While they used capital, like the merchants, yet they had to combine it with labour, and transform it first, not merely into saleable commodities, but also into instruments of production embodying the latest achievements of a changing technology. And about it all there lay the heavy hand of a hostile State and an unsympathetic legal system, which they had to transform, as they had to transform so much of the rest of their environment, in the process of creating their industrial capitalism (Pollard, 1968, p. 17).

In this, Pollard is following Weber's argument that what distinguished the modern factory was 'not the implements of work applied, but the concentration of the ownership of workplace, means of work, source of raw material in one and the same hand, that of the entrepreneur'. Weber argues that this combination was '. . . only exceptionally met with before the eighteenth century' (1927, p. 202). Court accepts that 'the central event of the Industrial Revolution was the novel handling of resources by individuals' (1967, p. 97).

Having established the distinctiveness of the efforts of the entrepreneurs there arises the question of their distinctiveness as a social group. Gough (1969) shows that most of the very early entrepreneurs were members of the aristocracy or the upper classes. His study concentrates on the period earlier than that generally regarded as the Industrial Revolution, however, and when we look at studies of the later periods we find authors like the Hammonds pointing out that many entrepreneurs of this period were from yeoman stock, among these, Peel, Fielden, Strutt, Williamson, Wedgewood, Darby, Crawshay, and Radcliffe (Hammond and Hammond, 1966a, p. 21). Owen had early on been apprenticed to a retail shopkeeper and Brotherton had been a schoolmaster (*ibid.*). Bendix's review of the evidence leads him to accept as having a factual basis 'the common opinion that *most* of the early manufacturers came from working-class or lower-middle-class families', although he warns against generalising too broadly (Bendix, 1963, p. 23). But what is clear about the social origins of the early entrepreneurs is that the contempt in which they felt that they were held by the traditional ruling class strongly increased their consciousness as a group. Bendix sees this as sufficiently important to warrant regarding them as a social class: 'the opposition of ruling groups in English society to the rising entrepreneurs was an important stimulus to the formation of this social class' (*ibid.*, p. 16).

Bendix's emphasis on the importance of the aspirations of the new manufacturing class fits well with Israel's analysis of an earlier period of English history where he shows how, since the reign of Henry VIII, England had the 'most permeable class structure in Europe' but that the aspirations held by many Englishmen were unrealistically high (1966, p. 591). Consolidation of various 'occupationally diverse proto-industrial groups . . . was promoted by their clear perception of having a common foe, the Establishment' (*ibid.*, p. 591).

Opposition and conflict with previously dominant social groups played an important part in creating a consciousness of common interests among entrepreneurs. This conflict was, in a sense, a motor helping to propel the change processes which were to create the new economy and form of society. But one of the characteristics of change in Britain after the Industrial Revolution was the adaptability of the traditional ruling groups and the formation of what can be seen as new coalitions of interest. The Hammonds point out that in the mining industry the capitalist class had come in part from the aristocracy (1966a, p. 22) and that the landowners in Lancashire were happy to make money from land rented for industrial purposes (*ibid.*, p. 23). More importantly though, Hobsbawm writes of a 'continuity' and 'carefully moderate adjustment' rather than a 'disruption' in the patterns of dominance (1968, p. 82). He does point out, however, that 'absorption into an aristocratic oligarchy is, by definition, available only for a minority' and that this left many others to form a self-consciously 'middle' class who, after 1830, could pursue their own interests as they saw them. What is important here is that those interests dependent on capital, investment, manufacture and employment became the dominant ones through the access gained by the most successful pursuers of such interests to the institutions which would ensure an eventually hegemonic role.

Rationalisation

The arrival of members of these new social groups in positions of power did, of course, depend on their prior success in the creating of wealth on a scale and in a manner which had not been seen before. This takes us back to the distinctiveness of their efforts and to a consideration of the means which were employed to achieve this success. Fundamental to the changing *ideas* which have to be understood to enable an appreciation of the nature of these means is the notion of *rationalisation*. Schumpeter saw rationalism as fostering the growth of commercial activity by 'placing before men, and legitimatising, the goal of self-interest' whilst 'nascent capitalism seizes upon the rationalist spirit' and 'implements it with certain tools, especially the profit-and-loss statement as an index of success'

25

(O'Donnell, 1973, p. 205). But this analysis derives from the seminal work of Max Weber and his tracing of the process of increasing rationalisation of life in the West from the Reformation onwards. Bendix argues that the concept of rationalisation, in no way to be understood as an evolutionary process, is the central theme of Weber's work (1965). And it is to be taken here as a factor of basic importance. Within this process the world is increasingly subjected to science, calculation, technique and rules, all aimed towards the methodical attainment of given ends. This implies that

> one can, in principle, master all things by calculation. This means that the world is disenchanted. One need no longer have recourse to magical means in order to master or implore the spirits. . . . Technical means perform the service (Weber, 1970, p. 139).

Unlike Schumpeter, Weber is highly equivocal about this process, differentiating between the *formal rationality* by which activity is based on rationally calculable principles and *material rationality* which refers to the extent to which such calculable rationality furthers the achievement of actual human goals or values. The tensions between the two rationalities and the fundamental problems for modern civilisation arising from these tensions will be treated in detail at a later stage. For the present, we must examine the centrality of the growth of formal rationality to the understanding of the problem of labour in the developing industrial capitalism.

Ideas like those covered by the notion of formal rationality are not seen here, any more than they are in the work of Weber himself, as having any independent causal status. Within my general theoretical scheme ideas are created or seized upon by interest groups, and particularly by the 'spokesmen' associated with them, in the process of articulating and furthering the interests of that group. As Weber himself puts it:

> Interests (material and ideal), not ideas, directly govern men's conduct. Nevertheless, 'views of the world' created by 'ideas' have frequently acted like switchmen indicating the lines along which action has been propelled by the dynamics of interest (quoted by Bendix, 1965, p. 17).

Elsewhere Weber used the term 'elective affinity', borrowed from Goethe, to express the dual aspect of ideas: that the individual creates or chooses them (elective) and that they fit in with his material interests (affinity).[1] Hence the relationship between the 'Protestant ethic' and the rise of capitalism.[2]

This need to relate manifestations of formal rationality to the interests of particular individuals and groups is of great importance.

The methodological position being adopted here precludes any acceptance of the traditional view that the division of labour, the development of technology and its application in factories, the techniques of hierarchical control, and the rest came about because of any *intrinsic* 'technical superiority'. Such conceptions, like that of 'efficiency', imply the existence of certain *ends* and this leads to the question of *whose* ends? The point that has to be made here is that, in Forbes's words, 'formal rationality is wholly suited to the needs and interests of capitalists' (1975). Such an argument has been forcefully put, with the regard to the division of labour and the development of the factory system, by Marglin (1971). The division of labour was not, according to Marglin, as Adam Smith argued, the result of a search 'for a technologically superior organisation of work, but for an organisation which guaranteed to the entrepreneur an essential role in the production process, as integration of the separate efforts of his workers into a marketable product'. Similarly, the factory developed through the capitalist's choice of 'substituting his own for the worker's control of the work process and quantity of output', and the hierarchical control of production was adopted 'to provide for the accumulation of capital' (*ibid.*, p. 4). Such a view is not to be interpreted too simplistically, but it is of prime importance that formally rational techniques are not themselves reified and treated as being an independent 'force' in social change.[3]

Having indicated the role of interests in the development of formally rational techniques in work organisation and thus suggesting some causal factors behind social change processes, some closer attention can be given to particular manifestations of formal rationality which developed as part of the growth of a new type of society and a new mode of integration. Hobsbawm puts it neatly:

> Arithmetic was the fundamental tool of the Industrial
> Revolution. Its makers saw it as a series of sums of addition
> and subtraction: the difference in cost between buying in the
> cheapest market and selling in the dearest, between investment
> and return. For Jeremy Bentham and his followers, the most
> consistent champion of this type of rationality, even morals and
> politics came under these simple calculations (1968, p. 69).

As this would imply, the development of money and the techniques of accounting to allow the calculating of profits and losses are necessary prerequisites of modern capitalism. Giddens points out that 'in Weber's view, rational book-keeping constitutes the most integral expression' of the modern form of capitalistic enterprise (Giddens, 1971, p. 179). But these techniques have to be combined with a series of other prerequisites, according to Weber, including the detachment of the productive enterprise from the household, the

27

absence of restrictions on economic exchange on the market, the existence of legally 'free' wage labourers and a technology, 'constructed and organised on the basis of rational principles' (*ibid.*, p. 179). Bendix describes the widespread enthusiasm for technology which existed among the rising entrepreneurial class and indicates how such an interest was actively propagated by organisations and by particular spokesmen (1963, pp.-27–9). The new methods brought about by technology are often used to explain, if not to justify, the detachment of production from the home and its moving into the factory but we must nevertheless recognise that, in Fox's words, '(t)he emergence of the factory system owed as much to the drive for closer coordination, discipline, and control of the labour force as to the pressures of technology' (1974, pp. 179–80). And this relates back to the points made by Marglin about the division of labour in production, a fundamental aspect of the new formally rational organisation of working life and a central precept in Adam Smith's *Wealth of Nations*, the most significant document of the 'English System' (Nisbet, 1970, p. 24).

The division of labour described by Smith has spread in all industrial societies beyond the matter of simple task specialisation within manufacturing units. Processes of increasing specialisation of activities on a societal level were seen by Durkheim as processes which transformed societies (1933) and functionalist sociologists since then have characterised modern processes of social change in terms of 'functional differentiation' (Smelser, 1959). As we shall see later both of these aspects of 'differentiation' create a range of problems in which personnel specialists become involved. But, for the moment, attention has to be paid to a related aspect of these changes, that of bureaucratisation. As Miewald points out, the growth of bureaucracy was, for Weber, another manifestation of the process of rationalisation: 'the true essence of bureaucratisation feeds upon that which will make the affairs of men more amenable to rational calculation' (1970, p. 66). It was this aspect of the extension of the division of labour which, in Marx's analysis, led to the expropriation of the worker from his means of production (Giddens, 1971). The growth of a state administration carried on by salaried officials did in part precede the major processes of economic rationalisation, but the prerequisites of modern capitalism which Weber set out could not, as he indicated, exist without such a rational administration of the modern state (*ibid.*, p. 179).

It was the activities led by the entrepreneurial and associated groups which was primarily responsible for increasing the scale of organisation. With this increase in scale it became increasingly difficult for the entrepreneur who, typically, 'wrote his own letters, visited his own customers, and belaboured his men with his own walking-stick' (Pollard, 1968, p. 232) to continue without a managerial, clerical and administrative staff. As Bendix says, 'seen historically bureaucratisation may be interpreted as the increasing subdivision of the functions which the owner-managers of the early enterprises had performed personally in the course of their daily routine' (1963, p. 211). These functions cover labour management and the various mercantile functions like purchasing, sales and finance. It is this structural differentiation of the employing organisation which we see, at a later stage, producing what became the personnel department.

With the growth of specialised managements we see a whole panoply of formally rational techniques becoming applied to the efforts of employees, and particularly to manual workers. Many of these techniques are usually described in terms of 'scientific management', the origins of which can be seen as early as the beginning of the nineteenth century in the Soho factory of Boulton and Watt (Roll, 1930). As the Hammonds comment, 'Boulton was an adept at scientific management' (1966b, p. 119). But it was towards the end of the nineteenth century that we see on a larger scale the increase in measurement, speed-up and rationalisation which led to a more and more pervasive low discretion type of work and the prevalence of what Fox calls the low-trust syndrome (1974, p. 191). The trend reached its high point with the appearance of the industrial engineers and efficiency experts, followers of F. W. Taylor and the like. Taylor, whom Weber describes as a 'pioneer' in this area (1964, p. 261), saw management becoming increasingly systematised:

> Many of the elements which are now believed to be outside the field of exact knowledge will soon be standardised, tabulated, accepted and used, as are now many of the elements of engineering. Management will . . . rest upon well recognised, clearly defined and fixed principles instead of depending upon more or less hazy ideas received from a limited observation of the few organisations with which the individual may have come in contact (1911, quoted in Sofer, 1972, pp. 32–3).

This movement was challenged by the so-called human relations movement which is not unconnected with the growth of personnel management itself and, indeed, many of the problems with which personnel specialists deal can be seen as consequential to the acceptance of many Taylorist principles. Such ideas, if in more sophisticated forms, are still central to managerial practice. As Albrow says,

> The growth of sciences of decision making, of operational research, of schools of management, amounts to the intensification of the importance of science in administration – of formal rationality (1970, p. 66).

Labour as a commodity

All these techniques and aspects of the spread of formal rationality are to be seen as part of the *means* by which the dominant groups in the new capitalist society created and maintain the advantage which they enjoy. However, we must now concentrate on one aspect of their rationalised control of production which was fundamental: its dependence upon the existence of a free market in labour and a situation in which people without property would have to sell their labour to make a living. Indeed it is this aspect of capitalism which Marx takes to be its defining feature. To Marx, capitalist society is one in which the productive process depends on the exchanging of labour power in the market against capital. It has been seen earlier that the entrepreneur is essentially involved in the 'mixing' together of economic resources. Human labour is one of these resources and is necessarily a *cost*. And the more a cost can be calculated, controlled and hence kept as low as possible, the more closely can the capitalistic employer follow the logic of market society – the society which is of his making and upon which his advantaged position depends.

Under industrial capitalism labour becomes a resource of a productive system and one of the major requirements which the employer has of this commodity is *tractability*. The employer must buy labour power when he needs it, use it in the way he requires to and dispose of it when it does not yield the surplus which justifies its purchase. But, however equal the relationship between buyer and seller may be claimed to be by the ideology of the new bourgeois liberalism, a structural requirement of the new type of society which necessarily results from this new mode of production will be a fundamental inequality. The propertyless do not have 'free access to the means of turning their capacity to labour into productive labour. Having lost this part of their powers to those who have the land and capital. . . . This constitutes the net transfer of part of their powers to others' (Macpherson, 1970, p. 32). And hence we see developing a basic inequality in control of resources, with the growth of one group of people who possess the resources to employ labour and the growth of another group who lack such resources and must therefore sell their labour power. In the widest sense of the notion of 'social group' then, we see two potential such groups, centring on the two conflicting objective interests which we would expect to see between the buyers and sellers of any commodity. As Moore says, from an economic point of view,

the interests of capital in any concrete situation are likely to be in the lowest possible labour cost consistent with continued production. From the same point of view, the interests of labour are likely to be in the highest wage consistent with continued operation of the industry (that is with the continuance of employment) (1951, p. 160).

The treatment of labour as a commodity does entail far more than simply its buying and selling in the market, however. It also involves a wholly new degree of specificity and control in the process of its utilisation. What has to be realised is that what is often taken for granted in contemporary managerial circles is something which was far more visibly problematic in the early stages of industrialism; that is, the necessity for the user of labour to counter human criteria of custom, tradition and spontaneity. However unpleasant pre-industrial work may have been, the controlling, pacing, co-ordinating and speeding up, with all its associated disciplines and penalties, was experienced as a newly transparent control of men by men rather than as a reaction to spontaneous needs, the seasons, the requirements of domestic animals, and so on. This was so much so that the early decades of industrialism saw labour needs being met to a considerable degree by women and children rather than by men (Bendix, 1963, pp. 34–6; Hobsbawm, 1968, pp. 85–9; Hammond and Hammond, 1966b, chs 7 and 12).

Labour: the problem of control

In a great deal of the study of industrial relations, management, economics and personnel management, the existence of a labour force is taken for granted. One of the aims of this present analysis is to argue that it is *essentially* problematic. Moore, in one of the few studies which diverges from this pattern, commented that, 'it is noteworthy that the whole scholarly literature on the development of economic individualism and the rise of capitalism pays very slight attention to any problems associated with the shift of workers to industrial employments' (Moore, 1951, p. 155). Moore documents the pressures which pushed people into industrial employment and characterises economic change as, for many, a 'choice among evils' (1965, ch. 3), backing up historical evidence with corresponding examples from contemporary industrialisation processes (*ibid.*, pp. 119–21). Wilensky and Lebaux introduce their review of the evidence:

> It is not an exaggeration to say that in the early period of economic development coercion has everywhere played the main role in labor recruitment. People have been *pushed* into the factories and plantations, more than they have been *pulled* by the great opportunity before them. The coercion has been both direct and indirect, open and concealed (1965, p. 50).

31

And, as Pollard adds, analysing the specifics of the early industrial-isation in Britain

> The very recruitment to the uncongenial work was difficult, and it was made worse by the deliberate or accidental modelling of many works on workhouses and prisons, a fact well known to the working population (1968, p. 190).

Although there have been arguments attempting to contradict such a view of labour recruitment[4] there is overwhelming evidence to indicate the necessity of the development of new forms of power to cope with the problems of utilising a large proportion of the population as a 'labour force' – as assets or resources. Coercion has severe limitations in the context of industrial employment:

> Although coercion may yield a large initial labor supply, it is a highly inefficient way of keeping people at work. Laborers recruited by coercion require too much supervision in the workplace; and their recruitment often leads to political instability. Above all, it takes more than coercion to develop habits of industrial work and discipline (Wilensky and Lebaux, 1965, p. 55).

To a great extent the fiercest wrench from the past and, in fact, the central management problem in the Industrial Revolution, was the 'rational and methodical management of labour' (Pollard, 1968, p. 189). The nature of the new markets that were being created required the production of standardised products, and the traditional craftsman's mode of working at a leisurely pace with spurts of great intensity was highly inappropriate. In modern industry the worker had to 'adapt his sense of accuracy to the requirements of standard-isation' (Bendix, 1963, pp. 203–4). The need was now to get compli-ance with general rules and specific orders in order to achieve the necessary execution of tasks according to design and in such a way as to facilitate co-ordination of the tasks which were increasingly organised on the principles of the division of labour. And here is a problem still central to the tasks of all managements: getting employees to carry out tasks which are closely specified by manage-ment and supervision without their descending to the blind following and literal interpretation of rules (the 'working to rule' which is such an effective sanction when used by organised labour). Bendix (1963) in his study shows the importance of developing managerial ideologies as one of the strategies designed to cope with this problem, but the point being stressed here is that we see in this a central tension in employer–employee relations under industrial capitalism, a tension with which personnel and other managers are constantly coping.

32

If we see, in the process of recruitment of labour and the subjecting of employees to disciplines of supervision and economic dependence, the growth of a new form of power in society, we must also expect to see some resistance, opposition and conflict. The very nature of the economic relationship between the buyers and sellers of labour is one where we can perceive an objectively existing conflict of interests. It requires the conversion of these objective interests into subjective interests to activate latent conflicts into actual ones. The growth of a class consciousness was a transforming aspect of the dynamics of industrial capitalism and a major challenge to the dominant groups of the new social order. Common experience was such that the identity of experience was bound to lead to some consciousness of what we conceptualise as 'class':

> . . . class happens when some men, as a result of common experiences (inherited or shared), feel and articulate the identity of their interests as between themselves, and as against other men whose interests are different from (and usually opposed to) theirs. The class experience is usually determined by the productive relations into which men are born – or enter involuntarily. Class consciousness is the way in which their experiences are handled in cultural terms . . . (Thompson, 1968, pp. 9–10).

The nature of employment, then, is a factor of major significance to the growth of the structuring of capitalist industrial societies on a 'class' basis. The relations behind this have been described above largely in terms of the relationship between employers and employees, despite the fact that I have indicated the importance of the growth of 'managements' as part of the bureaucratisation process. I do not wish to examine the issue of the extent to which control of enterprises is now in the hands of managers rather than owners until the last chapter of this study. But, for the present, the managers fit into the model of the developing industrial capitalist order in their role as *agents* of those social groups who are most advantaged in that developing order. Their role came about as an aspect of the means by which that order was created – the rationalisation process. Whether or not the managers – some of them or all of them – are part of the dominant groupings in the contemporary order is partly an empirical issue and will be a matter of significance in chapter 9.

Tensions, conflicts and contradictions

A concept of pivotal importance in the analysis so far has been the Weberian one of rationalisation. A whole set of ideas and techniques which were developed as part of the growth of industrial capitalism have been described as *formally rational* and these have been interpreted as acting, to a large extent, as the means by which certain social groups built a new social order. Although Weber's use of various concepts of rationality are 'opaque and shifting' (Lukes, 1970, p. 207) it is in his notion of rationalisation and particularly his distinction between formal (or technical, instrumental or functional) and material (or substantive) rationality that his major contribution to an understanding of modern society lies. Giddens sees this distinction in Weber's work as 'focal to sociological analysis' and suggests that the application of it to the course of development of modern capitalism is critical in his interpretation of the dilemmas faced by contemporary man (Giddens, 1971, p. 183). To express the distinction in simple terms: the criteria of *formal* rationality are met when abstract principles, rules, techniques or calculations are applied; the criteria of *material* rationality are only met when particular goals or values are achieved through the use of rational calculation. Thus, one is a rationale of *means* and the other is a rationale of *means related to ends*. Formal rationality is a necessary but not a sufficient condition for material rationality. And it is the relationship between these two types of rationality which I intend to utilise to analyse the fundamental tensions and contradictions which underlie capitalist industrial society. This will enable us in the chapters that follow to examine the ways in which personnel specialists play a part in maintaining a particular societal 'mode of integration' by helping to cope with these fundamental strains.

The increasing rationalisation of Western societies in the hands of certain interest groups involves the increasing application of calculatively based techniques whereby those groups could further their interests. Indeed, the general increases in levels of output and the growth of wealth would indicate the effectiveness of these means. But within any society of human beings, all of whom necessarily exist in an 'ethically irrational' world, there exists a paradox of consequences (see above, pp. 15–16). As a result of this there will always be an inevitable tension between the two rationalities: the formally rational means are liable to defeat the purposes (goals and values) which they were originally intended to fulfil.

Conceived at the level of the society as a whole, Weber saw a threat to civilisation in the spread of formal rationality. Ironically, it led to a distinctive *irrationality* as means rather than ends (conceived from a value viewpoint) became ends in themselves (Loewith, 1970, p. 114). This coincides with the Marxian view of capitalism as irrational as money, means of production, employment and so on become ends in themselves rather than means towards the satisfaction of human needs. As O'Neill says, the modern corporate economy, viewed from a Marxist point of view, 'promotes the most highly rationalised forms of production process, business administration and market control while simultaneously, and on the same principle, undermining the culture and humanity of the social order it professes to serve' (1973, p. 25).[5] Yet Weber, despite his concern with ethical neutrality, did end up describing capitalism as more materially rational than socialism, largely because the latter would depend, he believed, on an even greater degree of formal rationality.[6] Nevertheless, a critique of the forces and unfreedoms of modern society in terms of what Weber called formal rationality is inherent in both Marx's and Weber's value positions. In the contemporary period, the most explicit critique of modern society on these lines is that of Ellul (1964).[7]

It is not appropriate here to pursue the ways in which modern society may be materially irrational at the level of goals and values seen as basic to Western civilisation. The concern is, instead, with the mode of integration of capitalist industrial society. And this has been conceptualised in a model in which certain social groups are seen as advantaged and dominant, using formal rationality as means in the fulfilling of their interests. Therefore where the tensions and contradictions between formal and material rationality become a problem of particular relevance to this analysis is inasmuch as they are problematic to those wishing to maintain the pattern of advantage underlying that social order. Thus, where managers are seen as coping with material irrationalities, then these are irrationalities from the point of view of the interests of the dominant social groups. I shall now look briefly at some of the basic forms that the problems ensuing from the strains between formal and material rationality take in industrial capitalist society. What this analysis will indicate, in very general terms, is that the *means* which the dominant groups of society (and their agents) use are potentially liable to defeat the *ends* of those groups.

One of the major formally rational techniques underlying the organisation of capitalist industrial society is the division of labour. Even its most famous early proponent, Adam Smith, saw countertendencies within its 'efficiency'. The division of tasks is generally liable to encourage a lowering of interest, commitment and therefore effective compliance of the employee with managerial requirements (*cf.* Friedmann, 1961). The need to bring the employee under close task specification to produce the standardised product required by the market can lead to resentment and to 'low-trust' relationships and, hence, low-trust industrial relations with all that that implies (Fox, 1974). Bringing large numbers of employees together in factories or other large units may also encourage the perception and articulation of common interests among those who are selling their labour, with the resulting increase in class consciousness (e.g.

Lockwood, 1958) or at least trade-union consciousness, thus encouraging the growth of organised opposition to employer interests. Here we have what was interpreted as one of the central contradictions of capitalism by Marx and Engels: the 'socialisation' of production occurring within the anarchy of the market economy, thus creating within capitalism the seeds of its own destruction.

The tractability of the commodity of labour, another prerequisite of formally rational methods of production, necessarily requires a pool of 'free' labour. This recruitment of a mobility of labour (understood in the widest sense of 'mobility') is difficult to encourage without the consequential demands for political freedoms growing among those being 'freed' to sell their labour power. Employing classes therefore face a potential challenge through the political institutions of society. And the use of money rewards to buy the necessary compliance on a competitive market may lead to the 'unprincipled inequalities', economic instabilities and social and political tensions accompanying the phenomenon Durkheim described as *anomie* (see Goldthorpe, 1969).

The growth of bureaucracy, a development which Weber saw as the height of formal rationality, is notoriously liable to involve the defeating of ends which inspire it (Albrow, 1970). The structures devised to co-ordinate the increasing complexity of tasks in increasingly large-scale formal organisations could be self-defeating as the rules, devised as means to ends, become ends in themselves and subgroups within the organisation pursue goals of their own which conflict with those of the designers of the structure (see, for example, Merton, 1957).[8]

Some wider responses

I have indicated above some of the major problems which exist for the 'integration' of capitalist industrial society. One of the responses to these problems has been, in the employment sector, the growth of personnel management. But to keep that institution in perspective as an integrative mechanism, it is necessary to give some brief consideration to other significant factors which can help explain what Worsley called 'one of the most striking phenomena of modern times', namely, 'the uninterrupted, albeit modified, dominance of the property-owning classes, in a society which has long been the most highly "proletarianised" in the world' (Worsley, 1964, pp. 22–3). The ways in which the state has gradually been modified in Britain throughout the nineteenth and twentieth centuries, coping with the economic difficulties and social costs of industrial capitalism on the one hand and acceding to demands for political representation on the other, has been of major importance. Worsley examines the ways in which dominant groups established the legitimacy of rule in their favour (*ibid.*) and Bendix discusses other subtleties of the 'incorporation of the Fourth Estate into the political community' (1961). The growth of 'social security' measures has been a major feature of all industrial societies (Mishra, 1973), and Rimlinger, in his study of the relationship between welfare policies and industrialisation, has stressed the importance of welfare measures in the provision and maintenance of manpower supply:

> Aside from being a means to enhance welfare, social security programs also are measures that affect the quantity and quality of a country's manpower resources. The poor laws constituted a manpower policy that was fairly well suited for a time when labour was abundant and mostly unskilled (1971, p. 9).

And at the later stages of industrialism,

> it became profitable, from the point of view of productivity, to develop and to maintain the capacity and the willingness to work. The workers' physical strength and good will had become important assets. Social insurance became one of the means of investing in human capital (*ibid.*, p. 10).

The increase in educational provision can be seen in a not dissimilar light and it can also be seen as providing an important 'safety valve' in its contribution to a degree of social mobility (Parkin, 1972). The increase in economic rewards and the appeal of material goods clearly plays a major role, developing ideas of 'economism' and 'instrumentalism' (Goldthorpe and Lockwood, 1969, Mann 1973) while religious beliefs have been of importance in the growth of a political consciousness not inimical to capitalism (Parkin, 1972, Thompson, 1968, Moore, 1974). And related to all these points has been the growth of the trade union movement with its associated reformist Labour party and the institutionalisation of industrial conflict, leading, as some put it, to the 'incorporation' of the working class into a capitalist order (Mann, 1973, Cousins and Davis, 1974).

This cursory survey of factors outside the direct influence of the managements of employing organisations is important in setting a context in which we can see the part that one specialist group plays in terms of a societal contribution. I shall now turn to this group – the particular institution with which this study is mainly concerned: the personnel occupation.

The welfare movement and the emergence of the personnel occupation

What can nowadays be described as an occupation, that of the personnel specialists, has to be seen as something which emerged only gradually from its roots in the industrial 'welfare movement'.

37

This movement can be understood as part of the reaction to the problems discussed above but it was, at the same time, very much the creation of a clearly identifiable number of individual men and women. As Niven comments: 'The welfare movement came in answer to the need of the times and was strengthened by the work and beliefs of the pioneer employers, who played a fundamental part in its growth' (Niven, 1967, pp. 20–1). The welfare movement, out of which an eventually recognisable occupation grew, was initiated by members of the entrepreneurial group who were considered earlier. These were the men who had been introducing increasingly formally rational techniques to fulfil their interests. But by the late nineteenth and early twentieth century there was some realisation that, taken too far, such techniques were potentially self-defeating and that the meeting of criteria of material rationality (profit, growth, or whatever) would require measures which, at first sight, might appear to contradict formally rational calculative criteria. These were 'welfare measures'. The issues were not seen in these terms, of course, although, as we shall see shortly, such a view, if not in the same words, became popular before very long. The pioneering employers in the welfare movement were motivated to an important extent by religious thought and feelings of conscience. These were men who sponsored welfare activities and employed the first welfare workers, and they did show an undoubted concern for the people whom they employed. Crichton says, 'The first personnel specialists were . . . welfare workers appointed to express the concern of the paternal employers for the conditions of their workpeople and the society in which they found themselves' (1968, p. 18).

In my analysis of these employers and the welfare workers whom they employed, I shall be following my theoretical scheme by seeking relationships between *interests* and *ideas*, again making use of the notion of *elective affinities*, thereby making irrelevant any suggestion of insincerity on the part of the pioneering employers in their benevolence. It is a matter of a convenient consistency between their humanitarian values and their entrepreneurial interests. As I have pointed out earlier, I am not giving an historical account here – this has been excellently done by Niven (1967), McGivering (1970), Crichton (1968) and others. I shall illustrate my thesis from the cases of two particular individuals, Seebohm Rowntree and Jesse Boot, making brief mention of American parallels later on.[9] American evidence provides useful comparative material and is important in that personnel management in Britain has, over the years, been increasingly influenced by the American experience.

Seebohm Rowntree was perhaps the most important single individual in the history of personnel management, if not in management as a whole, in Britain in the first half of the present century

(McGivering, 1970, p. 177). He followed his father's 'enlightened' views, uncharacteristic in their time but in the tradition of Owen, Salt, Lever and Cadbury (Chapman, 1970, p. 207) and his social philosophy 'grew naturally out of his religious upbringing and teaching' (Briggs, 1961, p. 12). It was the Rowntrees who appointed the first industrial welfare worker (as distinct from an extra-mural visitor), Miss Mary Wood, in 1896 (Niven, 1967, p. 21) and Seebohm played a central part in the welfare movement through his initiation of various meetings and conferences of those interested in welfare. But of great significance is the role he played in the involvement of the state in industrial welfare policies during World War II. He exerted enormous influence as Director of the Welfare Department at the Ministry of Munitions – a job given to him by Lloyd George (Briggs, 1961, pp. 117–18).

Jesse Boot is an individual of very different demeanour who is of interest here not only because he played a significant part in the welfare movement but because the firm which he founded is a major employer in the area of the country in which the empirical part of this study was carried out. He was a first generation entrepreneur

> a typical Victorian Entrepreneur and . . . one of the Napoleons of industry that transformed the structure and policies of whole industries during the course of the last century. As an entrepreneur he seems to represent quite a number of the characteristics of his class: he had little education, lacked social polish, was Nonconformist in religion and ideology, ascetic and irascible (Chapman, 1974, p. 190).

He was deeply influenced by his Wesleyan beliefs,[10] justifying his aggressive salesmanship by the benefits which he was bringing to the poorer classes (*ibid.*, p. 51). Chapman sees a 'strange ambivalence' in Boot's thinking on matters of welfare (*ibid.*, p. 159): he acquired a reputation among his employees for being 'rough and hard' (*ibid.*, p. 65) yet he felt the 'strongest attachment to the working class' whom he claimed, once, to represent in the House of Lords as the 'son of a man who belonged to the lowest ranks of workers' (*ibid.*, pp. 175–6). As Chapman puts it,

> On the one side we see the single-minded and tireless entrepreneur, impatient if not ruthless with any person or organisation that stood in his way; on the other side it is not difficult to recognise the idealistic Nonconformist and Liberal, eager to search for practical means of realising the Liberal-Christian ideas of industrial harmony, profit-sharing and co-ownership, and apparently ready to spend any amount of time and energy in these pursuits (*ibid.*, p. 159).

Boot recruited Miss Eleanor Kelly, one of the leading figures among the welfare workers, in 1911, and he was 'receptive to her ideas' (Chapman, 1974, p. 168). Of the early professional industrial welfare workers in Britain in 1914, four out of the sixty employed were at Boots and, unlike a large proportion of their colleagues elsewhere, these four 'had real standing' among the managers (*ibid.*, p. 169). Boots contributed to a welfare section at a trade exhibition in London in 1913 the success of which event, it has been suggested, led Seebohm Rowntree to help with the foundation of a welfare association (Niven, 1967, p. 32). Boot's son John was at the conference which founded what was to become the Institute of Personnel Management, in 1913.

I have now introduced two men who are of major significance in the history of personnel management. Their cases illustrate the importance of the individual entrepreneurial contribution to the welfare movement as well as the combination of religious thinking with interests in efficiency and profit. I shall now return to the question of the part that the welfare movement of which they were a part played in coping with some of the strains and conflicts underlying the now powerful and established industrial capitalist order. By the arrival of the twentieth century, organised resistance to employer policies was growing apace with the increasing strength of the trade union movement. Supporters of the welfare movement often had an interest in welfare which 'was inspired by a hope that in binding an employee more closely to the firm it would weaken both the attractiveness and the cohesion of the trade union' (Fox, 1974, p. 202). But Rowntree was willing to encourage collective bargaining and advocated what he called the 'joint control of industry' (Rowntree, 1921, ch. 5).[11] He was willing to consider the demand for a 'share in the determination of the working conditions' but felt it necessary to ask, note, 'how far it can be granted without interfering with business efficiency' (*ibid.*, p. 131). Given the fundamental conflict of interest which necessarily exists between the buyer and seller of labour, there is clearly an interesting ambiguity in this attitude. Such an ambiguity is even greater in the case of Boot who paid election expenses for a militant Liberal parliamentary candidate pledged to vote with the Labour party on labour issues (Chapman, 1974, p. 178). Boot also maintained a long friendship with the Labour politician John Burns, indicating what Chapman calls 'a soft spot for labour and trade unionism', a soft spot which did not prevent him from resisting any 'rival centre of power' in his own concerns (*ibid.*, pp. 171–2). The threat of the welfare movement to trade union and employee interests was clearly perceived by trade unionists, as several writers have shown (Niven, 1967, pp. 42, 64; McGivering, 1970, pp. 194ff.). And it was the increase in labour unrest and the growth of the shop steward movement during World War I which led to the state's encouragement of collective bargaining through the setting up of Whitley councils in 1917 (Niven, 1967, p. 46).

This involvement of the state in encouraging collective bargaining illustrates the importance of non-managerial initiatives in coping with the tensions and conflicts of the new type of society, as was shown above (pp. 36–7). And legislative action was a pressure of enormous importance in the development of the welfare movement, as it has been on the growth of personnel management ever since. The nineteenth-century Factory Acts played their part (Niven, 1967, p. 16; McGivering, 1970, p. 172) and the pressure was increased by the 1901 Factory and Workshop Act (Crichton, 1968, p. 19), the extension of the Workman's Compensation Act (Niven, 1967, p. 21), and all that followed up to the Health and Safety at Work Act and other such measures of the 1970s.

The influence of the state on personnel management has never been greater than during the two World Wars. With the advent of World War I there was a noticeable falling off in interest in welfare *per se* (Chapman, 1974, p. 169, for example) but with the new stress on efficiency resulting from the enormous pressures on, particularly, arms manufacture, the various aspects of the embryo personnel management assumed a new and major importance. Rowntree's influence was considerable here. He brought together the interests shared with others in the welfare movement and a concern with certain elements from F. W. Taylor's 'scientific management', showing, as Briggs put it, that he was 'anxious from his new vantage point to reconcile the claims of efficiency and welfare . . .' (1961, p. 119). State encouragement advanced research in the field of industrial psychology during World War I and this produced another strand which was to be pulled into the growing personnel specialism (Crichton, 1968, p. 22) – a specialism which was boosted by the growing interest in administration and organisational structure, another result of the influence of the American scientific management movement (Fox, 1966a, p. 14).

The personnel occupation did, to a considerable extent, languish in the interwar years as labour supply became far less problematic for employers, and personnel specialists became vulnerable to accusations of 'soft-heartedness' and acting as 'buffers' against authority (Crichton, 1968, p. 26). Rationalisation and the influence of the efficiency expert became more important than welfare (Niven, 1967, p. 73; McGivering, 1970, p. 177). But personnel management for the first time came into its own with the outbreak of World War II, when greater demands than ever before were put on an inevitably reduced workforce. The development of various techniques, ranging from those of selection and training to those of

41

conciliation, accelerated rapidly, and great efforts were put into the training of personnel specialists themselves (Niven, 1967, ch. 7; Crichton, 1968, pp. 35–6). The significance of the Second World War on the growth of personnel management is that it was in this period of history, when labour was controlled more tightly than it ever had been before and formally rational techniques more rigorously brought to bear on labour management, that it became really established. One breakthrough was its acceptance by the trade unions.[12] The personnel function was now established with a role which involved both applying and furthering formally rational techniques in the sphere of labour utilisation whilst, at the same time, having to cope with the contradictory or self-defeating aspects of these and other formally rational devices of human management. We can thus see an essential ambiguity underlying the personnel function itself – something which I will examine closely in the next and ensuing chapters when I look at the contemporary situation.

The interest in welfare had now become integrated into management itself, partly as a result of the efforts of the would-be personnel managers themselves – those former welfare workers who saw the only opportunity of gaining influence within organisations in taking on administrative and management roles proper (Crichton, 1968, p. 20). They were heirs to what had grown out of the elective affinity between conscience-based concerns for employee welfare and employer interests: the very identification of welfare with 'efficiency'. This identification is made very clearly in Cadbury's influential volume on industrial organisation:

> The supreme principle has been the belief that business
> efficiency and the welfare of the employees are but different
> sides of the same problem. Character is an economic asset;
> and business efficiency depends not merely on the physical
> conditions of employees, but on their general attitude and
> feeling to the employer. The test of any scheme of factory
> organisation is the extent to which it creates and fosters the
> atmosphere and spirit of cooperation and goodwill, without
> in any sense lessening the loyalty of the worker to his own
> class and its organisations (Cadbury, 1912, p. xvii).

Seebohm Rowntree, who wrote in 1907 that the Christian ethic forbids one to treat human beings as 'instruments for the accomplishment of our ends' rather than as 'ends in themselves', was writing in 1912 that the welfare supervisor was a 'human engineer who goes into the factory to see that all the human machines are working at their highest potential' (quoted by Fox, 1966a, p. 14). The equation of efficiency and welfare was very much the message Rowntree put forward in the war years and a leaflet on welfare supervision issued by the Home Office in 1919 saw the provision of the best conditions of employment as an 'essential part of efficient management'. Welfare is described as a duty owed to employees; it is 'not merely . . . a means of efficiency and maximum production' (quoted in Niven, 1967, p. 56). Lee, a leading management writer, advised that to 'cultivate industrial welfare is to cultivate efficiency' (Lee, 1924, p. 22) which echoed what Hagerdorn calls the 'favorite allegation' of the American welfare propagandists, that it 'paid to treat workers like valuable human beings' (1958, p. 137).[13] Hagerdorn illustrates the connection between an interest in welfare policies and managerial *control* by pointing to the high proportion of pioneering companies in America who manufactured goods where high standards of workmanship were required (*ibid.*, p. 135) seeing this as just one aspect of how the welfare movement was 'a way of dealing with persistent managerial problems, not yet solved, nor even bypassed' (*ibid.*, p. 134).

The background from which the modern personnel management occupation grew, then, is one in which initiatives were taken by a few of the entrepreneurs and leading managers of the early twentieth century – by people like Seebohm Rowntree and Jesse Boot. These initiatives helped to counter some of the conflicts and strains which were becoming apparent in the new economy and society which their class had created. As these strains became enormously exacerbated by the requirements of war production in two World Wars so the welfare movement became more systematised and its adherents and recruits integrated themselves as far as they could into management itself. The self-conscious efforts and organisation of the personnel workers and how they differentiated their own interests from those of their employers and patrons will be returned to in a later chapter when I look at the issue of 'professionalisation'. In the next chapter I shall look at how the conflicts between the interests of employers and employed and the tensions between formal and material rationalities create considerable strains and ambiguities which underlie the contemporary personnel specialist's job.

3 Personnel management: conflicts and ambiguities

The occupation of personnel management is one which is primarily concerned with the contribution of labour to the operation of employing organisations. In the previous chapter I set out to show how labour as a resource used in the meeting of certain goals is *essentially problematic* at a societal level. Capitalist industrial society is one which is work-based and which makes use of labour – or rather is one in which certain groups make use of the labour of others – and this labour is necessarily treated as a commodity, something which has to be tractable or, in the widest sense, mobile. But, of course, labour as a commodity is a peculiar one – like other resources it is there to be exploited but, unlike other resources, 'it' has a will of its own. As Moore put it: 'the free laborer is a peculiar kind of industrial expense. For the labor force in modern industry provides more resistance to efficiency of exploitation than do natural resources, capital funds, and productive machinery' (1951, p. 163). Consequently, those groups which have been in positions of power within this type of society or 'mode of integration' have allowed a process of accommodation to occur in political, economic and employment spheres to cope with the essentially contradictory nature of the social order: one in which the means used to further the interests of the dominant-group members are continually liable to subvert or at least divert those ends.

Human resources and organisational goals

As I stressed earlier, the industrial capitalist type of society did not just 'come about'. It was the result of the efforts of particular people and the bringing together of the interests of these groups with ideas and, particularly, with that whole range of ideas and techniques which have been characterised as *formally rational*. A central aspect

44

of the overall growth of formal rationality is that of bureaucratisation which has occurred to such an enormous extent that people's lives are increasingly lived within or are considerably influenced by large organisations. I have suggested above that personnel specialists are primarily concerned with the contribution of labour to the operation of such organisations. The Institute of Personnel Management's booklet *A Career in Personnel Management, what it is and how to train for it* states:

> The aim of personnel management is to bring together and develop into an effective organisation all the men and women who are employed, enabling each to make his or her own best contribution to its success, both as an individual and as a member of a working group. Where other kinds of management deal with functions such as buying, production, accounting, marketing and selling, personnel management is concerned with the human and social implications of working and the organisation as a whole (I.P.M., 1974a, p. 3).

But what is meant by the 'success' of the organisation? The standard answer here is that 'success' refers to the meeting of the organisation's goals. But to reify the organisation in this way would be to fail to meet this study's theoretical criterion of using the social-action framework. Since we cannot study the personnel job and its contribution without considering the goals of the organisation in which it is performed (as the one's very justification is frequently seen in terms of its relationship to the other) we need to clarify this issue of organisational goals. To this end I offer the following definition of an organisation, one which retains the purposive aspect of organising without reifying the structure:

> An organisation is a social and technical arrangement in which a number of people come or are brought together in a relationship in which the actions of some are directed and co-ordinated by others towards the achievement of certain specific tasks.

Individuals coming together more or less accept that their efforts are co-ordinated by certain of their number. This co-ordination leads to the structuring of the organisation in two ways: *horizontally* in terms of a division of labour (task specialisation) and *vertically* by a control structure. This vertical structure is a power structure with those nearer the top of the hierarchy exercising more discretion than those lower down. The organisation itself not being capable, logically, of possessing goals or defining tasks, it must be to those at the top of this hierarchy that we must look to locate the overall tasks which have to be fulfilled to produce 'success'. Child has brought together various concepts and insights relevant to this issue and I follow him in seeing the *dominant coalition* within management as the ones who make the *strategic choices* in terms of which the organisation is structured and operates – albeit within the exigencies and constraints of the environment, constraints which, nevertheless, the dominant coalition may manipulate (Child, 1972).[1]

Personnel work as a component of all management

Personnel specialists play a part with regard to human resources in achieving the successful meeting of goals set or defined by the dominant coalition. But this raises an important issue: that of the relationship of the personnel function to the management of the organisation as a whole. Textbooks on personnel management frequently point out that personnel management is, in the words of one major text, 'a major component of the broad managerial function and has its roots and branches extending throughout and beyond each organisation' (French, 1970, p. 3; see also Strauss and Sayles, 1968). The I.P.M. definition says that personnel management 'forms part of every manager's job' as well as being the particular concern of the specialist (1974a, p. 3). This very important point means that I must go out of my way to stress that, although I am putting forward the thesis that the personnel occupation plays a *particular* part in coping with the conflicts and tensions underlying the employment of people as human resources within industrial capitalism, all members of management are involved in coping with these problems in a *general* way.

The whole range of formally rational techniques which management uses are liable to have self-defeating consequences. Sofer points out how there is 'a persisting strain in all work organisations towards the maintenance or increase in rationality or efficiency with which resources are related to ends' (1972, p. 224) and later on points out the large number of ways in which this strain towards rationality 'is limited, tempered and countered in a number of ways' (*ibid.*, p. 225). These constraints range from those of complying with societal values to those of retaining staff, accommodating the conflicting interests of groups of employees within the organisation with that of the necessity of maintaining a certain level of 'morale'. Child, in his important study of management thought, detects tensions similar to those suggested by Sofer's analysis and relates these to the dual nature of management as both a 'technical function' and a 'social grouping' (1969a, pp. 16–18).

One of the best known, if not 'classical', conceptualisations of what I see as managerial aspects of the strain between formal and material rationality is that of Barnard. Barnard differentiates between effectiveness and efficiency:

> An action is effective if it accomplishes its specific aim . . .
> it is efficient if its satisfies the motives of that aim, whether it
> is effective or not, and the process does not create offsetting
> dissatisfactions. We shall say that an action is inefficient if the
> motives are not satisfied, or offsetting dissatisfactions are
> incurred, even if it is effective (1938, p. 20).

Barnard sees an organisation as needing to be more than simply successful in achieving its goals: it has also to pay constant attention to the needs of the individuals whose co-operation is needed for the 'equilibrium' and long-term survival of the organisation. It may well appear at first sight that this formulation is the same as the Weberian one which I am adopting. This is not the case, however. Barnard's overall model is an equilibrium one which is not in effect sufficiently useful *sociologically*, in that it does not relate the problems of organisation to the underlying structural problems of the particular societal order. It tends to locate problems in terms of the psychological concept of 'needs' – something which is essentially problematic to the sociologist and inappropriate, because question-begging, to sociological analysis (*cf.*, Silverman, 1970, pp. 85–7). Barnard's insights are useful, however, and emphasise the 'long-term' versus the 'short-term' dilemma which is also central to the 'formal' versus 'material' dilemma. The solution to the dilemma, according to the school of managerial economics which follows Barnard, is that the businessman or manager 'optimises' or 'satisfices' rather than maximises. But simply to say this underestimates the extent of the problem as experienced by those in management since, within complex organisations, the criteria of short-term and long-term are often brought to bear on the individual manager at different times or in different situations or more likely – and even worse in terms of strain – at the same time by others in different functions within the managerial hierarchy. What I would suggest is that the imposition on the individual manager of conflicting criteria creates a strain, ambiguity or ambivalence which is fundamental to most aspects of the managerial occupation. A typical example here would be the production manager who is pressed by his immediate superior for more output whilst, at the same time, being forbidden to work overtime in his department by the personnel manager who is attempting to comply with, perhaps, a union agreement or a company-level policy of cost control.

Campanis, a sociologist employed at the time of writing his article by a large commercial organisation, paints an almost horrific picture of the moral ambiguities and demoralising strains suffered by the manager. Campanis shows the manager caught between the pressures of two conflicting philosophies which operate within the organisation; the 'production ethic' and the 'human relations ethic', the one being 'tough-minded' and the other a 'softie approach' (Campanis, 1970). This analysis will become very pertinent later on when I look at the relationship between personnel specialists and 'line' managers. For the present, I wish to return to the personnel specialism within management, reiterating the general point that, because personnel management is an integral part of all managerial work, the problems which I am going to argue are present in the particular case of personnel people, are not wholly peculiar to that specialism. It is, rather, that they impinge on the occupation and are experienced by those in it in particular and, in some cases, peculiar ways.

Personnel management as an occupation

Personnel management as a general component of the management of complex organisations is concerned with

> recruiting and selecting people; training and developing them
> for their work; ensuring that their payment and conditions of
> employment are appropriate, where necessary negotiating such
> terms of employment with trade unions; advising on healthy
> and appropriate working conditions; the organisation of people
> at work, and the encouragement of the most appropriate climate
> of relations between management and work people (I.P.M.,
> 1974a, p. 3).

But additional to all these being part of every manager's job, the Institute of Personnel Management statement goes on: 'it is the special concern of those employed as specialists on the management team, whether their job covers all the above aspects, or whether they specialise in one of them' (*ibid.*, p. 3). It is these specialists that I have assumed, throughout what I have written so far, to be members of an *occupation*. Although the variable 'occupation' has its problematic aspects (Gross, 1959) I am using it in a fairly straightforward way to suggest (largely) full-time employment on a part or the whole of a range of tasks which are identified under a particular heading or occupational title by both those employed on those tasks and by a wider public. Before one can be said to belong to an occupation one has to share some common identity with others doing similar work. And this identity has to be recognisable to a substantial public outside this group. The fact that one can, as I have found in my researches, telephone almost any large employing organisation and, successfully, ask for the personnel manager or officer is in itself sufficient to warrant the use of the title 'occupation'. One indication of the currency of the personnel occupational title with the widest of publics is the existence, at the time of writing, of a television 'situation comedy' series based largely on a 'personnel officer' character.[2] But such evidence does not necessarily indicate the extent of the *coherence* of the personnel occupation.

Despite the growth of the Institute of Personnel Management as a 'professionalising' body – a factor also clearly indicating the existence of what can justifiably be called an occupation – it might well be claimed that there are many officials in a variety of organisations who do in fact specialise in those areas listed by I.P.M. as aspects of personnel management but who would not see themselves in terms of the 'personnel' title. These would include local government organisations, the civil service or, most obviously, the military. Employees here would see themselves first and foremost as local government officers, civil servants, or soldiers. Yet when one examines these areas a very strong trend towards 'personnel consciousness' can be detected.

Many of those whom I interviewed in the local government field spoke of the demise of the 'estabs man' (establishments officer) and his replacement by personnel people. Fowler, in his book *Personnel Management in Local Government* (1976), sees this as a reaction against the bias towards quantitative staffing controls which was supported by the Haddow and Mallaby reports of 1934 and 1967 and which was rejected by the Bains report of 1972 (H.M.S.O.). The Bains report not only called for the development of personnel management as such but went as far as to argue that 'the human problems of management in local government are no different from those in industry' (quoted I.P.M., 1976a, p. 3). Just one consequence of the implementation of this report is the high proportion of the student members of I.P.M. to whom I have spoken who are working in local government, hospitals and so on.

The reorganisation of the civil service following the Fulton report (H.M.S.O., 1968) has seen a developing situation where, as the head of the civil service put it to an I.P.M. conference, the 'establishments man . . . has gradually been giving way to the personnel manager' (Armstrong, 1971, p. 2). Both of these developments are reflected in the growth within I.P.M. of a Public Services Group which is seen as important to the role of the Institute. As the President of the Institute said in 1973, the year after the group was formed:

> By providing training for this new body of specialists in the public sector and by assimilating them at every level of our organisation, we shall ensure that the Institute continues to speak for the whole personnel function in this country (Lyons, 1973, p. 7).

The case of the military is perhaps the extreme one here in terms of occupational identity and the I.P.M.'s membership survey of 1974 indicated that 19 per cent of members of I.P.M. work in 'public administration and *defence*' (I.P.M., 1975a, p. 3). One of my interviewees, a personnel manager and member of the T.A.V.R. explained how he had been recruited to the 'Pioneers' whom he described as 'the army's personnel people' through an advertisement in the I.P.M.'s magazine. The army was actively seeking trained personnel specialists, he explained.

All of these trends can be interpreted sociologically in terms of Weber's rationalisation thesis. All the above areas of employment involve large-scale utilisation of labour resources and all are under similar pressures to use these resources 'efficiently'. As one local government personnel officer said to me:

'We've got the same problems as anyone else who employs people on a large scale. We've got increasingly militant unions. We've got people up the top always demanding more stringent cost control. We've got the same discipline problems, motivation problems and all the rest. And we recruit from the same labour markets.'

And in all these settings the constraints on formal rationality and efficiency are similar. When I started my interview programme I saw it as an issue that would be clarified by a comparison of interview responses as to whether the problems experienced in personnel work would be essentially different in various sectors of the employment world. One of the present findings of this interview programme is that it is often difficult to see any significant differences in responses across the range of types of employment. There is, in fact, a coherence within the occupation which is far greater than I expected when I set out to investigate areas of employment some of which were, until then, unfamiliar to me. To find personnel officers and managers in banks, engineering companies, co-operative societies, council offices and so on, speaking in such similar ways on aspects of their jobs was a considerable surprise to me. To present evidence or qualification for such a general and indeed qualititative conclusion is hardly possible. But it will, I hope, become increasingly apparent as I cite cases and quote interviews from the range of areas in dealing with the various issues which arise in this and ensuing chapters.

There is another aspect of the 'coherence' of the occupation which was of equal surprise to me. This was the corresponding difficulty which I have found when examining answers to specific questions in detecting common patterns between, say, those specialising in training or, say, those dealing largely with industrial relations. And, more importantly, the pattern of responses of people operating in any one of these specialisms within personnel management is often not to any significant extent different from the general patterns. I mentioned this emergent pattern to a training manager whom I interviewed towards the end of my programme and he commented:

'There's been a marked trend for training jobs to incorporate other elements of the personnel role. I get involved in recruiting, for instance, and promotion policy and appraisal. It's all part of this human resources thing. It's a definite trend. And when it comes to the unions, believe me, I'm as hemmed in as Roberts, our I.R. man. Training's as political as anything. And talking about I.R. – they're always on about legislation and tribunals and things. I say to them: now you're like us with our I.T.B.s and always having to justify ourselves to outsiders.'

This account highlights two trends – the increasing influence of trade unions and the growth of employment legislation – both of which put specialists within personnel management increasingly in touch with each other and increasingly under similar constraints and pressures. The recruiter has to check with the manpower planner, the salary expert with the industrial relations officer, the training officer with the job evaluator and so on. And, as my evidence shows, any one of these is as liable as any other to find himself at odds with the 'line manager', who may be anything from a factory production manager to a site foreman or a social security office manager.

To add to all these points which indicate a commonness of experience among those doing personnel jobs, I have to point out that I was similarly surprised to find, in many cases, very similar answers being given to questions by directors in large organisations to, say, junior personnel officers in small ones. The overall pattern in my interview material is such, in fact, that I shall treat the one hundred as a homogeneous category of personnel specialists. This is not, however, to ignore the considerable differences between individuals. But since the differences in responses are often more closely related to individual differences rather than to categories such as age, level, industry and so on, I shall allow the differences to emerge from my reporting of individual cases.[3] On the point of the level of the individual's job in the hierarchy, I would argue that, whether the personnel specialist has the title of personnel director, officer, manager or even personnel assistant, he is to be seen as part of management. All personnel specialists are involved in the managing of human resources, however junior they may be.[4]

One of the most important factors which I have found to be contributing to what might be described as a common consciousness among personnel specialists is the generally felt and frequently re-iterated need for them to establish their status within organisations. As Anthony and Crichton have put this: 'the history of the personnel specialists as a group is the history of a struggle for status to become full members of the management team' (1969, p. 165). This theme will come out time and time again throughout this study as we see personnel specialists attempting to refute the oft-quoted attack on personnel management of the popular management writer, Drucker who saw their work as 'bankrupt' and 'partly a file-clerk's job, partly a housekeeping job, partly a social worker's job, and partly "fire-fighting" to head off union trouble or settle it' (1954, pp. 275–6).

The personnel specialist and the formal versus material rationality problem

As I have indicated before, the early roots of the personnel occupation lie in the realisation by certain employers, increasingly pushed by governments, that the formally rational techniques of utilising human resources could be counter-productive were not other criteria considered. But members of the embryo occupational group which resulted from this saw that the only way they could establish themselves was to become more involved in the direct management process. This paradoxically meant involving themselves in working in terms of formally rational criteria. This becomes very apparent in much recent writing on personnel management. For instance, when the I.P.M. launched their new 'learned' journal in 1971 they invited an eminent American writer on personnel management to write on the 'changing role of the personnel manager' and, after reviewing current trends and pressures on the function, he concluded:

> The major points outlined in this paper suggest that personnel
> managers *will* be or become more effective in their
> organisations if they *earn* the respect of their top and middle
> management by their ability to help them in the development of
> human resources to achieve organisational objectives (Myers,
> 1971, pp. 6–7).

These objectives would be profit or whatever is appropriate to non-commercial organisations, he said. This was stated even more forcefully by the editor of *Personnel* Magazine in a review of the development of personnel management published in the *Financial Times*:

> . . . if the personnel manager of today is to carry real weight
> inside his organisation, he must be a profit-minded
> money-talking businessman who is clearly and measurably seen

to contribute to the profitability of the firm (Winsbury, 1968, p. 21).

This point has been taken up and we see it reflected in an increasing range of articles appearing in the personnel journals with titles such as 'Profits must justify personnel decisions' (I.P.M., 1975b), 'Why Investment is your Business Too' (Taylor *et al.*, 1976), 'Cost Effectiveness: the Training Officer's Lifeline' (Roberts and Stone, 1975). And this has been accompanied by a whole range of formally rational, calculatively based techniques, particularly manpower planning, psychological testing and human asset accounting. This latter technique is an especially interesting one, interest in which 'has been stimulated by an I.P.M. and Institute of Cost and Management Accountants' report' (Robinson, 1973, p. 31). The language here is very much in terms of the 'efficiency of the use of human assets' (see Giles and Robinson, 1972 and, for a critical review, Cannon, 1974). Attachment to this type of ethos is in clear contradiction to the one which has long been a motivating factor in personnel management, if not its basic rationale. This is recognised by many writers on personnel management. It is clearly brought out in the I.P.M.'s own textbook where the author shows that the identification of the personnel function with management generally (and its goals) 'has worried many personnel managers and those who write on the subject' (Thomason, 1975, p. 20). And it is reflected in the I.P.M.'s prize-winning essay of 1974, the author of which comments:

> There is a very real danger that in attempting to express people in measurable money terms, we may de-humanize and alienate the very resources we are striving to conserve and develop (Rogers, P., 1974, p. 42).

These trends towards a more calculative or technically rational approach have been discussed and debated within the occupation and blows are regularly struck for one side and then the other in the correspondence columns of the I.P.M.'s journal. An editorial in this journal headed 'Are manpower planners human?' called for a détente between those who are often criticised as 'number crunchers' and their rivals, alternatively criticised as 'woolly psychologists' or 'mere welfare workers' (Pocock, 1971, p. 3). But this debate within the I.P.M. between the supporters of the two theories underlying modern personnel management goes back some decades. This was brought out in a particularly significant article by the Personnel Director of the Burton Group in an attempt to review the personnel manager's role in organisational change (Stokes, 1971). [5] Stokes sees the personnel occupation as confused about what it 'stands for' and goes back to the I.P.M. Jubilee Statement which saw the scope of personnel management as 'the human and social implications of work and organisation'. The I.P.M. was then attacked by what Stokes calls an 'efficiency lobby' led by Professor Fogarty who, he reports, wrote in the Institute's journal:

> The first concern of the personnel manager is with value for money and the main consideration should be to teach him to think in this way – as the specialist in the economic use of human beings (quoted by Stokes, p. 33).

Stokes goes on to say that 'the efficiency bandwagon has been gathering momentum ever since' (ibid., p. 33). He illustrates this by referring to the, then, recently formed Manpower Society (partly sponsored by I.P.M.), whose objectives, he says, 'have a disturbingly dehumanised ring about them':

> Personnel managers planning and producing the right number of sausages, of the right size, shape and content, as the frying pans are ready for them! It is a far cry from the days when the personnel manager was seen as the channel linking management and employees, the sounding-box for the workers, or even the conscience of the company (ibid., p. 34).

British personnel managers are seen as preoccupied with techniques and making a 'mechanistic search for the latest all-purpose problem solving kit' and Stokes quotes the message given to an I.P.M. Conference by another senior executive, Parker,[6] who 'conceded that efficiency gives management its central initiatives in modern society but emphasised that "society will settle the larger questions ultimately of – efficiency, to what purpose and at what price?" ' (ibid., p. 34). The personnel manager should, according to the Stokes/ Parker view, look more towards the community and social change. Stokes asks 'Why should workpeople be expected to adapt to our industrial society? Why not adapt the industrial society to the workpeople' (ibid., p. 35). A not dissimilar return to what is identified with the old 'welfare' ethos is also called for by a senior personnel executive and influential I.P.M. officer, Kenny (1975).

The paradoxical situation underlying personnel management, with its two competing rationales, what Miller and Coghill call the 'welfarist' and the 'technicist' (1964), creates a clear problem for any attempt to articulate a clear ideology for the occupation. How can spokesmen for the occupation or profession as an interest group articulate the interests of the group? I will consider this issue in detail in chapter 7, but for the present will point out that the tendency which the I.P.M. has followed in handling this problem has been to conceptualise the conflict between the two rationales as one between 'efficiency' and 'justice' or 'fairness'. In attempting to make a definitive pronouncement in its golden jubilee year the Institute followed what Child (1969a, p. 190) called a 'question-begging' line by stating that, 'Personnel management aims to achieve both efficiency and justice' (I.P.M., 1963).

To the sociologist it is inadequate to conceptualise the conflict of rationales in terms of a conflict between efficiency and justice or between efficiency and welfare. These terms raise the question of efficiency in terms of *whose* ends and welfare for *whom*? Because, sociologically, we view the employment relationship under industrial capitalism as creating two objectively conflicting interests – that of buyer and seller of labour – we have to locate our personnel specialist as *in the final analysis* operating in terms of one of these interests. Although the individual himself may be selling his own labour power, he is, as a member of management (as I argued above), clearly an agent of those who are doing the employing or the buying of labour power. The real conflicts in which he is involved (I am talking here in a structural sense and certainly not a psychological one at this point) are therefore only between various of the *means* which are available for the fulfilling of the organisation's (i.e. the dominant condition's) goals. Because the personnel specialist is, in the final analysis, an agent of the employer he cannot be concerned with employee welfare, or social justice *per se*. He is, however, forced to be concerned with such issues in practice because ignoring them will lead to the eventual ineffectiveness of formally rational techniques as low morale sets in, industrial conflict breaks out, labour turnover increases dangerously or, ultimately, a potentially revolutionary situation results from the general disaffection of labour.

This study is looking at a managerial occupation, and in talking about problems for members of the occupation – problems in a structural sense – our concern is therefore with problems from a managerial point of view. But these problems have a major significance at the societal level, too. Any individual personnel manager is concerned only with meeting the goals of his own top management. But if managements generally were to fail to meet their goals by failing to cope with the unintended consequences of their managerial techniques, then not only would each organisation disintegrate but the whole industrial capitalist mode of societal integration would collapse. Having reiterated this societal issue I will now proceed to illustrate some ways in which personnel specialists can become involved in the constant tension between formal techniques and material interests.

One of the major aspects of the application of formally rational thinking to industrial work is, as I have stressed earlier, the division of labour. The so-called human relations school of industrial social science showed the inadequacies of many aspects of this and its later ally, Taylorist 'scientific management' (Roethlisberger and Dickson, 1939). Many of the ideas associated with the rejection of the orthodoxy of 'scientific management' were applied by Worthy and his colleagues, operating from the personnel department of Sears Roebuck. Friedmann points out how Worthy felt that the division of labour had 'gone wild' and had gone 'far beyond what is needed for productive efficiency' (Friedmann, 1961, p. 35). An anonymous pamphlet published by the I.P.M. in 1955 took up Mayo's human relations arguments and pointed to the 'paradox' of the fact that efficiency-oriented 'techniques' could contribute to the destruction of the necessary 'mutual trust' in industrial relations (I.P.M., 1955, p. 10). The growing interest of personnel managers in such new, less restrictive, techniques as job enrichment, job enlargement and the rest can all be understood as part of an interest in coping with the problems here (see Butteriss, 1971).

Formal rationality has also been manifested in the trend towards increasingly larger organisations with consequential 'economies of scale'. But such trends can have the unintended consequences of increasing trade union consciousness (see above, chapter 2), or of creating a whole series of bureaucratic dysfunctions which can lead to what personnel managers may see as communication problems. As a 'personnel services manager' said to me, in explaining the company's house journal for which he was responsible:

'You may see our company paper as a simple hangover from our old paternal image. But I'd like to see it as one way in which we [the personnel department] can help overcome the old perennial of one department or plant working against the other or even in ignorance of the other.'

But it is in the industrial relations sphere that the personnel man is most often involved in coping with one of the 'costs' of organisational size. This has been variously described to me as the 'wage-drift problem', 'salary consistencies', 'leap-frogging claims' and so on. In the company where I was employed, one was continually referring line managers to the problem of what the company called 'read across', pointing out that to meet some small wage claim in one department could lead to claims amounting to vast sums across the company. There was an apocryphal claim for 17s. 9d. in one small area which had cost in the end, a figure variously quoted to me as £250,000, £500,000, or even £750,000.

If the phenomenon of wage-paid labour itself is seen as a basic formally rational technique then this can present a whole range of consequences with which the personnel specialist may become involved. These problems can be interpreted as deriving from what sociologists have labelled the *instrumental orientation to work*. A training manager said: 'I'm supposed to get shop-floor blokes trained for both efficiency and safety. But you try getting them to slow down a bit for instruction when it means losing bonus.'

An engineering personnel director told me,

'This constant demanding of cash by the unions just cannot go on here. It'll break us. We've got to find other ways of motivating people. When I talk about participation my line people say "not bloody likely". Yet they realise we can't go on like this . . . only getting through to people through the pay-packet.'

And a personnel manager in the same organisation referred to 'the rubbish these blokes turn out' –

'I don't know what's happened to quality control here. I stuck my neck out the other day and collared a bloke who'd left rough edges and things. He wasn't bothered though. "Why should I care", he says. He gets paid you see.'

The few personnel managers who talked about industrial democracy in a positive sense tended to see it as something which, in their industries, personnel would have to 'sell' to the line, as one man put it, 'if we're going to do our bit in keeping the place going'. I did not find public administration personnel specialists talking of participation, but a not untypical comment here was that of a civil servant involved with recruitment: 'I just can't get people like we used to have who would come and show some loyalty. They just come for the money. It's no good talking to them of public *service*.'

The personnel function increasingly finds itself utilising one formally rational technique to counter problems created by the application of other techniques based on such criteria within general management. Yet this may lead to the personnel function suffering from the clash of the two rationalities internally. A case of this which has been mentioned to me in both manufacturing industry and in the civil service is that of appraisal or career development schemes. These represent a technique whereby the treatment of employees in administrative or managerial jobs as units of labour (with the demotivating consequences of them among 'more qualified' people) is meant to be countered by procedures which ensure that the individual's progress is reviewed and the existing talents of staff are best matched to the available jobs within the organisation. The middle-class type employee, in return for commitment, is thus rewarded by a 'career'. But the personnel function, in setting up a scheme which is 'fair to all', necessarily creates a complex system of paperwork and procedures. As Henstridge has pointed out, such procedures may create expectations which, however, 'can no more

57

and no less be met *after* the introduction of such procedures than they could before. Disillusionment leads to a marked lack of co-operation in pointless procedures' (Henstridge, 1975, p. 49).

One personnel manager pointed out to me,

> 'I tried to improve our foremen's motivation by bringing them into our appraisal scheme. But, as I now realise, what careers are there here for bloody foremen? The foremen now see me and my department as bigger shit-bags than they ever did. And that's no good – to me or them or the firm.'

These are a few examples of the type of contradiction or conflict in which the personnel specialist can find himself. These are specific manifestations of a structural problem inherent in practically all personnel jobs.

Conflict, marginality and ambivalence

The structural problems inherent in the personnel jobs leave the personnel specialist in a position where he is likely to experience considerable ambiguity and tension in his work. The great paradox which underlies this position is that members of the occupation have increasingly undertaken a range of organisational tasks which would help them generally achieve managerial status within organisations and, having gone a long way towards achieving this aim, find themselves as much if not more than ever in conflict with members of the general management 'team'. The extent of the personnel executives' 'arrival' is indicated in the figures provided by salary surveys which, prior to 1975, regularly showed personnel salaries as below those of other managers. Figures quoted in December 1975, however, show personnel executives earning an average of £6,500 compared with an average for other executives (excluding managing directors and equivalent) of £6,000 (Swannack, 1975, p. 3). Another survey quoted in the same journal shows personnel board members earning more than finance directors (I.P.M., 1975c, p. 5).

But it is some of the major factors lying behind this change which put, if not the newly highly paid directors themselves, the personnel managers and officers into an increasingly marginal or conflictful relationship with general management. Swannack, a director of the consultancy company which undertook the first of the surveys cited above gives various reasons for the personnel executives' 'improvement in position' regarding salary and 'status' but picks on two in particular: 'the extra demands being made upon him as a result of Government legislation and the change in the employer/employee power ratio . . .' (*ibid.*, p. 3). Both of these forces are important sociologically because they represent challenges to long-term survival of the organisation and they represent ways in which the structural contradictions of industrial capitalist society are coped with by, on the one hand, representatives of organised labour and, on the other, by democratic institutions following the British reformist method of coping with societal strains. But both of these forces represent deflections or constraints upon the members of general management. And to a considerable extent these constraints are mediated by members of personnel departments, thus creating a conflict between the personnel manager and the line manager. I have tried to represent this situation in Figure 3.1 which includes various other factors which contribute to this effect.

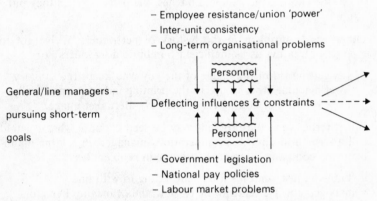

FIGURE 3.1 *Constraining influences on managers' use of labour, mediated by members of the personnel department*

The individual personnel specialist is therefore put into a position of considerable ambivalence. This is reflected in the answers which I received in reply to my question: *What is the biggest difficulty faced by the personnel manager?* The overall impression which is given by reading through all the responses here is that the ambivalence that is created by the personnel specialist's relationship to general management is one from which he or she cannot escape. Where the personnel department is not well developed in an organisation, the personnel practitioner is constantly faced with overcoming his low status and credibility in order to influence managers. But where the personnel department is well established, the specialist may find a situation developing where, as one interviewee put it,

'they come along and dump any "people problems" on us. When we try to get them to do something or see something in a wider perspective they say "that's your pigeon – that's personnel – nowt to do with us".'

59

In answering the above question, something like half the respondents gave an answer on the lines that the biggest problem is 'gaining acceptance', 'establishing credibility', 'selling the service' or simply 'persuading'. Whereas some of these responses were not specific about with whom they were seeking credibility, or implied that it was a general problem for those in personnel, we find a significant majority suggesting the problem is with regard to management. Sometimes management itself is blamed:

> 'the problem is getting an agreement with management to a policy or going down a particular avenue. The greatest problem is not with organised labour but with disorganised management . . . the cliques, the personal bitches, the petty barriers they put up.'

Others see a problem in the history of personnel: 'We've got to stop them treating us as inefficient bumbling do-gooders', or

> 'It's getting rid of the image of the guy who keeps the sanitary towel machine stocked up. In the printing industry, specifically, it's a question of getting rid of the old paternalist image.'

But, alternatively, the problem may be seen as more what I would call a structural one. A 'remunerations manager' in a large manufacturing company thought that the main problem was

> 'knowing just what his job is and fitting in with line management. He tends to be close to the Managing Director and is therefore bound by the constraints of the business as a whole. But the line are not aware of the general company position – they're not aware of the totality of the problem.'

It might surprise laymen to find members of what is an essentially managerial occupation being more worried about its relationship with management than about anything else. They might well expect a significant concern to be about, say, employee resistance to management or with trade union activity. However, only four respondents mentioned industrial relations conflicts in a unilateral sense: as a problem arising from union initiatives (e.g. 'the new militancy of the unions in the public sector').[7] The seventeen others who saw the greatest difficulty in terms of industrial conflict saw it in bilateral terms, for example: 'It's having to try to equate opposing demands all the time: what different groups want and others can give.' The general relationships of personnel specialists to managers is that of the staff department to the line. The personnel manager paradoxically does not *manage* (apart from his own subordinates who may include canteen staff, etc.). As the I.P.M. statement on personnel careers puts it:

It is not the personnel manager's job to manage people, but to provide the specialist knowledge or services that can assist other members of the management team to make the most effective use of the human resources – people – of the organisation (I.P.M., 1974a, p. 3).

This means that the role is officially an advisory one and this contributes enormously to the ambiguity of the personnel manager's job. He can officially only advise, yet for reasons ranging from the pressure of trade unions and the growth of employment legislation to the overly parochial or short-term concerns of line managers, he is forced more and more towards interventionist action. This ambiguity is reflected in many of the accounts given in response to my question *How do you see the role of the personnel department in the organisation – what role does it play?* Thus: 'It's advisory. The line manager must run the shop. But with all the correct legislation it's advice which *must* be followed.' Some respondents appear partially to welcome a more executive role:

'You have to accept being basically advisory – however much you want to get things done. But because of this – the need to get your teeth into problems – we are increasingly taking on executive responsibilities. We have to.'

The extent of the potential conflict with general management is apparent in the following account:

'. . . there's always the union pressure requiring consistency. This is all tending to push personnel managers into a line role. This is the route to industrial disaster because you're taking away from the poor bastards the only thing they've got left to manage.'

Whereas the responses to this question on the role of the personnel department tend not to follow any particular pattern in terms of respondents' age, industry, level and the rest, there is an apparent tendency for that type of account which sees an inevitable, if sometimes reluctantly faced, usurping of line authority, to come from those who have a high industrial relations component in their job.

The accounts of the personnel department which saw it primarily as there to 'help people', 'develop individuals' or to act as the 'conscience of management' – reflecting an older personnel ethos – also tended to come from respondents at all levels, at all ages, in all sub-specialisms and so on. There were fourteen responses of this kind, and I would not wish to overstress the difference between these and the most popular type of account, given by a quarter of the interviewees, where the personnel role is described as 'providing a service

to management', 'assisting the line' or 'providing the right environment for management to do its job'. The difference between those
appearing to give emphasis to management and those mentioning
'people' is less than it might seem since the latter group of accounts
often add that it is through helping people that management is
served. The general availability of the two accounts reflects the
general ambivalence of the occupation, I suggest.

There is one remaining group of accounts which can be seen as
containing a common emphasis, and this is the group of twenty
accounts which saw the personnel role as based on 'communications'
or being a 'placator', 'oiler of the works', 'a buffer' or 'a safety
valve'. I am very reluctant to rely too much in my analysis on a
technique which draws into categories what are in effect individual
accounts. I simply do this for indicative purposes. In this latter case
I suggest that we can see an indication of some popularity in a view
of the personnel specialist as, to use a commonly used phrase, the
'man in the middle'. Knowing that such a conception does exist
within the personnel occupation, I included in my interviews a
question specifically raising this issue. The idea of the personnel
specialist as a marginal man or woman looking 'two ways at once'
is a view which reflects what I see as the essential ambiguity in the
role. The responses to my question of this will be considered together
with a much more detailed consideration of the range of issues
arising from the relationship between personnel and other managers
within organisations in chapter 8.

What I have attempted to do in this chapter is to establish the
existence of a common type of problem which underlies the occupational situation of all those working in personnel management at a
range of levels, ages, and qualifications and in a variety of sub-
specialisms and types of employing organisation. I have argued for
the existence of these problems, which are to be seen throughout
management, albeit in a less specific way, by way of both a sociological or structural analysis and also by demonstrating certain ways in
which inherent problems for the occupation are reflected in the
personnel literature and in the accounts given to me by practitioners
in the interview context. All of this is informed, of course, by my
own observations and experiences as a former employee in the
personnel field. I have used words like conflict, tension, ambiguity
and ambivalence to characterise the situation of the personnel
specialist. Such terms are frequently used by other commentators.[8]
Henstridge, for instance, in his analysis of the 'phenomenon of
personnel management' comments that 'much has been written of
the confusion which exists over the Personnel Manager's role – both
his own sense of ambiguity and the uncertainty of line and top
management'. But Henstridge tends to explain these problems in

terms of the youth of the 'profession' and says, 'Problems of role . . . originate primarily in the lack of clear comprehension of the function and purpose of Personnel Management' (1975, p. 50). Thomason, in the I.P.M.'s textbook, finds 'a foundation for understanding the ambivalence so often associated with the function' in the 'two diverse origins' of the occupation, 'the one paternalistically orientated towards the welfare of the employees and the other rationally derived from corporate needs to control' (1975, p. 26).

Both the above analyses are valuable: it is reasonable to refer to 'misunderstandings', as most personnel workers would endorse, and my own analysis has indicated the importance of what Thomason calls the 'historically-associated differences of orientation' (*ibid.*, p. 39) within the occupation. But what I am concerned to emphasise is that the problems of tensions and conflicts are not to be understood as simply characteristic of a stage of development of an occupation with a certain history. Were the occupation to completely throw off its welfare image, for example, societal factors would nevertheless force members to operate within criteria which can still be conceptualised in welfare terms, as Kenny has emphasised (1975). The problems of conflict and ambivalence are intrinsic and essential ones, not temporary ones, as long as personnel management is centrally involved with the utilisation of human resources within a capitalistic industrial society. The members of personnel departments are forced to pay attention to both the formally rational criteria of productivity, profit, effectiveness and the rest as well as the human needs, interests and aspirations of employees which, if not attended to, may lead to the formally rational means subverting the substantively rationally conceived ends of the ultimate controllers of the organisations. The problem of ambivalence is thus one of what Merton and Barber call *sociological ambivalence* which refers to 'incompatible normative expectations of attitudes, beliefs, and behaviour designed to a status or to a set of statuses in a society' (1963, p. 95). Although I use a very different sociological paradigm and terminology from that of these authors, my theoretical analysis has attempted to do something similar to Merton and Barber's in that it

> deals with the processes through which social structures generate the circumstances in which ambivalence is embedded in particular statuses and status-sets together with their associated social roles (*ibid.*, p. 95).

4 Occupational entry

The personnel management occupation has been shown as emerging from a situation in which those controlling large-scale organisations sought to cope with some of the problems of utilising 'human resources' and where those undertaking such tasks became increasingly involved in managerial work itself. Such a situation together with recent societal changes which have involved an intensification of industrial relations activity and an increase in employment legislation has not only crystallised the personnel role, giving it a coherent occupational existence, but has made it an occupation whose members are faced with handling some of the fundamental tensions and contradictions underlying employment and management. Their own position is one involving ambivalence and conflict. At this stage in the present study the focus will be less on the societal or organisational aspects of the personnel occupation and more on the individual's experience within it. A major concern will be with how individuals cope with the ambiguities and conflicts which their work involves, although this will be even more central to chapter 5. Once the individual's orientations and 'adjustments' have been dealt with I will return to adjustments at the occupational level with an examination of the professionalisation strategy, in chapter 6. For the moment, however, attention will be turned to the processes whereby individuals eventually find themselves working within the occupation of personnel management.

Theories of occupational choice

There is now a considerable body of literature dealing with what is generally referred to as 'occupational choice'. The problem with this literature, with regard to its applicability to the problems with which I am concerned here, is that it is segmented into different approaches.

The approaches vary with the purposes which have informed their development and with the theoretical assumptions upon which they have been based, these assumptions not always having been made explicit by the various authors. Because all of the existing approaches have something to offer the present analysis I will review them briefly before going on to an attempt to counter their partiality by extending my own theoretical scheme to provide a framework for considering the occupational entry and orientations to work of personnel specialists. The nature of the existing literature in this area is, I suggest, a reflection of the situation in the sociology of work as I pictured it in chapter 1. Occupational choice, entry to work, or however it is conceptualised, has been tackled as a compartmentalised area, not only in many cases too far away from the main stream of sociology, but often, if not most typically, as if it were little related to other aspects of work orientation, organisation and experience. I hope that this will become apparent in the following brief review.

Taken as a whole, the literature on occupational choice equivocates on the question of whether there is, in fact, *choice* or anything like it. Different approaches within the literature have either emphasised the existence of choices or sought to indicate the lack of opportunity for what can realistically be called 'choice'. Pavalko writes of two general approaches:

> One approach emphasises the deliberate, planned, rational and purposive nature of occupational choice. The other characterisation views occupational choice as more spontaneous, non-rational and adventitious. According to this perspective, individuals are seen as 'drifting' into occupations by virtue of situational influences and pressures (Pavalko, 1972, p. 78).

Taylor points out how the early theories suggested that occupational choosing is characterised by 'rational decision-making' (1968, p. 193) whilst the trend then moved towards viewing it in terms of what Slocum calls 'a continuum of rationality, with decisions ranging from those made purely on impulse to those which may be regarded as fully rational' (Slocum, 1959, p. 143). One researcher, Roe, describes how, contrary to her expectations, her researches indicated how the 'subjects find themselves reacting to the external influences and contingencies in their lives without much sense of choice or responsibility' (Roe, 1964, p. 19). Examination of empirical studies of particular occupations reveals studies such as that of Sherlock and Cohen who, in the recruitment to dentistry, locate a 'strategy of occupational choice' (1966). In contrast, we find studies such as that by Katz and Martin of nurses stressing that '"situationally delimited" actions are deemed to be basic ingredients' in the process of embarking on a career (1962, p. 154). I wish to argue that this equivocation within the literature results from the inadequacy of the extent to which the research and theorising is set within a satisfactory sociological framework. By this I mean a framework which allows for the essentially dialectical relationship between individual action and structural constraint. Only when we have such a framework can we cope with *both* what Ford and Box call the *purposive* and the *adventitious* aspects (1967, p. 287). As Sofer shows, there are fundamental problems in deciding what is purposive or rational, outside an 'action' frame of reference (1974, p. 36). Such a framework has not, generally, been used in studies of occupational entry.

One could hardly expect such a framework to be used in one of the most influential approaches, that which Roberts labels the 'developmental theory' (1975, pp. 134-5). This approach draws on the perspectives of developmental psychology (Roberts, 1975; Zytowski, 1968, pp. 119-20) and the best-known writers here are Ginzberg *et al.* (1951) and Super (1957). This type of approach sees the individual passing through a series of stages during which process a self-concept grows as his or her abilities, aptitudes and interests develop and, in the light of various situational factors, an appropriate occupational choice is eventually made. Roberts indicates a fit between this theory and the growth of a vocational-guidance occupation in America and argues that when one looks at evidence now available, one can see that the theory is 'quite simply . . . wrong' (1975, p. 138). I would hesitate to condemn this approach quite so totally and would point out its value in stressing, together with early sociological writers on the topic (Miller and Form, 1951), the processual aspect of the individual's approach towards employment. The main criticisms of the developmental theory, however, are of its ability to do justice to the *extent* of the objective constraints on the individual's development and ultimate career entry.

Sociological approaches in questioning the extent to which one is free to choose do not have to make career entry entirely adventitious. As Dunkerley points out, what the individual sees as an 'accident' can involve as much 'determinism . . . as in the situation where the individual can claim to have made a rational decision about his occupation' (Dunkerley, 1975, p. 10). But it is precisely over the issue of determinism that many sociological theories can be attacked. The widely criticised functionalist theory of stratification (Davis and Moore, 1945) contains an implicit theory of career choice and, like all functionalist approaches, is liable to be criticised as giving an 'oversocialised conception of man' (Wrong, 1961). Musgrave's more recent attempt to develop a sociological theory (1967) is open to the same criticism (cf. Coulson *et al.*, 1967). Perhaps the most valuable among the sociological approaches is that of Roberts (1968; 1975). His structure-opportunity model shows how job opportunities are cumulatively structured and how young people are placed in varying degrees of social proximity with different ease of access to different types of employment. And, as Sofer puts it, 'according to Roberts, it is careers that determine ambitions' (1974, p. 52). The value of this approach is that it lays stress on the constraining factors in the social and economic structure of society without ignoring the psychological processes involved in what is, in effect, an adaptation of aspirations to perceived realities. Here people are not role-playing puppets (see Coulson, 1972) yet neither are they free to pursue whatever ends they may wish. As Timperley has commented, however, a limitation of the model may be that it concentrates on entry into employment and does not deal with subsequent job choices (1974a, pp. 87–8) and this is a point to which I shall return shortly. The model is well supported by its value in empirical analysis as it is utilised by Roberts and, theoretically, can be seen as compatible with a social action frame of reference. *Occup Choice*

The social action framework and the claims for it with regard to the sociology of work is generally associated with the writing of Goldthorpe, Lockwood *et al.* (1968) and their notion of the individual's *orientation to work*. Their analysis stresses the importance of the way workers choose their employment and how this has to be understood in terms of 'what *meaning* work has for them' – this having to do with 'the way in which workers order their wants and expectations relative to their employment' (1968, p. 36). These insights are of prime significance for the sociology of work but their particular formulation by these authors is open to various criticisms as I indicated earlier (p. 12). There is the danger of over-emphasis on 'prior orientations' (Beynon and Blackburn, 1972; Wedderburn and Crompton, 1972) and another of being insufficiently *dynamic* – of paying too little attention to situational factors within the work experience (cf. Daniel, 1973; see also Brown, 1973). Further, there may be insufficient stress on the structural context at the societal level: as Mackenzie argues, community and kinship relationships are important in shaping prior orientations – 'But the crucial fact remains that community and family structure are shaped by the industrial and therefore the occupational structure of a particular area or region' (1974, pp. 242–3). It is ironic that this is just the point that the earlier work of Lockwood had emphasised (*ibid.*) and this brings me back to my earlier point that the various approaches to work entry or choice have tended to have been developed within the context of tackling specific issues or with particular purposes. This part of the Goldthorpe, Lockwood, *et al.* study was concerned to refute one specific existing approach within industrial sociology: the 'technological implications' approach. The generality of the relevance of the analysis of these authors is thus reduced by their concern to illuminate the experiences and meanings of manual workers in the light of an alternative analysis of similar but workplace bound issues. My intention is to take over their insights and use them in a more general model.

Silverman, in his attempt to indicate the appropriateness of an action approach to the study of organisations, brings out one weakness of the approach of Goldthorpe, Lockwood, *et al.*, this being that

> one may miss the way in which people's views of themselves and of their situation is the outcome of an on-going process i.e. never fully determined by one or another set of structural constraints but always in the act of 'becoming', as successive experiences shape and re-shape a subjective definition of self and of society (Silverman, 1970, pp. 184–5).

This corresponds precisely to my requirement for a notion of *dynamic orientations*, and Silverman finds the required emphasis in the Chicago school within the sociology of work and occupations and the work of, particularly, Hughes and Becker. Yet as I have argued (p. 8) and Silverman indicates (1970, p. 185) this tradition has operated relatively autonomously within the sociological study of work, organisation, etc. Particularly useful within the Chicago approach are the concepts of career and the idea of adjustment to ongoing situational contingencies. This scheme, as I develop it below, will be such that it can incorporate insights from the Chicago approach, but the ideas of people like Hughes and Becker will be more explicitly utilised to help with the problems tackled in chapter 5. This work has not influenced the study of occupational choice a great deal, although we can see its relevance in Haystead's utilisation of Glaser and Strauss's notion of 'awareness contexts' (Haystead, 1974; Glaser and Strauss, 1964). Glaser and Strauss's work is generally relevant here in that it takes the concept of *career*, which is valuable in its bringing together of the subjective and objective aspects of work, and applies it in the *organisational* context (see Glaser, 1968). And this need is a very important one because little of the literature on 'occupational choice' has paid much attention to the work organisation – despite the fact that the bulk of work in modern society is within organisations. One of the few writers to come to terms with the importance of organisations here is Timperley (1974a, 1974b) who points out that it is through their control of entry that organisations exert, in an important respect, their power (1974b, p. 36). Although Roberts's important analysis concentrates on initial entry to work, he does, in his later article, quote the research of Freedman (1969) who examined the personnel records of five American companies and shows that 'once hired, individuals'

positions and prospects, and consequently their actual career movements, are substantially determined by the "organisational opportunity structures" in which they become enmeshed' (Roberts, 1975,
p. 141).

The above review of the literature on 'occupational choice' and
career movement does, I hope, indicate my overall argument about
the unfortunate subdividing within the sociology of work. But my
critique does not simply derive from an *a priori* dissatisfaction with
the discipline. Although what I have written above does not explicitly
discuss the case of the personnel specialist and his career, my points
are all informed by or, if you like, *grounded* in my empirical investigations. Similarly my own theory is reflexively related to my
research experience, neither one preceding the other. The distinctiveness of my contribution to the study of occupational entry processes
derives from my examination of the case of an occupation which is
characterised by being a bureaucratic one, an emergent one and one
whose nature is more ambiguous than many others. The case of the
personnel specialist will indicate the need for any general theory of
occupational 'choice' to recognise that occupations can be entered
at points in one's career later than the initial entry to work, that
career 'status passages' are very much influenced by organisational
structures and strategies, and that occupational socialisation and
identity is very much to be understood in terms of situational adjustments as well as 'prior orientations'. Having pointed this out I
shall now extend the theoretical scheme which has so far been
applied at societal and organisational levels to apply it at the individual level.

An alternative model

My theoretical scheme has already been established on the level of
social life in general, at the level of capitalist industrial society and
at the organisational level. Organisations result from the process of
bureaucratisation which is, in turn, part of the wider process of
rationalisation. Since the rationalisation process is to be understood
largely as a development of various *means* by which dominant social
groups establish themselves and maintain their advantaged position
in the social order, we can see that organisations are a fundamental
element of the political order in society.[1] Inasmuch as work is made
available by those controlling organisations, we can see that the
structure of opportunities is related to the political order of society
and hence to the type of society itself. I gave my definition of
organisations earlier (p. 45) and suggested that the individuals who
came together in an organisation (some to 'be directed and co-
ordinated by others towards the achievement of certain specific

69

tasks') more or less accept that their efforts are co-ordinated by certain of their number (this leading to a structuring *horizontally* into a division of labour and *vertically* into an authority or control structure). The individuals who seek employment in an organisation will approach it with (a) *different amounts of resources* (cash, materials, knowledge, skills, physical strength, etc.) and (b) *differing motives, interests and expectations* (to make a living, enjoy work, achieve power or status, etc.). What I would stress here is that both of these, the resources and the expectations will, to a large extent, be informed by the *social groups* from which he comes. Particularly relevant here will be his social class, family and educational experience. His educational experience will tend to be important in that it will mediate between his family and class background and the expectations which he will have of work. And because those social groups which are most advantaged have general ascendancy in the variety of institutional spheres of capitalist industrial society, stability with respect to the distribution of advantage tends to follow from this structured pattern of resources and expectations at the point of entry to employing organisations. Put simply, the higher in the hierarchy of social groups from which the individual comes, the more likely will he or she be to have both the resources and the orientations appropriate to eventual employment at the higher levels within the organisation. Thus the structure of opportunities in employment, both at the point of entry and with regard to the subsequent employment career, are closely related to the overall social order and, particularly, to the class structure and its ramifications in the spheres of family, socialisation and education. Such an insight is fundamental to a *sociological* model of occupational entry and career passage.

The possession of resources relevant to employment, together with a set of interests and expectations, contributes to the making of an *implicit contract* between the employer and the employee.[2] I treat this concept as fundamental to the employee's definition of the situation with regard to his employment. It is fundamental to his *orientation to work*.[3] The employee's orientation to work involves a balancing of a variety of positive and negative factors as suggested in Table 4.1.

Any individual entering an employing organisation, whether he is the chairman's son with a business degree or an unqualified young labourer, can be seen, in the light of the resources he brings to the organisation and the expectations and motives deriving from these and his family, education and community background, as defining his situation in terms of a balance between factors of the type shown in Table 4.1.[4] Whilst this model recognises the importance of *instrumentalism* and the cash-nexus it does take us further by bringing into the analysis other factors which will inform the nevertheless essentially calculative or rational process of occupational decision making. The model is firmly within an action frame of reference but puts the 'purposive' in the context of the 'structurally constraining'.

TABLE 4.1

Costs (−)	Rewards (+)
(a) Effort (physical)	(a) Wage/salary and fringe benefit
(b) Effort (impairment etc.)[5]	(b) Intrinsic rewards (fulfilment)
(c) Surrender of autonomy and acceptance of control by the employer and/or his agents	(c) Security
	(d) Power, enhanced autonomy (esp. through exercise of power)
	(e) Status/prestige
	(f) Potential advancement (career)

The model also allows us to recognise the dynamic aspect of orientations in that, despite the fact of the conditioning by extra-organisational and biographical factors, the implicit contract is constantly balanced on a knife-edge. The slightest shift in market situation, the smallest technical change or any other way in which those controlling the organisation (and, lower down, their agents) alter their requirement of the individual, so may there arise a defined imbalance between the two sides of the 'equation'. Redefining may be influenced by changes internal or external to the organisation and very often the redefinition may result from the articulation of interest with regard to any changes by spokesmen associated with any group to which the individual belongs.[6]

Entry to the personnel occupation – four modes

I shall now turn to my interview material to examine the ways in which personnel specialists can be seen as entering their occupation and establishing careers within it. At this stage I shall follow a procedure which corresponds to the 'biographical approach' used by Krause (1971, chap. 2). I have closely examined the answers given to me by the respondents to a set of questions relating to occupational entry, and I have then allocated each of my respondents to one of four different modes of entry. In reporting cases of each type I shall here be incorporating into each case descriptive material included in response to the questions in Section 2 of the interview schedule. (See

Appendix 2.) My grouping of individual cases is, again, hesitant, pointing to the indicative purpose of such an exercise which inevitably involves a degree of arbitrariness – each account being, in fact, unique. The four modes of entry, each with sub-modes are as follows:

I Initial choosers

Personnel work is more-or-less the initial career

(a) in response, primarily, to an advertisement
(b) after a process of eliminating other possibilities ('negative choice')
(c) as a first choice ('positive choice')

II Employee-initiated career change (positive)

Occupational entry during career largely at employee's initiative with career advancement a major motive

(a) from manual work
(b) from clerical/secretarial work
(c) from supervisory/manual work
(d) shift in career setting

III Employee-initiated career change (negative)

Occupational entry during career largely at employee's initiative with rejection of or incapacity in previous work

(a) dissatisfaction with previous work
(b) health problem in previous work

IV Organisation-initiated career change

Where an employing organisation has initiated the employee's move into personnel

(a) asked to join the organisation to do personnel work
(b) development of previous job
(c) general

The numbers of people falling into each category are given in Table 4.2.
Before commenting on or interpreting this pattern I shall illustrate each of the categories.

TABLE 4.2   *Four modes of entry to personnel work (total 100)*

I *Initial choosers*		II *Employee-initiated change (positive)*	
I(a) advert response	4	II(a) Manual	7
I(b) 'negative' choice	7	II(b) Clerical	5
I(c) 'positive' choice	13	II(c) Supervisory/managerial	13
		II(d) Career shift	4
Total	24	Total	29
III *Employee-initiated change (negative)*		IV *Organisation-initiated change*	
III(a) dissatisfaction	17	IV(a) asked to join organisation	2
III(b) health	3	IV(b) development of previous job	4
		IV(c) general	21
Total	20	Total	27

I Initial choosers

The 24 respondents here are all people who entered personnel work as more or less their initial career. The first sub-category (Ia) are those who were looking for jobs and 'came across' advertisements for personnel jobs. All four of the members of this category were women. A typical example is a 24-year-old personnel assistant in an engineering company, whose father is an accountant and whose mother had been a secretary.

She did not think of any particular job when young, but when taking 'A' levels at the local further education college decided that she 'fancied teaching'. Consequently she went to a teacher training college but did not enjoy the work and left. At this point, she says, 'I didn't want to be a secretary. I wanted a bit more. But there aren't many opportunities in the town.' She then saw an advertisement for the present job and, thinking it 'a bit different' applied. She had associated personnel work with industrial relations and with clerical work and record keeping. An initial appeal was 'the contact with people' but the large amount of clerical routine in the present job and the location in a divisional as opposed to a plant office means a lot of boredom. Her ideal job would be in personnel management but in a *plant* where there would be 'involvement'. 'One part of me wants lots of responsibility but the other half is not ambitious,' she comments.[7]

The people in the second sub-category (Ib) are of both sexes and all 7 are graduates, in their twenties and thirties, who, in the pattern of their occupational entry, follow a very similar pattern. I have called them 'negative choosers' following the comment of a typical member of this group who said, 'It was a negative sort of choice really – like for a number of people I know who came into Personnel at the same time I did.'

An example here is a 29-year-old male sociology graduate, the son of a sales director. He 'didn't have much idea of what he wanted to do' when at school and 'therefore went on to university'. On graduating he considered 'either Personnel about which I knew nothing and Marketing about which I learned something and didn't like what I found.' He asked himself, 'What am I to do with a sociology degree? I didn't want to teach and so I tried Personnel.' Although the industrial relations work appeals a lot ('because of the constantly changing situation'), he finds 'the routine side boring'. His ideal job would be 'something involving a lot of foreign travel – Marketing, perhaps, but it would have to be at a high level; none of the foot in the door stuff.'

A 25-year-old female personnel officer whose father is a civil servant and who, as a child, wanted to be a ballet dancer or air hostess, but studied languages at university on leaving school said:

'It was a choice after university. I didn't want to go into teaching or to use my degree in any direct way. I thought vaguely of social work but saw the danger of getting too involved. I thought of industry as one of the more "humane" fields. It could fulfil the same desire to help people. I thought recruitment would be particularly interesting. And it was a good field for women. I didn't want a job telling people what to do. And I wanted a job where I could improve things.'

The third sub-category of the 'initial choosers' (Ic) consists of a group of 13 people about whom we can perhaps most realistically talk of occupational *choice*. I shall illustrate this largely graduate category with two examples. The first is a 27-year-old industrial relations officer in electrical manufacturing who had, as a child, wanted to be a doctor and, later, a minister of religion, something which led him to take a social sciences degree. It was whilst he was an undergraduate that he came upon personnel management:

'I discovered Personnel basically by chance I suppose. I had to do a project on my degree. This brought me into this company

74

to collect material. I was overwhelmed by the experience. I
liked the problems, the involvement with people at a high level
and, in fact, I got hooked.'

His ideal job 'would be in Personnel although, if I could fantasize,
I'd like to run a field centre in the Lake District'.

My second example here is one of the 3 members (of the 13) who
are aged over 35. He is a senior personnel executive in a very large
group. He is aged 45 and his father was an accountant. As a child he
wanted to be a pilot. 'This lasted through the war and then I wanted
to be a radio announcer. Later I was confused and tried teaching for
a term after leaving school. This wasn't challenging enough so I
thought of industry. The army changed my ideas and gave me the
idea of Personnel.' After the army he took a degree, specialising in
sociology and 'clearly decided to go for Personnel in industry.
Welfare had nothing to do with this but I was slightly "left of centre".
The appeal was in motivating people and influencing things.' His
ideal job would be as the Personnel Director of a medium-sized
company.

II Employee-initiated change (positive)

This is the largest single category and includes all those who came
into Personnel from other work and who, as far as I can judge, did
so largely at their own as opposed to the employer's initiative
(although inevitably there is always an element of both: the distribution between this and the 'organisation-initiated' category is ultimately based on the emphasis given in the respondent's account). As
with all the material being dealt with at present we have to remind
ourselves that these are 'accounts' which people are giving of their
biographies – with all the elements of rationalisation and justification
that to the ethnomethodologists would warn us to expect (see Scott
and Lyman, 1968, and, also, Mills, 1967). The first sub-category
(IIa) are those who started in manual work. My first example is a
labour officer in an ordnance factory, aged 44, and ambitious to
become a senior industrial relations manager. As a child, in Durham,
he wanted to work in something where he 'could wield power for
good' –

'My parents insisted that I wasn't to go into the pit. They
wanted me to go into a clerical job. . . . My father was an
aspiring type of working man. I went into steel, though, and
was active in the union. I trained with the union for full-time
union work. But then I failed to get into Nuffield and saw
redundancies coming in steel. So I got into this business. I took

exams here to get onto the clerical side but was lucky enough to get "boarded" for this job, which I got.'

My second example here is a 27-year-old factory personnel officer in the food industry. His father is a 'production manager'. This man had wanted to be a chef or butcher as a child and on leaving secondary modern school went into a butcher's shop. He studied part-time to improve his qualifications and 'worked up to shop-manager, then onto a management traineeship on the manufacturing side. I got on well with people here and liked helping people. They offered me a training officer's job. This appealed to my ambition and from there I've got onto this job.' He gets 'a lot of job satisfaction' in the present job but, ideally, would like to be a social worker.

Here are two different types from within this sub-category; one whose 'advancement' was connected with union work and another whose main concern was a straightforward one of career advancement (career opportunity being perhaps a more realistic possibility in retailing than in more factory-based manual work).

The second sub-category (IIb) are 5 women who are all very similar to the hosiery industry personnel officer, aged 37:

'As a kid I'd wanted to be an air hostess. . . . I got engaged at 19 which changed all that. I'd been doing clerical work to fill in before going to train but once I saw this becoming permanent I got fed up with it. So I "temped" to look around and met this super woman doing a super job – Personnel. This encouraged me to get a secretary's job in a personnel office. I got this because of my Red Cross training. . . . After I had the kids I thought it would be good to get a personnel job – they might like a more mature person. So I got in here . . . I've a lot of sympathy for the workers but I have high aspirations. I want to be part of THEM – the management.'

Ideally she would like 'a combination of my present job and the Directors!'

The IIc sub-category include several working in local government who, with the reorganisation to which I referred in the previous chapter, took the opportunity, as several put it, 'to get up a grade':

'I'd been in O and M and saw my chance to get up a grade on reorganisation. Salary was my main motive here. The vacancy was for a senior personnel assistant and I got the job instead of better qualified people with less knowledge of local government. The boss knew me and what I could do.'

Four of the members of the category had been draughtsmen. One of these, whose father was a civil servant, is now the personnel director of a major industrial organisation:

'At 14 I remember thinking I'd like to do something flexible, something dealing with strange situations where I could use my qualities. I went into engineering by sheer chance and, being very practical, worked as a draughtsman. I liked the job. I was gifted at it and became the training draughtsman. I met a central personnel man and I saw a chance to get off the board. I said that I would like his job. So I got into Personnel.'

Prior to this his impression of Personnel had been of something 'tatty, down at heel'. The idea of being in business for himself appeals to him although 'I'd be happy in anything; a surgeon or a judge.'

The remaining sub-category here (IId) includes one man who came into personnel work after an army career, another one after an RAF career (both of these saw their military jobs as very personnel-oriented), whilst a third entered from a colonial police career. The fourth was a WRAC officer from an army family, the army being her 'first love'. She is currently a job evaluation manager.

'I left the WRAC to get married. I had always got on well with people and when I applied for a personnel job it was because I saw it as an outlet for my enthusiasm. I did a crash I.P.M. course to become fully professional although I could have got in on my WRAC experience. . . . I want a job in senior management. I want to see equal opportunities for women, and equal status, but by the right way – not by all this women's lib.'

III Employee-initiated change (negative)

Three out of this category of 20 were people who entered personnel work because they needed a less physically demanding job than they had been in, for reasons of health (IIIb). One of these was a nurse who had been injured in a car accident and another had been a railway operating manager who, by the time his health made such work difficult, was 'too old for accountancy training, so it had to be Personnel'. Although the ex-nurse would ideally return to nursing, the ex-operating-manager is now an enthusiastic personnel man and an I.P.M. 'activist'. The main group within this category (IIIa), however, consist largely of employees within large organisations which enabled them to internally transfer and thus leave work with which they were less than satisfied. Several were local government officers taking their chance to get away from clerical or management services work on reorganisation and, in industry, we find a number of engineers and chemists who were looking for work outside the

77

career in which they felt they had become trapped. Two others came into personnel work from teaching careers, having felt that they were in teaching only because of the way, as one put it: 'the school channelled you. You were good at French and so you read French at university. And then what do you do? Teach, of course.' One man, now a personnel director, and with an ambition to be a managing director of a firm 'of 5000 and no more', had been in line management with which he became dissatisfied:

> 'I went onto the personnel side largely because I saw such a desperate need for training. I could get things organised and all the jobs I've had since then have been in Personnel and they've all been ones I've been invited to take – "head-hunted", you know.'

IV Organisation-initiated change

The size of this particular category, 27 people, is to be understood, I suggest, as related to the emergent nature of the personnel occupation and the fact that the growth in the occupation has been a concomitant of the rapid increase in the problems and demands of the large-scale employment of labour. In examining this category of entrants to personnel work I shall look at the range of entrants across the category to show the extent to which organisations have had actively to seek out staff for their growing personnel functions. The Industrial Training Act of 1964 saw employers being pressured to appoint training officers and several members of this category came into personnel in this way. We find a former accountant being asked to go into training by his management, a college lecturer being 'recruited by the company' and a departmental manager who had 'always been a good persuader' being 'reorganised into a training job'. Several of those in the civil service and in banking had been, as one put it, 'more or less drafted into the growing Personnel side'. Although many people have told me, during my researches, that a lot of people are 'pushed' or 'shunted' into personnel work to 'get them out of the way', I came across only one or two cases where I gained an impression of this having happened (nobody, not surprisingly, admitted to this having happened to them!). I suggest that in several cases people were moved into personnel work to the convenience of both the personnel area and the area which was losing the individual but there were other cases where people were moved primarily because of particularly relevant skills or experience. A good example is that of the industrial relations manager of a very large company which has only felt the impact of unionisation in recent years:

'I've got no great interest in Personnel other than I.R. I'm not looking for promotion in this field. I was a line manager and found personnel people an interfering lot. . . . I was the manager of the only part of the company that had any real trade union activity – I was at the sharp end of the growth of unionism here. The company wanted me in this job, as the "expert". I didn't want to leave line management but they were running down my area so I gave in. I like I.R. – find it fascinating. There's a lot to be done. . . . I've no ideal job. I used to want to run a small shop of my own but I am very absorbed and interested in this job.'

There are three members of this category who had applied to large employers for unspecified employment and had been allocated to personnel work early in their appointments. One of these was a graduate who had been doing temporary manual work before joining the National Health Service whilst two others were men who applied to the same company for work, one on leaving and giving up his course at medical school and the other on leaving a Catholic seminary.

Entry to the personnel occupation – generalisations

The theoretical scheme which was set out earlier assumes rationality on the part of the person approaching an occupation. He takes into account the resources which he possesses and, in the light of these and his interests and aspirations, he moves towards an implicit contract with an employer who can offer work which is consonant with his expectations and ability (the availability of jobs itself being a factor informing the expectations). Both his resources and his prior orientations are related to the social groups to which he belongs and, particularly, to his social class and educational experience. We can now examine the patterns of occupational entry and career in terms of the variables which the model suggests as relevant.

I have analysed the overall sample by social class of origin, basing this on father's occupation, as follows. Middle class I includes professional, managerial, administrative and business workers; Middle class II includes routine clerical, junior non-manual, shopkeepers, publicans and salesmen. The remaining group is subdivided to give an Intermediate group. This includes all those respondents whose fathers were 'upwardly mobile' from manual work into supervisory or 'own account' work during the respondents' upbringing. The main Working class group are those whose fathers are or were manual workers who were not mobile. The class-origin distribution of the sample is shown in Table 4.3.

TABLE 4.3 *Personnel managers and officers by social class of origin*

| | Personnel managers | | Personnel officers | | All |
	No	%	No	%	No/%
Middle class I	28	46·6	14	35	42
Middle class II	12	20	8	20	20
	40	66·6	22	55	62
Intermediate	8	13·3	5	12·5	13
Working class	12	20	12	30	24
	20	33·3	17	42·5	37
Not known			1	2·5	1
	60	100	40	100	100

It is important to stress that this sample is not a random one, although I would add to this the point that I am unaware of anything in my selecting of interviewees which would be likely to cause any particular bias on this issue. I have compared this distribution with that of the Pahls' study of managers – one of the most recent of the relevant studies available and found a not dissimilar pattern (Pahl and Pahl, 1972, p. 69). Of the Pahls' managers 57 per cent are of middle-class origin, for instance, compared with 66·6 per cent of my personnel *managers*.

The theoretical scheme would lead us to look for some relationship between level of achievement within the organisation and social class of origin. Such a connection is suggested by the fact that 42·5 per cent of the *officers* are of Working class/Intermediate origin, whereas only 33·3 per cent *managers* are. This, however, does not take into account the likelihood that some of the present officers will become managers in the future. The proportion that will be promoted cannot be predicted, but some indication can perhaps be gained by assuming that, on current general trends in higher-level employment, those with degrees or who have qualified in personnel management would be more likely to be promoted than others. What we find here is that of the 14 graduate personnel officers only 2 are from Working class/Intermediate backgrounds (Table 4.4). And of the 17 officers of Working class/Intermediate origin not one is qualified in personnel management (in the overall sample only 14 people have gained I.P.M. membership by *examination* or have taken a college diploma in personnel management. All of these are Middle class by origin).

TABLE 4.4   *Graduate personnel officers by social class of origin*

Middle class I :	7
Middle class II:	5
Intermediate :	1
Working class :	1
	14

These figures would tend to support further the relationship between social class background and career level achieved as suggested in the model.

The respondents who come from manual backgrounds were broken down into two categories in Table 4.3 to indicate what proportion of them come from homes in which the father was socially mobile – i.e. the Intermediate group. It is interesting that more than a third of those whose fathers were manual workers at some stage in their upbringing experienced their fathers' being upwardly mobile. It is indicative of the nature of the British class structure that of 100 people in a middle-class occupation (and remember that a proportion of these are relatively 'junior' employees) only 24 per cent were from strictly (i.e. non-mobile) working-class homes.

Having looked at the organisational levels of the sample and the social-class background, I shall now return to the issue of the processes whereby people made their entry into the occupation. This is moving back to more qualitative material and the relative arbitrariness inherent of the allocating to categories of 'accounts'. Tables 4.5, 4.6 and 4.7 indicate some of the features of category I, that mode of entry into personnel work where the job was chosen more or less as the initial career.

TABLE 4.5   *Initial choosers by social class of origin*

Middle class I	17
Middle class II	6
Intermediate	1
Working class	—
	24

This clearly indicates that those who have entered personnel management as a first career are predominantly the younger, better-qualified people from homes of higher social status. One is tempted

TABLE 4.6   *Initial choosers by degree qualification*

Graduate	19
Non-graduate	5
	24

TABLE 4.7   *Initial choosers by age* (*at time of interview*)

30 and below	16
31–40	5
41–50	1
51 and above	2
	24

here to look to these figures as supporting the view that it is more realistic to refer to occupational *choice* in the case of middle-class employees than it is in the case of working-class employees. But we have to be cautious here because my sample is of people in one particular and perhaps atypical occupation. And, further, of the 24 initial choosers, we have seen that there was a degree of adventitious-ness (the advert responders – 4 cases) and a degree of acceptance of what work was available on the principle of elimination (the 'negative choosers' – 7 cases). It is, however, worthwhile to look at the features of the sub-category who, out of the 100 people interviewed, are those most appropriately described as having made initial occupational *choices*. And the result of such an analysis is quite striking, I suggest. Of the 13, 9 are graduates, 10 are under 35 and 9 are from Middle class I backgrounds. So those most clearly choosing personnel careers as their initial employment are very predominantly young, qualified and from high-status homes. This can tell us something about occupational choice and social background, but it is also, and more importantly perhaps, indicative of a trend in the personnel occupation. In so far as the occupation is attracting young people as an initial career choice, it would appear from this sample to be attracting people of a particular background. The professionalisation issue and the occupation's improving status (and level of reward) may well be relevant here – a point to which I will return in chapter 6 when I discuss professionalism and personnel management.

Analysis of the other modes of entry into the occupation does not indicate any particularly striking patterns. To go into detail on what patterns there are would be methodologically unsound, my sample not being random (therefore precluding tests of significance) and the categories being inevitably somewhat arbitrary. I am only happy to cite the above patterns because they are sufficiently striking to counter the arbitrariness to some extent. But I would stress once again that their value can only be indicative. Taking all these reservations into account, together with the point that the personnel occupation has grown very fast, in size and status, only in recent years, we can, I suggest, see in my overall findings clear indication for the prime importance of the *structural context of opportunities* in the process of occupational entry. The evidence on social-class background indicates one aspect of this, and another aspect, that of the type of work that employers make available, is clearly indicated – perhaps most forcefully by the fact that 27 per cent of my sample (category IV) came into this occupation at the initiative of employing organisations rather than through their own choice. Both of these factors, the social class/family/education one and the 'available-work' one are very much related to the type of society with which we are concerned: one where the social structure is very much bound up with the organisation of work, this organisation being most influenced by social groups most advantaged in the social order.

One danger of the type of analysis which I have just performed is that in attempting to locate structural mechanisms at a societal level, one tends to lose sight of the individual and the uniqueness and richness of each individual biography. I hope I have given some indication of this other side of the picture in the profiles which I presented earlier. At this point, and as a further antidote to the above reducing of individuals to components of a sociologists's 'structure', I will reproduce some accounts given to me by one of my respondents. I have not chosen him for particular reasons of 'typicality' but because his own insightfulness and self-analysis is a particularly useful illustration of the fact that people are not the manipulated puppets of much sociological analysis. Like many of those I interviewed, this local government employee, a 29-year-old student member of I.P.M. and a miner's son, clearly recognised the constraints inherent in social life and the processes of rational compromise that characterise personal adjustments and accommodations.

'The first job I got interested in was being a draughtsman. This was because I was interested in maths at school – a technical grammar school. Other things at school weren't highlighted. My father used to help me with my maths. My mother helped with the literature. I ended up doing management services work here eventually. . . . My parents insisted that I had to do something at managerial level. My father saw me as an extension of himself rather than as a person, I sometimes think.

83

Being a mining family they were desperate to get at least one of us to Grammar school. . . .

Part of the appeal of working in management services was the redistribution of wealth aspect, but that's now become irrelevant – the bonus schemes don't give the employee a real return anymore. . . . It's all too technique-oriented now: you know, the American idea of the instant answer. . . . The appeal of Personnel is, I suppose, mixed up with emotion. Employees need to be represented at the management decision level. It's not a social service though. . . .

I feel that my working-class experience is important to me. There is always some *hidden channelling* in one's life. One is not always free to make choices. I always remember a chap I used to work with, a very conservative, conventional sort of bloke. He was getting pretty dissatisfied and one day he just said, "I've been programmed. I've been bloody well programmed." He had wanted to be an artist but had been steered into something more respectable by his family. Very middle class they were, it seems.'

Throughout the accounts given to me in the biographical section of my interviews one sees people being pushed away from manual work by parents; others encouraged to work in something 'secure' or 'professional' by their parents; we see people studying school and degree subjects which they were 'best at' rather than 'interested in'; we see people 'drifting' into engineering because 'the factory was down the road'; we see people unable to train for careers because 'the grants weren't available in those days' and we see people doing the job that their employer needed, wanted or persuaded them to do. The sociologist would seem to be justified to talk of 'determinism' in the light of these patterns.

Yet more than a third of the sample were fairly emphatic in denying any connection between their present career and their upbringing, some seeing a positive reaction against their families. More than a third of the sample, again, are in a higher social-class position than were their parents and since practically half (49) of the sample have been categorised as entering personnel management by the two 'employee-initiated' modes (II and III), after achieving a more satisfactory or advantageous implicit contract, we can see another side to the same coin. Men do make their own histories even if not as they might wish. It is not a matter of either choice *or* determinism: there is a dialectical relationship between human effort and social constraint. The analysis of personnel specialists performed here indicates this, if nothing else, and any theory or model of occupational entry is inadequate if it fails to recognise it.

5 Orientations, values and adjustments

This whole study of the personnel occupation and its members is based on the 'social action' frame of reference, an approach which I see as necessary for a successful sociology of work and employment – a sociology which will do justice to both the free-will and rationality of human beings and to the constraints and exigencies of social structures. The possibilities of such an approach have been indicated, with reference to the entry of individuals into the personnel occupation, in the previous chapter. The intention is, now, to apply further the model which has been developed above but still, for the present, primarily at the level of the individual experience.

Dynamic orientations

In my earlier discussions of the social-action framework and in my adoption of the notion of 'orientation to work', I have been anxious to avoid the danger into which some authors have fallen of placing too much emphasis on 'prior orientations' and not paying sufficient attention to ongoing situational and organisational contingencies. In my conception of the employee's orientation to work as based on a rationally conceived *implicit contract*, I have been keen to emphasise that this is constantly liable to shift as definitions, interests or requirements are changed by either party, thus leading to an *imbalance* and some form of *adjustment*.[1] It is here that I feel that certain insights of the Chicago school of sociological study of work and occupations are useful. One particular value is their stress on the importance of the influence of immediate situations on human conduct, something forcefully demonstrated in that major Chicago study, *Boys in White:*

> The proposition that immediate situations exert a compelling influence on individual conduct has pervaded our entire book.

. . . When we say that . . . we intend to distinguish that influence from the influence of factors outside the immediate situation (Becker, Geer, Hughes and Strauss, 1961, pp. 441–2).

The factors outside the immediate situation include such things as membership of groups whose values and standards may be influential, as well as the individual's personal 'generalised values'.

While both of these phenomena do exert considerable influence over human conduct, we contend that much of human conduct is oriented to the immediate pressures and social controls originating in the situation in which the person is presently acting, and that he will organise his behaviour so as to take account of and in some way adjust to them (*ibid.*, p. 442).

The value of such a perspective is also demonstrated by Freidson in his analysis of medical practitioners (Becker *et al.* were looking at medical students) and I would agree with his point that 'too much attention has been paid to the personal characteristics and attitudes of individual members of occupations and far too little to the work-settings' (Freidson, 1970, p. 88).[2] It is precisely in this matter that the concept of orientations is so important in sociology: it replaces the psychologist's notion of *attitude* which, although valuable in its suggestion of a *predisposition towards* conduct, does tend, from the sociologist's point of view, to overemphasise the variable of *personality* (as a relative constant) at the expense of individual adaptability. I believe that one requirement which we should have of a sociology of work (industry, organisations, etc.) is that it can provide an alternative to the predominantly psychologistic tendency of so much managerial writing.[3]

To see how this notion of situational adjustment is related to the valuable processual emphasis of the Chicago school, we have to be aware of the centrality of the concept of *career* to the theoretical framework which is general to that school. This is the *symbolic interactionist* framework in which the notion of career is often used far more widely than in its more common conception as 'a succession of related jobs, arranged in a hierarchy of prestige, through which persons move in an ordered, predictable sequence' (Wilensky, 1960, p. 554). The interactionist tendency is to use it 'to refer to any strand of any person's course through life' (Goffman, 1968, p. 119) emphasising the interplay between 'the personal and the public, between the self and its significant society' (*ibid.*, p. 119). The element of this approach which I wish to make use of here is the idea that one can view as one of these *careers* (as a strand of a person's course through life) the overall process of movement towards work, entry into work and adjustment and change within work. Thus, that strand of the individual's biography which is concerned with work can be viewed analytically as one process. This insight can be incorporated into my overall theoretical scheme as follows. The individual, throughout his life, belongs to a range of social groups (family, peers, colleagues, friends, etc.), his interests contributing to and deriving from these memberships, definitions being constantly modified and adapted as memberships develop and shift. As the child grows into the adult, there increasingly arise points in time at which decisions have to be made where one has to balance one's interests, values and aspirations with situational contingencies. (For example: I interviewed more than one person who wanted to be a doctor but who, because either they could not afford to or were not sufficiently qualified to enter medical school, studied and worked in pharmacy instead.) These contingencies may be to do with the resources which the individual possesses, the job-opportunities available or one's age, sex, health and so on. One's work-related career throughout one's life is one of adjustments in this way. In this chapter I am concentrating on individual adjustments, leaving until later consideration of occupational/professional or group adjustments and strategies.

The analysis of the processes whereby members of my sample of one hundred personnel specialists entered the occupation gives a clear indication of the importance of situational factors at that particular point in their work career. Now that a point has been reached in the biographies of my subjects where they are employed in the personnel occupation, I can turn to concentrate further on problems and adjustments which arise in the work career largely as a result of features specific to the personnel occupation. One of the problems which we saw earlier which particularly concerned personnel specialists was that of 'credibility' – this being to a considerable extent the result of the 'welfare' *history* of the occupation as well as a result of the fact the occupation is still perforce involved in fulfilling certain criteria of organisational performance which might be seen in welfare rather than hard-headed 'efficiency' terms. If an occupation has a 'credibility' problem – as seen by many operating in the field and many writing about personnel management – then one is bound to wonder about the image of that occupation to the potential recruit. To gain some idea of the situation here, I asked in my interview: *How did you think of personnel work before you became involved in it – what image did it have?*

Pre-entry images

The responses to this have to be treated with particular care because I was asking people to think back to an earlier time in their careers.

There might be a tendency for people to give, in retrospect, a more 'positive' response than would be accurate (to emphasise the rationality of their job choice perhaps) but there might equally well be a tendency to lean in the opposite direction, so conforming to the stereotype of the poor backward personnel function struggling to win its place in the management team. My feeling is that the latter is nearer to what happened. Sixteen respondents gave an explicitly negative image (although such an evaluation is implicit in probably the large majority of other answers here).[4] Thus, 'a terrible image'; 'a joke – women organising outings and giving gold watches to people'; 'an old man's job': 'a hopeless, interfering bunch of people' and so on. In contrast to this there were 11 accounts of the image as 'influential', 'an important part of management' and so on. There is no pattern that I can see in the characteristics of the respondents giving these two types of response. However, among those giving the latter type of account I do recognise that a number of them were among the few interviewees whom I felt at the time reacted to my interview with some reserve, speaking in a more 'official' manner and giving me what I felt was something of a 'public relations' treatment. This is a useful indicator, I feel, of a methodological point of major significance: the extent to which interview responses are conditioned by the interview situation and, indeed, the personal characteristics of the interviewee and the interviewer and so on.[5] Some 9 people said they had had no impression of personnel at all prior to their involvement and 10 had seen it as 'remote', 'distant', 'esoteric' or 'boss-oriented'. This latter group were predominantly people who, prior to involvement in the field, had worked in more junior manual or clerical jobs (5 of the 10 in public administration – which fits with the 'estabs man' background of personnel in that area).

The group of respondents whom one might expect to give a distinctive type of response would be the small group of 13 largely young and graduate respondents whom I characterised earlier as the 'positive choosers' of personnel careers. The pattern of their responses is not strikingly dissimilar to the overall one, however, and to give an impression of the flavour of the accounts I shall give the responses of this group:

'Estabs; powerful people who said what you could and couldn't do.'

'Recruitment, welfare and training. I never thought of industrial relations.'

'I first came across it as a student and was impressed by its importance.'

'Engaging staff and looking after their wellbeing.'

'A drop-out sphere with no status. Very limited.'

'A service function, not influential in industrial relations.'

'Hire and fire; welfare – especially where women were concerned.'

'Nice. Something nice. Dealing with people. Some glamour.'

'It hardly existed then, in 1939.'

'Welfare and mediation.'

'The science of people at work. I was influenced by sociology at college here.'

'Not welfare like many think, more motivation and bargaining.'

'Admin.; checking whether the coffee-machine's working. Not industrial relations.'

We have to remind ourselves again, here, that we are looking at a developing occupation and it is interesting to note that of the 13 accounts given above, 3 included the observation that they had not thought of industrial relations work, something currently central to the 'improving' status of the personnel function. To indicate what elements of the work were mentioned I have set them out in Table 5.1.

TABLE 5.1   *Elements of personnel work mentioned as part of pre-involvement image*

Welfare, sick visiting, etc.	25	Mediating, placating, 'go-betweens'	5
Dealing with people and their problems, etc.	13	Industrial relations, bargaining	4
Recruitment, interviewing, 'hiring and firing'	24	Training	3
'Administration'	10	Wages and salaries	3
		Motivating	2
		Organising, movements and promotions	2
		Total	91

Whilst accepting that personnel management has grown in importance only relatively recently we have to note that nearly a third of my sample are 30 years of age and under and will, therefore, have gained their pre-entry impressions in the fairly recent past. Yet many of those elements which are stressed as central in the personnel management literature: industrial relations, training, manpower planning, organisational design and development and so on do not appear, from my evidence, to figure largely in pre-entry knowledge. There is very likely a general point to be made here about people's knowledge of potential jobs but there is undoubtedly, I feel, a problem specific to personnel management. I shall return to this shortly in looking at 'personnel types'.

The above analysis of pre-involvement images provides an important background to the orientation to work of personnel specialists. It also usefully links the issues of occupational entry and occupational career. Against this background we can now examine what can be seen as aspects of, alternatively, the positive and negative elements of the *implicit contract* – the felt relationship between 'reward' and 'cost' aspects of the definition of the employment situation. To get an indication of the 'reward' side I asked the question *What appeals to you most about personnel work?* and, for the 'cost side', *What do you most dislike about personnel work?*

Personnel work: the appeal

I have indicated the aspects which are reported as contributing to the appeal of personnel work in Table 5.2.

In Table 5.2 I have put the total of 123 reported appealing aspects of personnel work into categories and then grouped together categories A and B to give a total of 48 'people-oriented' aspects and categories C, D and E to give a total of 65 'task-oriented' factors. I do this categorising of accounts with reservation, as usual, particularly pointing to the fact that the appeal of 'variety' may relate equally as much to the 'people' aspect as to the nature of the tasks. What I think can be inferred from this table, however, is that there is a shift in orientation in terms of what personnel work means to the individual between the pre-entry impressions, where the dealing-with-people/welfare aspects are stressed, and current employment situation, where there is a clear positive orientation towards what might be seen as the more managerial content of the work. Yet we have to be careful in this setting up what might be seen as two alternatively appealing aspects of personnel work. When one reads through the one hundred accounts of the 'appeal' of personnel management what can be seen is, I suggest, that what provides the personnel occupation with its essential problems and difficulties – its dual orientation to people as *people* on the one side and to people as *resources* on the other (welfare and efficiency, if you like) – also provides some of the basic reward of being involved in the work. The combination of satisfactions on the 'people' side with satisfaction of the 'efficiency' side is apparent in many accounts. A young training officer in a retail and manufacturing organisation said, for instance,

'I like the power, I suppose, the power to make worthwhile decisions. I'm given a lot of freedom to do my job. And training gives a lot of job satisfaction: you can see people perform better as a result.'

TABLE 5.2   *Aspects of personnel work which appeal to respondents*

A	Helping or developing people	16
B	Working with people, contact with people, etc.	32
		48
C	Involvement in the business, influencing decisions or policies; working at a senior level, the politics	39
D	The variety in the work	22
E	Organising	4
		65
F	Using my abilities, the challenge	5
G	Freedom from committing oneself	3
H	Nothing	2
		10
	Total	123

And an assistant personnel manager in a factory, a woman, commented

'I like being in a job where I can make a decision. You're in a privileged position of knowing about people's problems and helping them. I also like the senior management aspect of personnel work; the fact that even though you're not yourself particularly senior, you do mix with people at a higher level.'

This latter point is, I feel, of very great importance. Many of the younger personnel officers see a lot of their satisfaction deriving from the involvement in issues which, outside the personnel function, one only met once one has achieved a senior level.

This is connected with the personnel function's *essentially* managerial role and its involvement in longer-term or organisation-wide aspects of management (see above, chapter 3). It was this aspect of the work, and particularly in the industrial relations sphere, that I found gave me the most interest as a young graduate employee. It was noticeable to me, in a large company with a considerable annual intake of graduates, how the orientations to work of the younger graduates involved in industrial relations and other personnel jobs was generally very different from those in other functions – many, if not the majority of whom, tended to become highly dissatisfied with their junior status and their menial work (contrasted with their expectations as graduates in a 'blue-chip' company) and many of whom left the company within twelve months of starting. A contemporary of mine in that company, whom I interviewed in the present study, said of the appeal to him: 'It's the wide range of contacts, the face-to-face angle with clients. Also it's that you've got to know a hell of a lot about the business overall. And I enjoy the politics.' Interestingly that particular individual was very little involved in industrial relations and the tendency for people to find reward in the combination of human contact and efficiency elements is found across the range of industries, levels, ages and functions. I have quoted above a training officer in retailing, a generalist in manufacturing and, latterly, a headquarters personnel man in engineering. An older respondent, a manpower planning manager in the food, drink and tobacco industry, provides me with a further example:

'There are two things. Firstly, there's the face-to-face aspect which I enjoy. I used to be a backroom boy when I was an office manager and like most managers here found interviewing and things strange at first. Now I really enjoy meeting and dealing with people. And, secondly, it's being able to provide data for management one jump ahead of when they ask for it. . . . When they want figures on turn-over or the number over 60, I can do it. All this has been very important recently in dealing with the recent problems here.' [Generally relating to a problem of a fall-off in demand in the industry.]

Personnel work: the dislikes

When we turn to the dislikes which the interviewees report, there is a variety of types of response including the dislike of sacking people (a dislike qualified in all but 1 of the 5 respondents who stated this as their main dislike as, for instance, 'it's unpleasant but necessary'). There are the dislikes which one would expect in any managerial work, of 'frustration', 'too many constraints', 'being let down by people', 'people's bloody-mindness', 'over-work', 'insufficient resources' and so on. Five people spoke of their dislike of suppressing their ideals, or not being allowed to be honest to themselves – something to which I shall return later – whilst we get only 3 mentions of conflict or confrontation and just 1 explicit mention of trade unions. There are just two relatively large groupings of response. The first of these, cited by a fifth of the interviewees includes, 'administration', 'routine', 'paper work', 'keeping statistics', 'records', 'salary forms' and the rest. I would comment on this again from my 'participant observer' experience. This type of complaint was practically a standard one among personnel managers and officers of my acquaintance and often provided me with a useful rationalisation (or 'acceptable utterance') for paperwork neglected. My own boss, at one time, a generally highly regarded man, had the title of personnel and administration manager and he regularly uttered the words

'I like the Personnel but I hate the fucking Admin.'

I would suggestt hat a dislike for such routines is common to many occupations but it becomes a particularly poignant problem in an occupation where there is the contrast of the more active or extrovert work of bargaining, interviewing, counselling, instructing, 'politicking', and the rest. Not only is the personnel occupation one which provides these compensating rewards, but it also is one which is highly dependent on accurate record-keeping, absolutely precise wage or salary conditions, clear and unambiguous minutes of negotiations and so on. The formally rational techniques are immensely important.

The second major category of dislike, with another fifth of the respondents complying and, like the above responses, spreading across the range of the respondents, are those relating to the relationship of personnel to the organisation:

'It's the attachment of women to it – the welfare image.'

'We're not seen as part of management by management.'

'We're only used to fire-fight.'

'Having to draw back from using power you haven't got.'

'It's far more with management than unions.'

'Being treated by the line as if we were a philanthropic institution.'

'The lack of a clear personnel philosophy in the company.'

'Our lack of status and people and knowing what to do.'

'The weakness of management.'

'Everybody thinks he's a good personnel manager.'

'Being a service department; not being seen as contributing to the organisation.'

I have said that such responses came from across the range of respondents. This contradicts what might be expected: one might expect to see such responses coming from the less senior personnel specialists, those relatively less involved with the strategic level of management. Yet the tendency is, in fact, in the opposite direction. Two out of every three responses of this type come from a personnel manager rather than an officer and of the 12 directors or senior executives in my sample (remember, I treat these as a sub-category of the 60 personnel 'managers') 3 gave responses of this kind.

The conclusion that I draw from this material, is, as I indicated above, that the features which give personnel management its appeal are closely related to those which provide it with problems and dislikes. The sociological ambivalence in the personnel job, which I suggested in chapter 3, is reflected here at the level of subjective orientations. My evidence suggests that the issues of credibility, status, recognition and the rest are significant ones for personnel specialists. Yet these arise from the personnel workers' involvement in the unique, in the subjective, in the non-tangible, non-quantifiable, the ambiguous nature of human relations – the very things which appear to contribute towards making personnel work rewarding. How relatively rewarding a type of work is, how positive are orientations within it or how strong are individuals' attachments to it are things which are very difficult to judge. They cannot be measured, but my personal observation would be that my years of meeting and being involved with managers across the range of functions indicate a strong case for viewing personnel management as among the more rewarding.[6]

In answer to my question *If you can imagine it, what would your ideal job be?*, 54 per cent of my respondents unequivocally cited personnel work. Among those not citing personnel are people citing jobs at a higher level in general management (or in two cases teaching personnel management) which could be seen as a development of their current specialist period in management. Other cases were largely those who cited jobs like actor, artist, musician, surgeon, farmworker which were preceded, often, with 'well, if I may fantasise'. Two people would like to be social workers and another intended to go into the priesthood, an earlier ambition. Although my interpretation is a subjective one, wide-open to contradiction, I feel that this pattern of response gives some indication of a positive attachment, generally, to personnel and associated work.

There were only a handful of accounts suggesting any antipathy towards their present occupation: one of these was the former nurse who had been forced to leave her preferred occupation for health reasons and two others were people who were finding the 'rat race' distasteful. Even if my interpretation of a particularly positive orientation to work among personnel specialists is not tenable, I would nevertheless argue that the responses which I have reported so far, relating to developing stages of the individuals' work careers, indicate the importance of seeing the career process as one which involves dynamic orientations. To illustrate this simply, we see 54 per cent of a sample of occupational members seeing work in that occupation as providing an 'ideal job' despite the fact that only 13 per cent of the sample can be seen as positively choosing it as an initial career and in spite of the predominance of uncomplimentary or, alternatively, partial images of the occupation prior to involvement in it. Retaining this concern with the dynamic and the processual I shall now turn more directly to the problem of how the individual adjusts to a type of work which I have characterised earlier as based upon conflicts, ambiguities and ambivalence.

Role-conflicts and individual strains

I have characterised personnel work in terms of the structural problems to which it can, in many ways, be understood as a response. I argued earlier that the use of people as resources in large-scale organisations creates potential conflicts and tensions between means and the achievement of the longer-term ends of those controlling organisations. All managers operate in terms of conflicting criteria, long-term versus short-term, efficiency versus human satisfaction, and so on but those criteria are brought into conflict most overtly at that point where, typically, the personnel practitioner operates. The conceptual apparatus which is most often brought to bear on this type of problem by sociologists looking at occupational positions which involve conflicting criteria is that of *role, role-conflict, role-strain* and a whole battery of related concepts. Ritzer points out that 'much of occupational sociology has been dominated by role theory, although to many occupational sociologists this orientation was not explicit' (Ritzer, 1972, p. 116).[7] One of the most influential works on 'role conflict and ambiguity' is that of Kahn *et al.* (1964) who set up five types of role-conflict: role-overload, inter-sender, person-role, inter-role, and inter-sender. To this is then added *role-ambiguity* which occurs where the role receives an inadequate amount of role-related information. A temptation is that such concepts should be used here. Hall in his discussion of role conflict and ambiguity cites the case of personnel as one of those departments which are often in such conflict 'because of the nature of their activities' (1969, p. 63) and Ritzer and Trice in their study of personnel specialists, titled *Occupation in Conflict* uses role-theory as its conceptual and theoretical framework (1969). Ritzer and Trice use the theory of role-conflict resolution developed by Gross *et al.* (1958) and find that the personnel people studied do not resolve their role-conflicts in any of the ways suggested by that theory but, instead, by what they describe as 'independent action' (1969, p. 77).

I would argue that such a 'finding' could have been achieved without any of the complexities of 'role-theory' being brought in. Fox, in his discussion of adaptations to organisation with reference to those in the 'man-in-the-middle' type situation says, for instance, in the particular case of the middle manager: 'the adaptations of the middle manager . . . are likely to take the form of individual, unilateral action of the innovative kind' (1971, p. 85) and he goes on to give structural reasons for such an argument. This brings me to my primary objection to role theory: it tends to force analysis to the level of the interpersonal and to the expectations of 'others' at the expense of the deeper underlying structural problems. The tendency of the theory is to give an impression of the individual as more *other-directed* than autonomous or innovative – something which, as Ritzer and Trice found, may not be too realistic. And I would add to this objection the general point that role-theory tends to parallel the complexity of real social life with an unnecessary linguistic complexity (see Coulson, 1972). I suggest that the underlying assumptions of role-theory (Coulson, 1972; Coulson and Riddell, 1970; Dahrendorf, 1968) are quite different from those basic to this study and, for this reason too I choose to reject role-conflict type terminology.

As Dawe comments, this type of conceptualisation 'compartmentalises lives in a way which utterly violates the everyday experience of a total self, and thereby misses that vital area of analysis concerned with the self-integrating purposes participants in social interaction bring to the various sectors of their lives' (Dawe, 1973, p. 32). It is to these 'self-integrating purposes' that I would draw attention in my ensuing analysis, which covers the two basic types of problem where individual adjustment may be required. One of these is where there may be structurally based conflicting criteria of performance and the second where situational demands or pressures may potentially conflict with personal expectations or values. These two are only conceptually separable and the first question in my interview which was intended to provide information on the problems under examination here was a general one: *You have already given your views on the biggest problem facing personnel manners. But what do you feel are the greatest strains on the individual doing the job?*

Among the responses to this are many which could be expected in many other jobs, as indeed a number of respondents pointed out. We get, 'frustration', 'fear of mistakes', 'lack of time', 'lack of resources' and so on. There are others which are perhaps more specific to personnel work like, 'having to be nice to people all the time', 'interviewing', 'often having just to listen – playing the hollow oak', 'having to have a butterfly mind – jumping quickly from one type of problem to another' (as one manager said here, 'personnel managers get this to a more extreme extent than others; you're negotiating a redundancy one minute and dealing with complaints about girls' tights getting laddered the next'). But the two largest single groups of more personnel-specific strains are seen in the 17 accounts relating to personal relationships and emotional involvement ('dealing with sad problems', 'not getting too involved', 'being let down', etc.) and the 16 relating to relationships with the organisation ('trying to get through to managers', 'always having to persuade', 'always being opposed', 'being scapegoated'). Ten people found the 'conflicts' in the work a strain and I saw the greatest strain in issues relating to personal values and 'conscience' (I shall look closely at these points shortly). This data can only give an impression and I put it forward as background to the more detailed issues which I go on to confront. Before I do this I will quote one account given by a senior personnel man who was particularly concerned to analyse the essential problem in personnel work, something he referred to at several points in the interview as 'ambiguity'.

'In Personnel what you need is a high tolerance of things ambiguous. The greatest strain on the individual comes from tolerating so much ambiguity. This ranges from work in employee relations where there's often no apparent logic, to situations which are highly structured. You're always walking on a knife-edge. And there's a lot of strain in listening to people's problems where you know in the end that it's their responsibility. There's nothing you can do but you have to listen.'

And the case of this individual leads me to a general point about strain. In using such a concept it might appear that one is assuming some sort of pathology in the situation. However, paralleling my earlier argument about the difficulties of the work being related to the rewards, I would suggest that what might be reported as strains may well be closely tied to satisfactions. The individual whom I quoted above and who also saw 'ambiguity' in the advisory yet influential role of the personnel manager (*vis-à-vis* other managers), saw satisfactions here (in response to the question about the appeal of personnel work):

97

'I get satisfaction and pleasure in, well, how can I put it . . .
by nature, I'm devious and am a political animal. In this job
I've an advisory role rather than an executive one yet I like
power. It's not overt power, it's influence. I like influencing the
totality!'

Efficiency versus fairness?

To find out the extent to which the structural contradictions basic
to the nature of personnel work, and analysed here from a sociologist's point of view, are perceived by those operating in the field, I
asked the question: *Some people argue that there is an inevitable
conflict between an organisation being efficient on the one hand and
socially just or fair on the other, how do you feel about this?* As a
number of people commented here, it does depend on what you mean
by efficiency and what you mean by fairness. But my point is not to
find out anything about people's attitude to a single specific phenomenon, but rather to see whether any aspects of what I call 'structural'
problems are recognised by practitioners and, if so, how they
conceptualise them and see them being dealt with. It is important to
recognise that belief in a fundamental contradiction between
'efficiency' and 'justice' – an inevitable conflict – is not one that many
operating in the field might hold with comfort. As one personnel
officer said, 'If I didn't believe that the two were compatible, I'd be
too cynical to be in Personnel.' Such 'cynicism' is perhaps mandatory
on the part of the sociologist but it would be unrealistic to expect the
same emphasis from those actively involved in such situations. Of
the interviewees 55 did not believe that there was an inevitable
conflict between the two criteria. But throughout the answers here
there is the implication that such a conflict has to be actively avoided
by managerial efforts. A personnel manager in transport said:

'I know it's a hackneyed phrase but a happy ship is an
efficient ship. If people know what's expected of them and know
people will see what they give; if they know they'll be treated
fairly and justly and consistently in their society, they will
work efficiently. It is more important to provide a man with
the right tools than to butter him up and kick him in the arse.
We must create jobs in which people can be interested and they
will work. Bonus schemes tend not to work. There are no short
cuts with people.'

Although this respondent emphatically denied the existence of a
conflict between the two criteria, his response, like that of many
others, indicates that there is at least something here which is
problematic for management. Indeed 14 of the 55 people denying

the existence of an 'inevitable' conflict did see such conflicts existing *in practice*, for example:

'There doesn't have to be [such a conflict] but there often is.
The balance is not right. With the correct personnel policies
you can be as fair as you can and still be efficient.'

The belief appears to be that management can overcome the problem:

'There's no conflict if you can persuade people not to see things
in conflict terms. For instance, when you sack a man and the
union opposes it, it is possible to show that the dismissal is
right and can be in the interests of both sides.'

And Personnel, it is implied, is particularly involved in finding ways of resolving the conflict, by such measures as the introduction of industrial democracy:

'There is likely to be a conflict in a rapidly changing social
climate. This will be the domain of Personnel in the future.
We will get resistance from the line on the industrial democracy
that is to come. We always have had line resistance to unions.
Senior people are failing to see the point of industrial
democracy – it is a way, in fact, of resolving the conflict you
mention.'

Although I am well aware of the danger of the sociologist seeking verification of his structural analysis from qualitative interview-response material, it does seem to me that many of the responses which deny the fundamental conflict underlying personnel management, nevertheless give accounts which are compatible with a view of personnel work as having to cope with such conflicts.

An interesting case here is in a written account sent to me by a personnel director (whom I did not interview) as comment upon the early report on my findings where I pointed out that 55 per cent of the respondents denied the existence of a fundamental conflict. He felt that this was a lower figure than was desirable and argued that it was a failure of communication on the part of senior personnel people that led to some fairly extensive belief in conflicts of this type (although my evidence does not, interestingly, suggest that *level* is a relevant variable in the type of response here):

'One thing that your paper brought home to me was our failure
to communicate down through the Personnel function the
business considerations which help to shape solutions to
industrial relations problems. As a Board member I have not
seen an inherent conflict between efficiency and fairness,

whereas as a Personnel Officer I thought I saw a conflict clearly on many occasions. I think the reason is possibly that I now have access to information which I did not then. I realise much more clearly that without an increase in efficiency, contraction, redundancy and unemployment is inevitable. It is not difficult for me to see this as I get all the information about adverse cash flow, losses on contracts, penalties imposed by customers, and so on. I am sure my subordinates do not see things the same way, which is a failure on my part. As a Personnel Officer, I could quickly get steamed up about pay anomalies which were clearly overdue for correction. At my present level I think I can understand better the reasons why they cannot simply be corrected. The reasons will vary and I am not here talking in the context of Government pay policy. Most commonly the reason will be that any correction of the anomaly will start a round of leap-frog claims which will re-create the anomaly. On anomalies as between works and staff my experience here, for example, has shown that while certain occupations ought to be reclassified from works to staff, my attempts to do so would provoke inter-union conflict hurting everybody far more than the existing anomaly. One does build up a wealth of experience in industrial relations which junior people have yet to acquire.'

This account reveals how one man's orientations can be seen as having changed over his career but, in effect and in the light of the responses which I have received, I would suggest that similar perceptions to those involved in this account can be found at all levels. I refer here to what I regard as a perception of the part which personnel plays in coping with structural strains.

When we turn to the accounts of the 45 who agree with the idea of an inevitable conflict, something similar emerges. Whereas the tendency of the above type of account was to see possible *resolutions* of the conflict, the tendency here is to see a possibility more in terms of *coping:* 'There is such a conflict, and this is what we deal with in Personnel – we're always trying to bring the two together. But there will always be a conflict of loyalties.' Accounts here refer to 'keeping a balance' or 'compromising between the two'. Of the 42 respondents who thought that there was an inevitable conflict, 18 spoke in this way, leaving 24 who simply commented on the conflict (and remember that my question does not explicitly raise the issue of conflict resolution or handling). For example:

'Yes there is a conflict. A firm can be efficient and exploit the workers . . . especially female labour.'
'Oh yes, there is definitely a conflict. You see it clearly in a

100

redundancy situation.'
'There is . . . sometimes you have to be unfair but I hope I
don't do it obviously.'

But even in these accounts we can often get some insight into how
the individual sees such conflicts being handled:

'It is true. For instance, a company may have sick-pay rules
and so on. But they have to be rigid. They have to be and,
because of this, the conflict can arise – thus they can sometimes
be unfair. The only way is to be firm but fair.'

or:

'Yes. It's a matter of being efficient and *consistent*. The
difficulty is whether you are seeing yourself as an extension of
the social services or as an efficient organisation. It can't be
both. I've seen this in having to review our current problem of
high absence people. . . .'

To avoid some of the problems of interpreting discussions of such
abstract notions as efficiency and fairness and, at the same time, to
enable me to look at individuals' orientations in the light of situational contingencies, I raised the question of how the respondent
would cope with a redundancy situation.

The case of redundancy

It was the redundancy situation that was the example most frequently
cited in the respondents' discussions of efficiency and fairness and
my own feeling is that the redundancy situation is the one where,
potentially, the conflicts and tensions inherent in the personnel role
become most apparent. As one respondent said, 'I can see why
you're asking this question: this is where you find out where we all
really stand when it comes to the crunch.' There was practically
universal acceptance of the fact that redundancy could become
'inevitable' in an organisation – at least in the present way that
society is organised. My interests in responses to the question about
the principles which the individual would, personally, apply in a
redundancy situation are two-fold. First, I was anxious to see how
individuals saw themselves handling what I see as a situation where
rival criteria are likely to operate in a more visible way than is
normal, and second, I felt that it would be revealing to look at such
responses in the light of the individual's personal values and loyalties.
Before I look at the responses, however, I shall say a little more
about the ways in which redundancy situations can be seen as
involving conflicting criteria for action.

This most obvious conflict which is likely to arise in a redundancy situation is that between the interests of the employer and the interests of the individual employee. Fryer (1973) usefully discusses the problems here and Eldridge analyses the inter-group conflicts which may emerge, together with the possible existence of 'competing rationalities' where 'strong logical arguments are advanced on the basis of different value assumptions' (1968, p. 225). These issues are indeed ones of considerable importance but since the personnel specialists, with whom we are concerned here, are agents of the employers, then my present concern is with the extent to which a redundancy is problematic from the point of view of the management. And the conflicting criteria in which I am interested are those relating to formal and material rationality. Given the immediate problem which faces an organisation whose management had decided to lose employees, it is clearly logical for members of management to use formally rational criteria of performance, attendance, efficiency and so on, in selecting which employees to make redundant. Such criteria would clearly have the appeal of 'rationality' for those departmental managers whose own performance tends to be judged in terms of such criteria. Yet to apply such criteria may be materially irrational from the point of view of the 'organisational' interest. To make redundant those whom the management select as 'least efficient' or 'slackers' or whatever can lead to such a lowering of morale or a lack of trust of management on the part of remaining employees that the longer-term wider criteria of the employer are not met.

Given wider societal values of 'fairness' there will be pressure, particularly where employers are unionised, to pursue a selection policy which can be seen as 'fair'. But the most obvious criterion of fairness – selecting those who are best able to find alternative work – may produce problems for both management and employees. It is problematic for management because this may well mean their losing the staff whom they may most wish or need to retain. And from the point of view of employee representatives, it puts them into the invidious position of either allowing management or being willing themselves to make choices between fellow employees on such difficult and ambiguous criteria as chance of getting other work, family or personal need, general circumstances and so on. The compromise that is often sought, therefore, is one based on the more objective criterion of length of service – the last-in-first-out principle (LIFO). But in any organisation of any complexity this may create problems where there are, say, recently established departments or occupational groupings whose members are largely more recent recruits. So, even within LIFO, there may have to be negotiation to balance 'organisational effectiveness' with what is generally acceptable in terms of 'fairness'.

In so far as the personnel department is the area of the organisation where the problems of human resources are dealt with in a specialist way, then it is the management representatives here that will be in a position of having to handle these various conflicting criteria. Gill writes of the personnel function dealing with problems of 'organisational shock' and 'defensive retreat' and, in his analysis of 'organisational dynamics' in a redundancy situation, points to the ways in which decisions which 'may reach the immediate goal of resolving the redundancy but which may counter the long-range goal of survival and future profitability' (1975, p. 36). He sees 'a number of needs which a well-equipped personnel function would satisfy' which include counselling line managers on 'organisational dynamics', negotiating over various details, helping the individuals affected by the redundancy but: 'More critically, it should help line managers to decide who should go and to prepare to communicate bad news to employees' (Gill, 1975, p. 36).

My argument about the centrality of the personnel specialist in the decision-making process, should his function be a well-established and recognised one in his organisation, is not only based on the relevant literature, however. My own experience as a member of a personnel department in a company which found itself in a widely publicised crisis which led to a redundancy, has been very important in my overall thinking about the personnel occupation. It was the process of spending days and nights negotiating with both trade union representatives and line managers which brought home to me the underlying tensions of the work, which I later conceptualised in sociological terms. More clearly than in any other situation did one become aware of the conflict between the long-term and the short-term, between the calculable criteria of performance and the more abstract notions of morale and justice, between the treatment of people as resources and the recognition of the individual's personal needs and difficulties. One's sensitivity was considerably increased here by the awareness that should the company decide, at a later stage, to apply the same criteria to members of the personnel department as it was attempting to apply to the bulk of employees, then one would be out of work oneself! And, more than ever, one was aware of that ambiguity of being closely in touch with both the strategic decision-makers (the receiver's office in this case) and the trade unions whilst, at the same time as coping with demands from both of these groups, one was spending a great deal of time in coping with the demands of departmental managers – demands which often coincided with neither of the other two. If ever there was 'role-conflict' or 'role-strain' and a feeling of being the 'man in the middle', then this was it. Also, in carrying out the dismissals, one thought very hard about one's own values. Here were the normal problems of the personnel specialist magnified many times. I follow the requirement of *reflexivity* explained in chapter 1 in this account of my personal experience, both to locate the main tenor of my analysis in its experiential background and to indicate the importance which I attach to my question about what my interviewees would do in a redundancy situation. I shall now examine the responses to that question.

The question asked was, *In a situation where a redundancy is inevitable in an organisation, what principles do you personally feel should apply when it is carried out?* I explained that in each case I was not concerned with the employing organisations' policy on redundancy and that by 'inevitable' I meant a situation where the redundancy decision had been made 'at the top' and where other strategies like early retirement, 'wastage' and so on were not sufficient to lose enough staff quickly enough. By 'principles' I meant the criteria for selecting 'who goes'. From the responses to the question, I find that there appear to be three basic criteria for selecting 'who goes', as are shown, together with the prime consideration upon which they can be said to be based, in Table 5.3.

TABLE 5.3 *Basic criteria for selecting employees to be made redundant*

Criterion for dismissal	Prime consideration
Those best able to cope (e.g. those without dependents, those near to retirement, those best placed on the labour market)	Employee welfare
Bad performers/the least 'efficient' (e.g. 'slackers' 'deadwood' 'passengers' 'the rubbish', etc.)	Short-term organisation/departmental efficiency
Those with shortest service (LIFO) – often within occupational categories or departments or with special exceptions to protect organisational viability	Longer-term organisational performance, recognising the need for 'fairness' / 'acceptability' to employees

In asking the question on this issue I was very much aware of a hypothesis which I felt I was testing. In setting the scene for the question I was 'replicating' the type of situation I had experienced myself, where I had been aware of the pressures that are on the personnel function in such a situation. Bearing in mind the likelihood that a proportion of my interviewees would not have experienced the same extent of union pressure in their work (my own organisation was highly unionised) and that there would often not be the same pressures to defend occupational groups which one gets in an advanced technology large-scale organisation,[8] I hypothesised that the response would lean towards the third category: that of LIFO with varying degrees of application within groupings and with negotiated exceptions for key personnel. Table 5.4 gives the responses, there being six categories since the three basic criteria are sometimes mixed.

TABLE 5.4 *Respondents' criteria for selecting employees to be made redundant*

Criterion	Number supporting
Those best able to cope	8
Bad performers/least 'efficient'	18
Shortest service (LIFO) – including within categories	59
Mixture of shortest service and least efficient	12
Mixture of shortest service and those best able to cope	2
Mixture of least efficient and those best able to cope	1
Total	100

This pattern strongly supports the hypothesis behind my question. The hypothesis was based on the pressures of which I was aware both from personal experience and from the literature, combined with the theoretical position which expects the individual employee's orientations to be dynamic and, hence, his actions to be related to situational contingencies. This corresponds to Ritzer and Trice's finding that the personnel specialist will tend, in a 'role-conflict' situation, to follow a course of action which does not coincide precisely with the course towards which he is pushed by any one of the conflicting pressures or expectations to which he is open. Closer examination of the accounts reveals the extent to which the criteria cited are based on a notion of 'compromise' or 'balancing'. And the only pattern which I can detect in the responses, in terms of the various characteristics of the individuals, is one which my data does not allow me to follow up systematically. This is that those tending to avoid the straightforward criteria of 'best able to cope' or the 'bad performers' are most often those who have experienced redundancies, particularly in unionised situations, or have read about redundancy (possibly in connection with an academic course of study), or are or have been employed in unionised organisations where there is therefore an awareness of the type of employee pressure that would be exerted.

Those responses which indicate a mixing of criteria often refer to 'balance' or 'compromise'. For example, a personnel officer in the drug industry: 'Length of service must come in from the point of view of fairness. But from an efficiency point of view you'd have to look at the less able. You need to reach a balance.' Or, more calculatingly, from an engineering industry personnel manager with experience of carrying out redundancies:

'The survival of the company is the prime concern. You then write the rules of LIFO or whatever to suit the purpose. I'm therefore opposed to self-selection. You can't go for LIFO straightforwardly because you lose good people and you create an age gap. You therefore pay lip service, dishonestly, to LIFO. You make it look like LIFO and you lose the right people. In the end it's an individuals game you play, not a numbers game.'

The extent of compromise is best revealed, however, by the fact that of the 59 people who supported LIFO in some form, 20 made a point of stressing that this would not be their preferred course of action. People spoke of some form of LIFO as 'the only thing you can get away with' or 'in the end it's the only thing that is acceptable' whilst going on to indicate the ways in which modifications might be made. For instance,

'I'd like to select on competence in relation to the revised organisation pattern and demands. But there's no chance of doing it. LIFO is iniquitous in practice – I say this having handled two redundancies. You negotiate on the basis of opposing LIFO and you then concede it in return for them [i.e. the unions] conceding you the right to argue exceptions.'

The overall need, and justification for compromise is given in the following:

'Why should the personnel manager compromise? Surely the answer is that as a professional he would identify the overall best possible result for the enterprise as a whole. As "the greatest good" to which lesser goods must be subordinated. If he gets rid of those best able to get another job, then in no time at all there will be a further redundancy because the best men have gone, results suffer and the company has to contract further. If he tries to get rid of the least efficient, in conflict with the norms of society as well as the trade unions, he will have an enormous dispute on his hands, sanctions, disruption, failure to meet customers' demands and so on. This in turn will lead to a further redundancy. Quite logically, in his role as a personnel manager he goes for the best possible result. It may not be the most efficient in one sense or the most humane in another, but overall it is the best possible result.'[9]

This illustrates the grounds for compromise, adjustment and independent action with regard to the ambivalence underlying the position of the personnel specialist, in the case of one type of event. The next issue to be confronted is that of the possible needs for individual adjustment in terms of personal values.

Personal morals, ideals and values

One of the younger personnel officers said, in response to the question on selecting people for redundancy: 'as a socialist, I would say that those best able to get another job. As a manager, I would go for the least efficient. But as a *personnel* manager, I would compromise and go for "last-in-first-out".' This illustrates what I see as an interesting phenomenon revealed by my data: the way in which individuals holding certain ideals or values which are, logically, somewhat at variance with the situational requirements involved in managing people as resources, adjust and cope with these situations – again revealing, in my terms, the dynamic nature of orientations and the rationality underlying the way the individual copes with situational pressures. From my experience within the personnel management field (and my own case is quite relevant here, as I pointed out in chapter 1) I was aware of the existence of people working in the field whose orientations in personal value terms, at least in the early stages of their career, might be such as to differ from those most logically fitting a management role. Personnel management has a tradition, for instance, of recruiting a certain proportion of people from among lay trade union officials. Also the 'betterment' strand of the occupation's history – something which I have already shown to be important in the occupational images of potential recruits – may attract people who are interested in contributing through their work to social change. Indeed I would suggest that the dual orientation of the personnel occupation (efficiency and welfare etc.) creates a situation where it is often appropriate for organisations to recruit to personnel departments people who are 'sensitive to people' or sympathetic to employee interests. Yet, in the long run, such people are bound to operate in terms of the more calculative criteria associated with the utilisation of human resources – the treating of people as means rather than ends.

As I showed earlier, some individuals report that the strains which they associate with personnel work are related to problems such as 'going against one's ideals'. But to gain a fuller impression of the various aspects of this problem I included in my interview the

107

question: *Are there any religious, political or moral influences or interests which you feel may be relevant to your being in this work?* The general pattern of response is given in Table 5.5.

TABLE 5.5 *Political, moral and religious values: number of times each mentioned*

Value ('interest' or 'influence')	No. of mentions
Nothing, not relevant, etc.	26
Religious	16
Moral	39
Political (left) ⎫	22 ⎱ 25
Political (right) ⎭	3 ⎰
Total	106

One has to be careful, as ever, in grouping together responses to such an abstract question and one has to be aware of an obvious tendency for 'acceptable utterances' to be made in such accounts. Most of the respondents in the first category simply said 'No' to the question. Two individuals explained that they put aside such considerations in doing their work, another said he was 'more a logic man than interested in ethics' and a personnel man in banking said: 'All three certainly pass through my mind. But it has to be limited since this is a commercial institution.'

The majority of those mentioning religious influences saw this in terms of it giving them an 'awareness of right and wrong' or making them 'care about the individual' and so on. In more than half of the cases there was mention of Methodist or Non-conformist influences, which is perhaps interesting in the light of the historical background of the occupation. For example:

'Yes. The non-conformist liberal background gives me a sympathy for the employee side.'

'I'm a staunch methodist. I'm a descendant of Wesley. My non-conformist conscience is very strong – it makes me see people as individuals. I hate to see people as numbers. . . . I used to get into trouble for supporting people against authority. . . . I'm conscious of this problem in this department. Size makes people become ciphers.'

'I've a Calvinist sort of view of work – people should expect to work hard for a fair wage.'

Yet 3 of the 16 people mentioning religious influences went on then to deny that they let it actually influence their work:

'Despite my strong Methodist background and its influence on me, it would be abhorrent to me that the religious things as such influenced me at work.'

The category of responses which mention moral influences are largely in terms of a claimed concern for fairness, justice, helping people, giving people a chance to better themselves, seeing people get a 'square deal', acting as the 'company's conscience', 'service', and 'getting a fair day's work for a fair day's wage'. Of those mentioning a political influence, 3 mentioned Conservative allegiances whilst the remainder gave accounts which I have labelled 'left', either because of a mention of 'socialist' views or because of a stated political interest in 'increasing equality', 'changing the way the staff are treated – they're usually overlooked or ignored', 'being sympathetic to the unions' and so on. Out of the 22 here 11 did use the label 'socialist'. I am particularly interested in this group because if there are members of the sample whose orientations in value terms are such as to lead us to expect action more in favour of the employee interests than the organisational interests, then these would be the ones. The specific action situation on which I have data is that of the redundancy – and this, I have claimed, indicates that likely conduct is to be seen more in terms of independent action reacting to situational pressures than anything else. To test this further, I have examined, therefore, the ways in which those suggesting potentially employee–centred orientations (those indicating 'left' values) responded to the redundancy question. This analysis gives us Table 5.6.

To put such apparently precise figures against what are inevitably relatively arbitrary groupings of unique accounts can, of course, be misleading. But I suggest that this table does indicate that those who oppose political 'influence' or 'interests' from a tradition which might lead one to expect less acceptance of business or efficiency criteria of action, nevertheless do not generally appear to tend towards a kind of conduct which is different from others' in a situation where alternative criteria are, theoretically, available. And it may be important to note that the three individuals who did cite the employee-welfare oriented criterion (those best able to cope) – two directors and an officer – were operating in a co-operative society, a local authority and the health service, respectively, where the selection of such a criterion can be seen to relate to certain organisation-relevant values.

The general pattern indicated by Table 5.6 reminds us how important it is to see orientations in dynamic terms. It may be that

TABLE 5.6 *Criteria for selecting redundant employees quoted by those mentioning 'left' values and by the whole sample*

Criterion	Prime consideration	No of 'left' respondents supporting	% of 'left' respondents supporting	No/% of total sample supporting
Those best able to cope	Employee welfare	3	13·6	8
The least efficient	Short-term organisational efficiency	5	22·7	18
Shortest service (LIFO) – including within categories	Long-term organisational performance and 'fairness'	12	54·5	59
Mixture of shortest service and least efficient		—	—	12
Mixture of shortest service and those best able to cope		1	4·5	2
Mixture of least efficient and those best able to cope		1	4·5	1
Total		22	100	100

the *specificity* of actual situations where decisions are made makes those situations more salient than the individual's personal values. As Becker says, 'One of the most important reasons for the influence of immediate situational constraints lies in the fact that they are so much more specific than statements of belief and value usually are' (Becker, 1961, p. 442). He goes on to illustrate how the generality of one's value position or 'long-range perspective' leads to a considerable leeway between this perspective and how it can be implemented in any particular situation: 'It is in this area of ambiguity and leeway that situational pressures and constraints operate' (*ibid.*, p. 442). What I would add to this would be to comment that it is not a matter of *abandoning* ideals, and that what we might call *adjustments* of this type are often quite conscious and indeed *rational*

110

– their being dealt with in terms of the implicit contract. This suggested by the prevalence of people mentioning, in the context of discussing the 'man-in-the-middle' problem (see chapter 8), the fact that, in the end, you have to remember 'which side your bread is buttered on'.

Although I nowhere *explicitly* raised the question of the relationship between personal values and occupational actions, a number of those mentioning employee-oriented sympathies or values did volunteer comment on this issue of adjustment. For example, an industrial relations specialist in an engineering company said: 'I am a socialist – in my ideals – and this clashes to a certain extent with my job. One modifies one's ideas. You turn a blind eye to things which don't seem moral.' A local authority personnel officer said:

'the longer you are in Personnel, the more you get sucked into the system – political and moral things "go off". You start off trying to be independent – including independent of management – but you can't keep things up. You end up thinking like management a lot of the time.'

Some idea of the dynamics of the processes here is given in the account of a man who had done several personnel and training manager jobs in various industries:

'Early on political and moral ideas were very significant. I saw myself as a champion of the underprivileged. I saw people being constantly misled by promises being made to them. I wanted to play a Sir Lancelot role – getting some of the promises fulfilled. It wasn't a matter of management deliberately lying. Employees were saying what they wanted and managers would say yes – but then never got round to it.

'Eight years of management made me a management's man. I can't exactly locate the crossing point. But it was especially since I first became a personnel as opposed to just a training manager. It meant seeing things through managers' eyes. In the job you make the best of the job. Your political values are still there. But you take them home and you take them to the ballot box.

'I got excited by being a manager – having some effect. In personnel management you have to retain the confidence of your superiors, your peers and the workforce. You're not *seen* therefore as a managers' man by the workforce. You are someone who is more aware of their problems and situation. They want someone they can talk to with a little more hope.'

A particularly interesting case is that of the personnel director in a large co-operative society, an ex-miner, trade union and Labour party activist. Despite the fact that he felt that the co-operative movement was 'possibly the only management I could work in' because the 'social commitment of co-operation gives a purpose to my work', he nevertheless pointed out that 'in the end it's as capitalist as anything else'. He spoke of his 'views getting tempered as time goes by' and in replying to my question about what he most disliked about personnel work, he referred to 'the way it tends to change me. It makes me not the man I thought I was – having to come to terms with realism and therefore suppressing some of my ideals.' A written comment on my early working paper which included the above quotation saw it somewhat differently:

'I do not believe the job has changed me. I have learnt that some of my early ideals are just not attainable. I find nothing incompatible between making people redundant and my Christian faith. I am seeking to serve to the greatest good of the greatest number. Experience has told me that one's view of the greatest good does change as one advances through the hierarchy, but I believe that it is due to the wider span of responsibility and the broader view that it gives. It is not due to losing one's values and ideals.'

By quoting this series of accounts and by my earlier attempt to locate a more general pattern of relationship between values and situational requirements I hope that I have thrown some light on the general processes of individual adjustment to work. But I would argue that the pattern that I have located has a particular relevance to the occupation of personnel management. And my point here is in accord with my theoretical requirement to see work orientations and adjustments as part of the same process which includes the entry into the occupation. My point relates to a relatively widely held conception of the personnel occupation as one which attracts people with values and interests which might not be compatible with 'efficiency' or business-oriented management.

Personnel types

Managers operating outside the personnel area are often given to referring to the 'woolly-types' or the 'softies' working in personnel departments. This is one component of the problematic relationship between personnel specialists and other managers and it is not a concern at this point. I was interested, however, in whether any such typifications operated *within* the personnel occupation. I therefore asked the question: *Is there anything generally different or distinctive about people who work in personnel management: are they a type in any way?* I have not made use of the whole range of responses here since a large proportion simply answered in terms of the qualities they thought a personnel specialist *should* have. Where individuals do answer the question more directly there is a strong tendency for accounts to be given like:

'Yes, there are three types. There's the older 'soft-option' type interested in welfare or who has just been 'shunted in'. Then there are those who have worked their way up from manual or lower-clerical jobs and, thirdly, there are the younger professional types who choose Personnel as a career.'

This is a fairly typical account of this type and the third category – the more qualified 'professional' is often seen as the currently increasing group. There is no immediate suggestion in the above type of account of there being a particular problem of people with a 'soft'-orientation, the old 'welfare types' being replaced by the more qualified careerists. Yet when I selected out the accounts given to me by the few individuals whom I judged to be particularly involved, through the nature of their own jobs, with the selection and training of personnel specialists, such a suggestion does emerge. And interestingly, the suggestion is with regard to the younger 'professional-types' or the 'young graduates – especially the social scientists'.

It was suggested that there is a tendency for these to be 'unbusinesslike' or to be, as one put it, 'soft personalities who are nervous of conflict'. They are more concerned with making people happy than with taking decisions and they want to bring to work what someone called a 'misplaced softness'. Such a point was put particularly strongly, and with particular concern, by one man who had been teaching personnel management to 'post-experience' students on courses leading to both the Institute of Personnel Management qualification and to the more general Diploma in Management Studies. He argued that there was a clearly discernible difference in orientation between the specialist group and the generalist group – on the lines described above. One senior executive commented that such an unbusinesslike orientation might not be such a problem 'at the lower levels' and that it might change on promotion. Another explained that his way of dealing with the problem was 'to mix up the personnel professionals with appointments from the line'.

Such policies would not contradict my own analysis, which suggests that orientations do shift in the face of organisational requirements. But where such a recognition may tend to be less brought to bear, in practice, I would suggest, would be at the point of recruitment to the personnel occupation. I have no systematic evidence on this point, it not being an issue that could be raised with many interviewees, but the four people with whom I felt it was relevant to raise it did indicate some disquiet that they felt at the

113

proportion of job applications which they received from 'churchy sort of people', in one case, 'people who would obviously be better off in social work' in another and, again, 'young girls who think that Personnel is the place for women to make careers in industry'. I gained the impression that recruiters to personnel departments are tending to be very negatively predisposed towards job applicants who betray any religious attachments, an interest in social work or, very importantly, who are women. (My evidence here, I should add, does come from large organisations where recruitment to personnel work is done by senior members of the occupation.) This tendency is related, I believe, to the structurally and historically based problems of credibility with general management and the felt need to 'kill the welfare image'.

I shall deal with the issue of women in personnel management in chapter 8 on these lines but, at this stage, I would comment that policies with regard to recruits to personnel departments may be underestimating the phenomenon of dynamic orientations and adjustment to situational exigencies. In my own career within the personnel occupation and during the course of my academic researches I have come across and worked with several individuals with very strong religious attachments (including seeing the Church as an alternative career in two cases) and of people very interested in a possible move into social work. I cannot infer any typicality on the part of these individuals (each of them is currently in a relatively senior post) but I think that it is worthwhile to comment that I could see no way in which any one of them was any less 'hard-headed' or 'businesslike' than any other personnel manager whom I have observed at work or whom I have interviewed. Indeed, in two of the cases I would comment on a 'ruthlessness' behind some of their actions and statements which was relatively atypical of people in the field.

The range of issues analysed above all contribute, I hope, to indicating the ways in which individuals adjust and cope with structural problems underlying the personnel occupation. I would not deny the existence of psychological stress among those working in this field but my investigations do suggest to me the importance of individuals' 'self-integrating purposes', and this adapting of their orientations to work in such a way that the sources of strain in the occupation can also be seen as the rewards or satisfactions of the work. In the next chapter I shall turn to adjustments to the inherent problems of personnel management at the occupational level and look at the 'professionalisation' strategy.

6 Professionalism: symbol and strategy

The notions of professionalism and professionalisation can be of great significance to the spokesmen for occupational groupings. They appear to be a valuable resource which is available to those concerned to represent and further the interests of any grouping of people who operate within a sphere of work where there is sufficient specialisation to create a potential coincidence of interest centring on the way the work is performed and the rewards which can accrue from that performance.[1] Personnel management is being looked at in this study as an occupational grouping and it has been shown that both the history of the occupation and the structural problems which underlie it, given the nature of the tasks and the organisational positions with which its members are concerned, are such that a potential common interest can be seen to exist. The previous chapter has demonstrated some of the ways in which the individual practitioner copes with what can be seen from the outside as problems of ambivalence and contradiction. Adjustment and accommodation to situational exigencies, combined with the dynamic or processual nature of individual orientations, are central to that analysis. But, in so far as personnel practitioners face similar or shared problems, we can see a common objective (potential) interest around which a coalition of interest or social group might form. Such a group would operate to protect or further the interests of its members. The extent to which an occupational grouping has developed, converting an objective into a subjective interest and making use of the readily available concept and strategy of professionalism is the concern of this chapter.

The study of professions has constituted a popular area within the sociology of occupations. Its popularity may relate to a fascination on the part of the investigators and their audiences with areas of life like law and medicine which are so surrounded by mystique

115

and social prestige. Such a fascination might be coloured by a vicarious aspirational interest or, alternatively, by a sceptical, critical or debunking motive. Where the studies have not been of the so-called 'established' professions they have frequently been concerned with examining the extent to which this or that occupation is a profession – implicitly awarding the occupation a place in the league table of 'success'. Taking this approach has often produced one of the most blatant cases of the confusion of the topic and the resource in sociology. The notion of professionalism, a resource used by those being studied by sociologists and therefore an appropriate topic for sociological investigation, has often become a resource to be used by the sociologist – a sociological concept itself. Such conversion of lay typifications into sociological concepts or ideal types is an inevitable and intrinsic part of the sociological project, but one cannot help feeling that, in the case of professions, this has often been done in such a naive fashion that the observers have uncritically adopted the assumptions of the observed, so confusing propaganda and analysis.

In discussing this study with practitioners in the personnel field I have repeatedly been asked 'well, how professional do you think we are?' and a number of personnel managers have criticised me for failing, in a working paper, to construct a typology of personnel employees in terms of their relative professionalism. My experiencing of such pressures in the course of my research has given me some insight into the situation which Johnson describes, where 'the problem has been transformed into a largely sterile attempt to define what the special "attributes" of a profession are. These definitional exercises litter the field' (1972, p. 10). Such approaches may list 'traits' or trace the 'natural history' of the professionalising occupations (ibid.). The only full-length sociological study of the personnel occupation is centrally concerned to examine the extent to which personnel administration in America can be said to be 'professional', examining its development and the performance of its members against the attributes listed in this type of literature (Ritzer and Trice, 1969). The British Institute of Personnel Management is looked at in similar terms by Timperley and Osbaldeston (1975, p. 610).[2]

The concern with the professional credentials of particular occupations is in contrast to an older concern within sociology: a concern with the contribution which might be made on a societal level by organisations which regulate work on other than a business or profit-oriented basis. The medieval guild model clearly informed Durkheim's view of professional type bodies and their possible contribution towards social order and the countering of dangers of anomie (1933, Preface to 2nd Edition). Tawney (1961), Marshall

116

(1963) and, more recently, Halmos (1970) have followed up these issues. I would agree with Johnson that there has generally been a 'nervous withdrawal' from the value-laden notions implicit in such analyses and that, consequently, there has been a neglect of these large-scale problems by sociologists (1970, p. 12). Although I am primarily concerned in this chapter to look at professionalism and personnel management at the occupational level, this analysis will contribute towards the discussion of issues at the societal level in chapter 9 where I shall examine Halmos's suggestion of an ethical reorientation in society associated with a professionalising trend within managements (1970). Despite my sharing of Halmos's wariness about the tendency for the 'contemporary climate of opinion' to be 'radically and bitterly antiprofessional', I do not think that one would be departing sufficiently from the unsatisfactory nature of much current analysis by turning attention, as he suggests, to subdivisions of the 'complex and global notion' of professionalism (1973, pp. 5–6). Like Turner and Hodge I feel that the focus should be on the occupational group (1970). The existence of the 'profession', a 'semi-profession', 'quasi-profession' or whatever should not be taken for granted. Rather, ideas of professionalism can be seen as ideological devices, and the structures and practices which are associated with these ideas as aspects of occupational strategies. Such an approach is not new. We can see how, to an extent, the growth of the sociology of work and occupations itself has been dependent on a suspension of assumptions about professionalism. This is revealed in Hughes's account of the 'empirical beginnings in the sociology of work':

> In 1939, I began to teach a course on professions. People from various departments of the university and from many occupations came into the course; many of them wanted to write about the efforts of their own occupation to have itself recognised as a profession. It is said that our image of the devil – the Christian devil, that is – is based on the testimony in ecclesiastical courts of people possessed. From the claims and hopes of people in the many occupations seeking professional status, we learned what the concept means to people. I soon changed the name of the course to 'The Sociology of Work', both to overcome to some extent the constant preoccupation with upward mobility of occupations and also to include studies of a greater variety of occupations and problems (1970, p. 148).

My concern in what follows is to take up this interest in the meaning that the concept of professionalism has for personnel specialists. My analysis therefore takes heed of the arguments of the Chicago sociologists. But since their perspective is not one which concentrates on occupations in the way which Johnson argues to be important in

117

the area of 'professions', that is 'in terms of their power relations in society – their sources of power and authority and the ways in which they use them' (1972, p. 18), I shall incorporate such a perspective into my own more 'power conscious' theoretical scheme. This can then be applied to the personnel occupation.

A perspective on professionalisation

According to the general theoretical scheme which was set out earlier (pp. 16–17), every individual person is associated with a range of social groups, these being coalitions around shared interests. Whenever there is a potential advantage with regard to what is valued and scarce in society, there is a logically possible 'objective interest'. The recognition and articulation of ways in which people might act with reference to such an interest leads to group formation (through the growth of an awareness of 'subjective interests') and consequent group-interest-oriented actions. *Ideas* and spokesmen to express ideas are vital to such processes, not just to create the initial subjective group consciousness but thenceforward to maintain and develop a *group ideology* to retain internal coherence and defend and further group interests with reference to other social groups. The political aspect of the structuring of society is dependent on the relative success or failure of groups in this competitive process – the group's 'power' denoting its access to whatever benefits 'goods' or resources upon which its members' shared interest is focused. The notion of professionalism is, in advanced industrial capitalist societies, a useful *idea* which can be taken up by individuals who, as spokesmen for others in a given type of occupational position, wish to make and legitimate claims on behalf of that group for power in specific areas of occupational performance. The idea contains within itself possible actions which the group may take to reinforce its legitimacy and the legitimacy of the label.

The idea of the profession as a ready-made ideological resource is available to the aspiring occupational group of the twentieth century, the model with its key to prestige, autonomy and power having been established in the nineteenth century (see, especially, Elliot, 1972). The resource is available to members of an occupational group as one means by which they might contribute to a construction of reality – a reality which will be consonant with their own perceived interests. Becker, working in the tradition established by Hughes, suggests that the idea of a profession can be seen as a 'folk concept' or 'collective symbol'; it is not a scientific concept but a part of the apparatus of the society which we study (1971, p. 92). These 'professions' are 'simply those occupations which have been fortunate enough in the politics of today's work world to gain and maintain possession of that honorific title' (*ibid.*, p. 92). But the label, I would stress, is only a means, and not an end in itself. Elger has argued for the analysis of the 'sustaining and transforming processes' whereby *structures* 'are patterned by negotiation and interpretation among participants with diverse interests and resources' (1975, p. 114). Thus

professional status is not simply 'given' in consequence of some correspondence to abstract criteria, but is rather socially constructed and maintained in processes of negotiation and interpretation concerning the grounds and character of such status. These processes and hence the meaning given to professional status may vary among organisational locales and with changes in organisational arrangements, while the actual practices adopted by professional claimants also differ, with varying visibility and negotiability of performances (Elger, 1975, p. 120).

Elger cites, in the course of the above discussion, the work of Becker and Freidson which was cited in the last chapter when I referred to the importance of situational factors in work orientation and behaviour. The point to be made here is that the specific situation experienced by any particular occupation may influence which particular aspect of the general symbol of the 'profession' is utilised by the group members and their spokesmen. The findings of my own researches indicate the importance of this point with reference to the personnel occupation, as I shall indicate later on. Before I turn to the ways in which personnel practitioners have used the professional idea, however, I will attempt to clarify a little more what is meant by professionalisation and how the concept relates to power. I shall also raise the question of the relationship between self-interest and altruism in professionalisation processes.

Having argued that professionalism is a symbol rather than a scientific category, one must hesitate before attempting to find a working definition. It is useful, however, to indicate the general components of the type of process which an occupational group will tend to follow, recognising that in any specific case some elements will be more important than others. Freidson has offered the following:

Professionalisation might be defined as a process by which an organised occupation, usually but not always by virtue of making a claim to special esoteric competence and to concern for the quality of its work and its benefits to society, obtains the exclusive right to perform a particular kind of work, control, training for and access to it, and control the right of determining and evaluating the way the work is performed (1973, p. 22).

119

The ultimate goal of such a process is occupational *autonomy* – assuming that any 'professionalising' group wished to achieve this ultimate point. And autonomy is the key to power. As Hall and Engel put it: 'autonomy is power granted to someone or some group because of their presumed *expertise* and the absence of the ability on the part of the laity to gain such expertise' (1974, p. 327). But of additional legitimating potential is the other notion which, like that of expertise, is implicit in any notion of professionalism – that of 'benefit to society', 'service' or 'altruism'. Claims to expertise and to service, then, are part of the means whereby an occupational group can increase its power and hence its ability for members' interests to be defended or furthered.

expertise + service

Such a view may seem cynical and to involve a debunking and hence an automatic rejection of any occupational claim to service. This, however, is not what is intended, even though one is recognising the need here to be wary of occupational ideologies and their associated utterances. Daniels has referred to what she calls 'the difficulties of disentangling the ideology of service from the political advantages of the professional label' (1975, p. 307) and Freidson, in arguing that professional ideologies are 'intrinsically imperialistic', says that such imperialism 'can of course be a function of crude self-interest, but it can as well be seen as a natural outcome of the deep commitment to the value of his work developed by the thoroughly socialized professional who has devoted his entire adult life to it' (1973, p. 31). The point is that a professionalising ideology which claims a service orientation may not be merely hypocritical: the fulfilment of self-interest does not necessarily preclude service to others. Either one might be a means to the other. Therefore, in arguing in this chapter that members of the personnel occupation have made use of the idea of professionalism to further their common interests, I am not claiming that this will in itself settle, one way or another, the issue of the 'societal contribution' of personnel management. It will contribute, however, to the analysis which will be made at a later stage. For the present, I will turn to the early occupational organisation of personnel workers and the nature of their interest in professionalism.

ideology + reality

self-interest + commitment

Occupational organisation and development

In looking at the development of the personnel occupation one has to avoid too carelessly imposing on the past categories which are taken for granted today. I have argued in an earlier chapter the grounds for regarding employees in a range of activities as members of the one occupation. I am now looking at the processes whereby this occupation emerged and will refer to 'personnel' work even though, prior to World War II, such a term was little used in Britain (Crichton, 1968, p. 23). In applying this term to cover a variety of activities, I am not suggesting that practitioners across this range saw themselves as clearly occupationally related as they tend to today. In chapter 2 I located the origins of the personnel occupation in the welfare movement of the early twentieth century and argued that this movement necessarily became involved in efficiency issues as well as the welfare ones with which this might potentially conflict. As Crichton makes clear, some components of what we now see as the personnel function were, in the early days of specialisation, undertaken by individuals from entirely different backgrounds from the welfare workers (1968, pp. 20–3). Particularly important here were the employment and industrial relations officers appointed in various organisations. How the various groups were brought together is something we can look at once we have examined how the 'nucleus of a group with professional aspirations' (Crichton, 1968, p. 21) was created by those interested in welfare, at the earlier stage. My account of this and much of what follows is largely dependent on the historical account provided by Niven (1967), and I shall select points from that study, leaving my reader to refer to it to fill out the picture given here from the inevitably selective sociologist's point of view.

A significant problem which was faced by the early welfare workers was a difficulty in knowing precisely what to do to meet the general requirements of their employers to raise standards of welfare. The existing training given in university social studies departments was not helpful, as Crichton points out: 'their theoretical studies were about social philosophy and social economics, which encouraged them to be concerned about social justice, with the result that the employers found them very critical of management ideologies' (1968, p. 19). The fact that a potential occupational ideology originating in the university setting was one which might conflict with employers was not a promising basis for a group ideology around which action might develop. Hence the early meetings which occurred between welfare workers tended to be at the instigation of the paternalist employers of the welfare movement rather than the welfare workers themselves. These, however, increased the felt need for more links between welfare workers (Niven, 1967, p. 33). The first formal association, the Welfare Workers' Association was established at a conference called by Rowntree in York in 1913 and this contained two classes of membership: employers (either corporately or as individuals) and welfare workers. The wording of the minutes is significant: 'it was decided to form an Association of Employers interested in industrial betterment and of welfare workers engaged by them' (ibid., p. 36). It is doubtful whether an organisation containing employers and employees stood any chance of viability, there being as many potential conflicts of interest as coincidences. And given that one of the basic problems of the welfare workers was their relationship with employers, it is not surprising that within a few years a struggle commenced for the association to be one of welfare workers and not employers. Moves in this direction were inevitably delayed by the advent of the war in 1914 which saw the departure of many of the original welfare workers from their posts followed by the recruitment of hundreds of new welfare supervisors who knew nothing of the Association and its work (*ibid.*, p. 47).

The war-time recruits to welfare work, despite their ignorance of the W.W.A., felt the same need for association as had the pioneers, and local societies grew up in different parts of the country to cater for this need. Concerns were largely with training and the need to maintain standards (*ibid.*, p. 47). The anxiety which this trend towards independent groups caused led to the calling by three of the pioneer women members of the W.W.A. of a conference in Leeds in 1917. A significant problem which the welfare workers shared and which was discussed here was the hostility which was being engendered among trade unions as a result of what the conference chairman, one of the employer members, saw as various 'mistakes' which he believed were being made (*ibid.*, p. 48). The need was for a national association through which members could learn to avoid such mistakes.

Rowntree's contribution to the conference reinforced the recognition of such a need and he felt that interested employers would give financial support to aid the processes of establishing offices, engaging in research, publishing findings and so on. Although the need for a national association to represent common interests among welfare workers was clearly recognised, there was a weekend-long debate over the extent to which the aims of such an association would be weakened by employer financing. A decision to go for independence was taken. Employers could be admitted as associates to what was called a 'professional' body 'of all engaged in welfare work in industrial and business enterprises' (*ibid.*, p. 49). We now have what can be called an *occupational* association and this was called the Central Association of Welfare Workers. It brought together the pioneers with what became the 'branches'. Expansion occurred rapidly with a major stress on the need for training. An *objective* common interest, based at this stage on such shared problems as the relationship with general management, the relationship with trade unions and the need to establish and maintain standards of competence, had become a *subjective* one with the consequent mobilisation of effort.

Another component of the situation which my theoretical scheme would suggest as necessary is that of a group ideology to aid internal coherence and to legitimate the group activities and interests externally. Such a group ideology can be seen to emerge formally in June 1918, when a definition of welfare work was approved. The opening of this definition, which, Niven comments, was inspired by Miss Kelly and Miss Harrison ('spokesmen' in my scheme) was 'Welfare work is that part of management which deals with the well-being of those engaged in business' (quoted in *ibid.*, p. 51). Niven comments on this: 'The committee had taken the bit between its teeth. If welfare were indeed recognised as being part of management, many of the difficulties already encountered would vanish and the way would be free for the proper development of the work' (1967, p. 51). Thus we see an occupational association seeing itself as a professional body – to distinguish itself from employer patronage which might weaken its independence; we see it becoming very concerned to establish training and maintain standards, yet, less on the lines of the professional 'symbol', we see it attempting to establish its place within 'management'.

This, I suggest, is because occupations do not automatically follow 'professionalisation processes' as some sociological studies seem to imply. They tend, rather, to *follow occupational strategies appropriate to what they, or their 'spokesmen', perceive as their own specific interests.* Such strategies use elements of 'professionalism' as appropriate. In bureaucratic organisations, status and authority were seen as dependent on welfare workers becoming part of management. As I suggested in chapter 3, attention to criteria of formal rationality (or 'efficiency') was a necessary means to achieving anything in terms of 'welfare'. But if acceptance by managements was one of the shared problems facing welfare workers, so was acceptance by the increasingly strong trade unions. The now formally stated group ideology, which gave some assurance to managers and supervisors in the statement that 'The work of the welfare workers is purely administrative and advisory', attempted an equivalent legitimation *vis-à-vis* trade unions with the words: 'He or she claims no right to interfere between organised labour and the employers recognising trade unionism as the chosen means of self-expression of the workers'.

Niven records how Association representatives approached government departments with requests that it should take part in any process to decide on standards for official recognition of welfare workers (p. 51) and a similar approach was made to the universities on training schemes (p. 52). Given these activities, it was probably inevitable that it should be laid down that full membership be restricted to those doing duties as defined by the Association (*ibid.*, p. 52). The association appointed an organising secretary and, whilst relations with trade unions were being constantly discussed in

London, she travelled the country attempting to 'convert' employers. She found the greatest problems in the spheres of relations with supervision, recruitment of workers and trade union opposition (*ibid.*, p. 53).

Consciousness of group interests, the need for appropriate structures and, particularly, the presentation of an appropriate image, exercised the association's activists in a number of ways. At the 1919 annual general meeting there were reservations expressed about the term 'welfare' and, to avoid confusion with other types of welfare work, the association's title was adapted to Central Association of Welfare Workers (Industrial). A not unrelated problem was the tendency for local societies for men in industrial welfare work to develop, thus giving the impression that there were different kinds of welfare for males and for females. Such a division was seen as a threat to occupational organisation and negotiations took place between the various bodies leading to the formation of the Welfare Workers' Institute in November 1919. A journal began the following year.

Incorporation was the next step, but this only came about after an Enquiry which was necessary to cope with various objections from rival bodies. The licence of incorporation was granted in March 1924 and this official recognition, it was felt, would improve the status of the 'profession' and give it stability (Niven, 1967, p. 70). The title was now the Institute of Industrial Welfare Workers. This was something of a turning point in that the pioneers' 'generation' was coming to a close (*ibid.*, p. 70) and the employment situation which was developing at the time was hardly conducive to the development of welfare work within management. Welfare was less necessary as a means towards efficiency or productivity in a situation where labour was plentiful and the welfare supervisors had, as Niven puts it, the 'adaptability to turn course from welfare to labour and staff management in order to meet new and pressing needs' (1967, p. 71). But with a perceived need for the occupation to move in this direction it was recognised that the occupational organisation would again be weakened were it not able to include those who were already operating in the employment and industrial relations areas.

Crichton stresses the social class differences between many of those in the welfare-based institute and those (male) workers in the labour field (1968, p. 23). An extraordinary general meeting was held in 1931 to discuss the issue and the title was changed to the Institute of Labour Management, this being followed by an influx of graduate men and a number of individuals of some eminence in the labour field (Niven, 1967, pp. 84–5). As Niven's account of this period indicates, there was an increasing tendency to operate in terms of 'industry's needs'. The occupation was moving further and further from its philanthropic roots. In 1939 the decision was made to change the institute's name for the seventh time but it was only after the war period, during which time personnel work expanded enormously, that the title Institute of Personnel Management was officially adopted, in 1946.

The period of development of occupational organisations for personnel workers between 1915 and 1946 is, I suggest, a fascinating example of the way key individuals and small groups of activists can create a consciousness of common interests and structure relationships between people working in related jobs. The importance of group ideologies in developing such an occupational association is illustrated by the frequent definitional and statement-of-purpose debates which took place both before and after 1946 (the later ones are looked at in the next chapter) as well as by the importance attached to the title of the body. The development of the association is perhaps symbolised in these changing titles:

1913 Welfare Workers' Association
1917 Central Association of Welfare Workers
1918 Central Association of Welfare Workers (Industrial)
1919 Welfare Workers' Institute
1924 Institute of Industrial Welfare Workers
1931 Institute of Labour Management
1946 Institute of Personnel Management

The membership in 1913 was 35 and by 1946 had risen to 2,896 (McGivering, 1970, p. 197).

Throughout the history of the institute there had been a strong concern with training and qualification. Such a concern is something which would logically be expected of any organisation claiming to represent the interests of the members of an occupation: it not only increases the marketability of members through the development of skills but restricts entry, to members' advantage – and, very importantly, gives both the occupation and its representatives legitimacy and acceptability through its ability to claim 'improvement of standards' and hence service to 'clients'. An occupational organisation would need to be careful, however, in the point at which it attempts to close entry on the lines of the professional model. To restrict entry before a high proportion of practitioners see membership as valuable could be fatal to aspirations. The I.P.M. introduced its own examination scheme and regulations in 1955 but, when the entry of younger members was found to drop for several years, the rigour of the examinations was reduced. The new examination scheme devised in 1960 enabled colleges to provide courses to prepare people for the examination. Entry to the institute was still possible, however, for those over 35 with several years' experience (Niven, 1967, p. 155).

It was not until the 1970s, after the period which I discussed in chapter 3 when legislation and trade union pressure were increasing the recognition of personnel work within management and public administration interests were catered for in the institute, that further moves were made to restrict entry. Since January 1975, new membership is only available to those taking examinations in statistics, psychology, sociology, economics, general personnel management and one optional subject (training and development, employment and employee services or industrial relations). Further examinations have to be taken to gain higher grade membership. My survey of the I.P.M.'s literature during the period prior to and subsequent to the change suggests an increased tendency for the rhetoric of professionalism to be used. Particularly characteristic are the words which open an article about the examination changes in the *I.P.M. Digest* of February 1975:

> Professionalisation is gradually becoming history at the Institute. Although the welfare roots may seem further away than ever, personnel management's contribution to industrial, commercial and administrative life has become more important and respected, through the growing competence of its practitioners. The I.P.M. has been at the vanguard of this trend (I.P.M., 1975d).

The article refers to the new regulations as 'one of the most important steps in the process' and goes on,

> The significance of this development should not be under-estimated, since it both reflects the influence of professionalism today and ensures high standards of academic ability and practical experience from the members of tomorrow (*ibid.*).

The use of the notion of 'professionalism' here seems to be stressing competence and expertise rather than autonomy or community service – the latter having been more central to the use of the symbol by the pioneer welfare workers. The opening address to the I.P.M.'s annual conference, which took place several months before the introduction of the new regulations was given by the President of the Confederation of British Industry and he was anxious to stress the need for personnel managers to recognise 'above all the necessity for adequate profits'. These words were reported in the December 1974 *I.P.M. Digest* which printed in large letters on its front page (i.e. as an eye-catching headline) the following words from the same speech:

> The Institute of Personnel Management has developed into one of the leading and most powerful professional bodies in the

United Kingdom and has a well deserved reputation for progressive and enlightened thinking (I.P.M., 1974b).

This embracing of the symbol of professionalism by the institute as part of the group ideology can be understood as an attempt to attract people to a high-status occupation ('professionalism' being an indication of prestige) as well as an important means of gaining influence with national and state bodies. The I.P.M. president said at the time of the annual conference in 1972,

> As the Institute which represents the personnel managers of the country, we too have a role to play in influencing thought on a national scale; a role which is also a duty as well as a right. We constitute the majority of personnel managers who regard themselves as committed to tackle the most intransigent and critical problems of industry today (Lyons, 1972, p. 5).

This interesting statement entitled 'Presidential Philosophy' and printed at the beginning of the conference edition of *Personnel Management* claimed that the

> true function of a profession is not only to set and maintain standards of knowledge and performance. We must also determine matters of principle in fields such as industrial relations which are critical to the function of our profession and back up, by pronouncements on those principles, members of the profession who seek to maintain them in the course of their employment' (*ibid.*).

The principles he had in mind appear to look both to the government of the time and to the trade unions. The I.P.M. should approve of the framework of law of the type developed in the Industrial Relations Act, it is suggested, and should declare a belief in 'strong, effective and manly trade unions'. Employers are probably looked to in the requirement that unions should have a 'business-like relationship' with employers 'because they respect them as capable of making and observing agreements by which their members are as tightly bound as the agents of management are bound'. Such a view of unions, which is not inconsistent with what has been called a notion of unions as 'managers of discontent', could well appeal to employers. Thus, in a statement of a 'professional' philosophy, we can detect legitimations of group interests *vis-à-vis* the range of related interest groups.

However, my earlier analyses do indicate that, for the individual personnel practitioner, the group to which he has to look for acceptance and legitimacy most critically and most frequently is his own management. The questions must therefore be raised of the relevance of notions of 'professionalism' to the practitioner who, in solving the day-to-day problems of his immediate situation, may be less interested in the arguments which are made at national, occupational, level. The concluding justificatory comments of the above presidential statement does, I suggest, look in the direction of the hard-headed practical down-to-earth line managers.

> In the field of human relations a laisser-faire attitude may sometimes be paraded as sophistication. Similarly an absence of ethical standards may be confused with being realistic. Both as professionals and as an Institute we have to be sure that we are progressive in our wisdom and morally courageous in our pragmatism (*ibid.*).

The relevance of professionalism in the workplace

It is likely to be in the interests of personnel practitioners for their occupation to be officially recognised as influential and for it to be seen as 'professional' in the eyes of the public. But it can be questioned whether the same practitioners will be as anxious to appear as members of a profession, with ethical standards, mystique and the rest, to their fellow managers and bureaucratic superiors. I see a suggestion of an awareness of this problem in the above quotation which provides the institute member with a potentially useful defence of professional criteria against the over-pragmatic 'realism' with which he may find himself challenged at work.

The dangers here are very carefully explained and illustrated by Goldner and Ritti in their important article 'Professionalisation as Career Immobility' (1970). This article is particularly relevant to issues under consideration here because the case which they use to illustrate their thesis is a personnel occupation one – that of American labor-relations managers. The authors explain how these personnel specialists studied by Goldner resisted the professional label since 'To be identified as part of a "profession" would preclude concurrent identification as general management' (Goldner and Ritti, 1970, p. 473), and as Anthony and Crichton have said, in the British context, 'The history of the personnel specialists as a group is the history of a struggle for status to become full members of the management team' (1969, p. 165).

Arguments which reveal the dangers of professionalism for the personnel practitioner in his organisational setting have appeared in the occupational literature. Price in 1962, in an article 'Personnel Management – A Service not a Profession', which appeared in the I.P.M.'s journal, saw professionalism separating 'the duties of personnel management from those of general management' to the detriment of the latter (quoted in Crichton, 1968, p. 329). Petrie, in his contribution to a much more active American debate about professionalisation of the occupation, asked 'The Personnel "Professionals" – who needs them?', arguing that the professional personnel specialist is denying himself the opportunity of organisational advancement (1965, p. 70). Arguments given for professionalising by Miller (1959a, b) in two articles do, significantly, accept this separation of personnel from general management, arguing that 'the personnel job is different . . . in that it has to serve the needs not only of the employer, but also act in the interests of employees as individual human beings and, by extension, the interests of society' (1959b, p. 92). The personnel specialist is thus 'the custodian of the corporate conscience in the matter of "the human use of human beings" ' (*ibid.*, p. 91). Thomason, in the I.P.M.'s textbook, sees the existence of two currently existing alternative conceptions of the personnel role. One of these is the organisationally dependent *administrative* one in which 'the emphasis will be upon personnel management as a process of helping to design and implement control procedures through the whole manning spectrum from recruitment to termination' and the other is the *professional* role where 'the emphasis will fall more firmly upon the man-in-the-middle approach, with justice and fairness as animating criteria and reconciliation of conflict over ends and means being a more central concern' (Thomason, 1975, p. 39). Whether this latter conception is viable in practice is questioned by the pressures on practitioners of organisational exigencies, as shown in the previous chapter with regard to approaches to redundancy. At this stage it becomes appropriate to turn away from occupational 'spokesmen' of various kinds and look at the responses of my interviewees to questions about professionalisation, to see what the notion means to practitioners.

Practitioners' conceptions of professionalism

A great deal of the effort of writers on professions has gone into the locating of the essential or 'traits' of the professional occupation. My approach has been to regard the idea of a profession as a model which might be *used* by an occupational group, highlighting those aspects of the model which would be most pertinent to the situation and aspirations of members of the occupation. To see which aspects of the professional model appear to be most meaningful to the individuals in my sample, I asked the general question: *What does the idea of a profession mean to you?* I have examined the responses to this question to find the number of times specific 'traits' of professionalism were mentioned. The results of this analysis are given in Table 6.1.

TABLE 6.1 *Professional traits mentioned by respondents*

Trait	Number of mentions
Education/training towards a qualification	41
High skill, expertise, possession of knowledge	31
High status/prestige	15
Restricted entry	10
Maintenance of standards	9
Dedication	9
Ethics, integrity, etc.	5
Experience	5
Autonomy/working for clients for a fee	4
Based on a body of knowledge or theory	3
Service to the community	2
	134

There are various other features mentioned. Three people said a profession was a job which was a 'career', one said it was something one got paid for and another that it was work 'based on objectivity'. One account saw it simply as a 'claim for self-aggrandisement', another saw it as 'just futile', whilst another spoke of professions as 'a man's world' (this was from a lady personnel officer). Other occupations mentioned in this context are shown in Table 6.2.

TABLE 6.2 *Occupations mentioned in answering question: 'What does the idea of a profession mean to you?'*

Occupation	Number of mentions
Medicine	10
Law	5
Accounting	3
Nursing	2
The Church	1
Teaching	1
Dentistry	1
Engineering	1

This type of data has to be interpreted with care, not least because of the arbitrariness of allocating elements of individual accounts to categories. This was a general question about professions with no mention of personnel management. However, the respondents were speaking about professions in a context where the main topic was clearly the personnel occupation (and this question was asked at a relatively late stage of the interview). Also, we would expect the individual's own occupational experience to have coloured his or her view of professionalism – the personnel occupation being one in which professionalism is often seen as an issue.[3] I therefore suggest that we can use this data to get an indication of the features of the professional 'symbol' which are seen as most *salient* to personnel practitioners. It would appear that the most meaningful elements are those suggesting the acquisition of a high level of expertise, skill or knowledge through the pursuit of a programme of training or education which gives a qualification. Such an emphasis might be present in any sample of people being asked the same question.

What is perhaps more significant, I suggest, is that, despite the fact that the particular occupations which were mentioned in this context indicate the relevance of the classic independent fee-paid professions to the image, certain traits often given emphasis in the literature on professions, like autonomy, ethics, community-service and the importance of a body of knowledge and theory (see Millerson, 1964, p. 5) are mentioned far less often. I suggest that this pattern is to be understood in that the latter group of traits are less likely to be salient to those operating in what is a bureaucratically oriented occupation. Elements of expertise and qualification are, however, highly salient to members of such an occupation. Professionalism, then, in the context of personnel management practice appears to be primarily associated with competence or expertise. In the light of the general concern among practitioners with 'credibility' we can see some attractiveness in the notion of a profession to them.

TABLE 6.3 *Respondents' accounts of professionalism and personnel management*

Type of account	No.
Personnel management a profession	46 ⎤
Personnel management not a profession but becoming one	22 ⎬ 77
Personnel management not a profession but ought to be one	9 ⎦
Personnel management not a profession	23
	100

Practitioners' views of personnel management and professionalism

The most general conclusion that one can draw from the responses to the question *Do you see personnel management as a profession?*

(*Is it one or ought it to become one?*) is to say that over three-quarters of the sample appear to feel that a professional image is in some way appropriate for their occupation. Categorising responses into four types gives the pattern shown in Table 6.3.

Those saying that personnel management is not a profession (and do not say that it ought to be one or is becoming one) give various reasons including the problem of locating 'a skill which you can identify and teach', the belief that 'you could never enforce group standards' and that 'it's too wide a field'. But the majority of responses here refer to the problem of the relationship to general management:

'No, it's part of general management.'

'No. The I.P.M. is too introspective. People should be able to get specialised training but the place for personnel managers is in a management body, not a personnel one.'

'No. There is a lot to be said for the idea of having half of your personnel managers at any time as people from line management who are doing a spell in Personnel. It avoids insularity and it also helps credibility.'

'No. Well what is professionalism? In this place we've got senior personnel blokes who are engineers, chemists and the like. They're not personnel professionals. So I suppose professional personnel people are those who aren't acceptable to line management.'

These accounts all point to the existence of an awareness of the problematic nature of the professional model for those in a bureaucratic, managerial setting. But when we look more closely at those accounts which suggest that personnel management *is* a profession we detect a similar wariness:

'Yes. But I object to the idea of people committing a lifetime to it. People should be able to move in and out.'

'Yes. But it does have a place for the amateur. I'ts wrong to make it a closed profession like the older ones.'

'Yes. As long as you can still bring in people from other areas – people who have flair and ideas.'

A common theme, particularly among those in more senior personnel positions, is to see one way of handling the problematic relationship with general management in maintaining an interchange of individuals. Professionalism in a full sense would militate against this strategy and is therefore a potential threat. There is thus an apparent paradox in the attitudes to professionalism: it appears from examining the accounts here that personnel management is something that needs to be done by trained and qualified people yet which can be done well by people who do not have that training. In response to my pointing out this apparent paradox, several senior people have accepted the point, commenting that the appropriate policy is for the 'professionals' with the detailed knowledge and skills to be, as one man put it, 'mixed up with the flair appointments. This way something of each rubs off on the other'. A personnel director commented

'a lot of big organisations mix up personnel professionals with temporary appointees these days. The way I see it is that it is a way in which we can recognise that personnel management – which can be a profession for some – is also a part of general management.'

This view takes us back to my earlier theme of the ambivalence underlying the personnel occupation. I would suggest that the various facets of the occupation which I characterised in terms of ambiguity and ambivalence relate to what I see as a general ambivalence in the attitudes of personnel practitioners towards professionalism. It appears in some of the above quotations and we see it again in the following: 'we do need to be professional but I don't want to see it indulging in black magic type mystique in order to be seen as one,' and 'It needs a professional approach but it doesn't need the I.P.M.'

I would suggest that we need here to return to the idea of the professionalism notion as a resource which is used in the construction of realities. If it can be used to suggest competence and expertise it is to be embraced. But in so far as it implies separateness, exclusivity and possibly 'career immobility' it has to be rejected. *'Being professional' or having 'a professional approach' is the emphasis which is often preferable to 'being a member of a profession'*. Recognising shades of meaning and the 'indexicality' of words is important to understanding such reality construction processes. 'Being professional' means, we might say, what the speaker wants it to mean. Thus: 'Yes it is a profession, but only in the sense that it needs a high degree of skill.' 'Personnel people are professionals and they should be. But I don't mean it in the traditional sense but in the sense of being paid for expertise.'

It is in the claim of competence that the professional symbol appears to be most relevant to practitioners. This is implicit in the statement of an American personnel society ('Professional Standards for Personnel Work': Washington D.C. Society for Personnel Administration, 1956):

There has been considerable evidence in recent years of the professional nature of personnel work. It is not necessary to debate here whether or not it is a fully developed profession. It probably is not. However, it does have a number of characteristics which indicate that it is an emerging profession. . . .

The element most badly needed for the improvement of personnel work is professional competence. Full professional level performance will follow closely in the wake of competence. Although the needs of standards for entrance, performance, and ethics in personnel work is evident, the primary need is for educational standards which will result in an adequate supply of competent personnel workers. . . . (quoted by Vollmer and Mills, 1966, p. 34).

Personnel practitioners and the professionalisation process

My preceding analysis of interviewee accounts has concentrated on the 'symbolic' aspects of professional labels. But professionalism also implies organisation and, as I showed in my discussion of the growth and development of the Institute of Personnel Management, there have been recent moves for the British professional organisation to restrict entry on the lines of the more traditional professions. Of my 100 interviewees, 48 are members of the I.P.M. although only 14 of these gained entry by examination; 21 are student members. However, I asked all interviewees: *The I.P.M. appears to be attempting to make entry into personnel management more difficult. What do you think of this?* (explaining the situation of entry by examination, when necessary). The general pattern of response was as shown in Table 6.4.

TABLE 6.4 *Responses to I.P.M. restricted entry policy*

Direction of response	No
Approving	27
Approving with reservations	40
Disapproving	28
Equivocal	5
	100

Whereas, as I indicated earlier, it appeared that three-quarters of the sample see value in adhering to some notion of professionalism, only just over one-quarter unreservedly approve of the recent moves of the I.P.M. to confine new membership to those passing a series of fairly rigorous examinations. Those who do approve often point out that this is a logical or an inevitable step if personnel practitioners are to achieve professional status. There is no tendency for those who themselves gained entry by examination to approve of these moves any more than those who gained entry by other means or are not members, interestingly.

It is only a similar proportion, just over a quarter again, who unreservedly disapprove of the institute's policies in this respect, leaving the largest proportion equivocal or approving with reservations. And very important to the disapprovers and to those with reservations appears to be a concern about the dangers of excluding, as it is often put, 'those who are good at the job but simply aren't academic'. Respondents often referred to the cases of individuals who were very capable but who were not the types to pass exams. I would suggest that this position also reflects what I have frequently observed among British managers – a deep suspicion of the 'academic' or the 'theoretical'. Connected with this is a no doubt quite realistic recognition of the importance of interpersonal skills – an importance that will become particularly apparent when I look at the bases of power and influence in chapter 8.

A Fellow of the I.P.M., a man currently involved in teaching student members, said

'I am split on this. I'm in the institute and if it becomes more exclusive so my raw market value increases. I'm selfish enough to be in favour. But in terms of exams, membership structures and so on, I've grave doubts. It's a question of acceptability. It's O.K. if you've got your bloody bit of paper – but the whole area of motivation, personality, self-starting, innovation – the main determinants of effectiveness in the work situation – are not examined. Some have the ability but will never pass the exams. . . . The I.P.M. is battling for status and professionalism. We can get the people who are applied social scientists, diagnosticians as Lupton suggests, but how many organisations would know what the fuck to do with them?'

This account illustrates several of the grounds for ambivalence towards the 'professionalising' process being followed by the occupational association. To investigate further the significance of the professional body to practitioners I asked members why they were members, and non-members why they were not.

Membership and non-membership

The reasons given for non-membership are interesting in that they suggest that the majority of non-members of I.P.M. are not

135

necessarily antagonistic to the idea of membership. Of the 52 non-members, 10 actually said that they felt that they ought to be members or that they would in fact be applying. Others said that they had entered the field too late or were too old to be taking examinations whilst others pleaded lack of time for study or simply said that they had 'never got round to it' (7 said this). Three personnel managers had not considered membership because they envisaged returning to line management. We are thus left with only 9 respondents who expressed hostility either to I.P.M. or to professional bodies in general. This figure appears, at first sight, to be surprisingly low, especially in the light of the large proportion not willing to endorse too readily the 'professionalising' strategy of the institute. The explanation becomes apparent, I suggest, when we look at the reasons cited by members for belonging. It appears that membership of the institute is *useful*.

Among the reasons given for belonging to the I.P.M. are a few which mention such things as 'status', 'a professional outlook' or the security of belonging to a 'closed shop'. But the vast majority of the accounts can be characterised by their apparent instrumentalism. The instrumentalism appears to be of two types; long-term *career instrumentalism* and shorter-term *situational instrumentalism*. Noting that a number of respondents gave more than one reason for membership we get a good impression of the emphasis here from Table 6.5:

TABLE 6.5 *Reasons cited for belonging to I.P.M.*

Reason	No of times mentioned
Career instrumentalism	
To get a qualification	18 ⎫
To get a training/entry to a course	17 ⎬ 52
To help one's career	17 ⎭
Situational instrumentalism	
To make useful contacts	11 ⎫
To obtain information, publications or access to institute services	10 ⎬ 21
General	
Employer suggested membership	6
Status	3
Professional outlook	3
Security/protection	2
	87

Situational instrumentalism appears to be particularly important to the older or more established members and career instrumentalism is very much a feature of the accounts given by student members, many of whom appear to be more interested in gaining a diploma than in obtaining the membership to which the diploma relates. One student even spoke of photocopying his diploma and resigning from the institute once he had passed the examinations.

My suggestion is that the approach of the personnel practioner to the professional association is, like his interest in the symbol of professionalism itself, very much a pragmatic one. This may explain some aspects of what a president of I.P.M. once called the 'unresolved dilemma' of the different emphases in the interests of the institute at national level, with an emphasis on 'standards', and at the branch level where the concern is more with practical issues (Niven, 1967, pp. 155-6). Lack of interest in branch activity has been shown by surveys done for the South West London branch and the Merseyside branch (I.P.M., 1974c; Timperley, 1972), and several of the East Midland branch meetings which I have personally observed have involved both strong attacks on central I.P.M. policies on the one hand, and strong complaints by branch officers, on the other, about the generally poor attendance at branch meetings. At one A.G.M. which I attended the branch chairman spoke of the embarrassment which he had experienced on a number of occasions when very small numbers of members had turned up to hear guest speakers.

However, the pragmatism to which I refer is indicated by the fact that when the branch ran a meeting to clarify aspects of the complex Health and Safety at Work Act there was, the chairman said, 'standing room only. There's nothing like new legislation to bring the masses out.' The Merseyside survey showed that a quarter of the members had never attended a branch meeting and, like the London survey, found a particular lack of interest among student members (*ibid.*) – this corresponding with the type of instrumentalism which predominated among the student members in my own interviews. By far the most popular feature of I.P.M. membership, according to the Merseyside survey, was the publications (Timperley, 1972) – these being seen, as my own experience during the course of my research indicates, as a very useful source of job-related information, by members and non-members alike.

The sociological literature on 'professionals in bureaucracies' leads one to look for conflicting loyalties on the part of those employed by a bureaucratic organisation who, at the same time, are members of a professional association (see Scott, 1966, for example). Yet Ritzer and Trice found that 'personnel managers are committed to both occupation and organisation' (1969, p. 82). I would interpret such a finding, in the light of my own work, as a result of the fact that an interest in 'professionalism' on the part of personnel practitioners is not so much an *alternative* orientation to one which involves contributing to organisational 'goals' as a *means towards making* such a contribution. It is through operating in terms of administrative criteria that the individual will help his career – not through devoting himself to a profession. His membership of a professional body can help him with guidance on new techniques, help with new legislation and knowledge of what is occurring in other organisations. The collectivism of the personnel professional is a form of the 'instrumental collectivism' referred to by Goldthorpe and Lockwood (1969, pp. 26, 27). There is little point in asking how 'professional' are the personnel practitioners. Application of a social-action frame of reference with its emphasis on motives, meanings and situational factors indicates that, although the personnel specialist is happy to embrace what Patten has called the 'seductive soubriquet' of the professional label (1968, p. 47) and that he sees the point of being 'qualified' and belonging to a body which can help him with information and advice, he is, nevertheless primarily a bureaucrat – he is still an aspiring member of the 'management team'.

7 Ideas, knowledge and ideology

The rise and development of industrial capitalist society has been part of the process whereby life has been increasingly *rationalised*. This has involved the increasing application of calculation, rules and the growing pervasiveness of 'scientific' knowledge. Routinisation and application of knowledge has been increasingly important in the seeking and maintenance of power – whether we are considering the distribution of power at the societal level or the power of occupational or organisational groupings. It was argued in the previous chapter that such a concern with knowledge on the part of occupational groups is central to the professionalisation strategy followed by some of these groups. In the case of personnel specialists it was seen that there is an interest in membership of a professional organisation and that this interest is to a large extent to be understood in terms of a desire to be labelled as competent – partly implying possession of appropriate knowledge – and in terms of a perceived opportunity to keep up to date with such knowledge.

The appropriateness of this knowledge, however, is very much a matter of its contribution to the personnel specialists' success in meeting the *administrative* criteria basic to their works. An illustration of this lies in the strong interest among personnel managers in the implications and details of recent employment legislation, something which is reflected in the publication, course, seminar and branch meeting activities of the Institute of Personnel Management. The connection between ideas, knowledge and power is central to the Weberian view of modern societies in which the rationalisation theme is so important. Bureaucratic and professional behaviour is not differentiated within Weber's sociology in the way that it has been to an almost extreme degree in sociology, and particularly American work, since his time. As Johnson comments, Weber 'specifically linked the process of bureaucratisation with the development of specialised professional education. He saw both processes as expressions of the increasing rationalisation of Western civilisation' (1972, p. 15). Professional status is usually regarded as in a large part dependent upon possession of specialist knowledge. But, as Weber said, in his discussion of bureaucracy, 'Bureaucratic administration means fundamentally the exercise of control on the basis of knowledge. This is the feature which makes it specifically rational' (1964, p. 339).

The personnel specialists whom I interviewed saw the professional body as a useful source of knowledge and information but, when it came to the issue of rigorous entry examinations, there were considerable reservations. These reservations were often expressed in terms of the importance of *experience* to the personnel manager. Weber pointed out that the knowledge which was the basis of bureaucratic administration was partly 'technical knowledge',

> But in addition to this, bureaucratic organisations or the holders of power who make use of them, have the tendency to increase their power still further by the knowledge growing out of experience in the service. For they acquire through the conduct of office a special knowledge of facts and have available a store of documentary material peculiar to themselves. While not peculiar to bureaucratic organisations, the concept of 'official secrets' is certainly typical of them. It stands in relation to technical knowledge in somewhat the same position as commercial secrets do to technological training. It is a product of the striving for power (*ibid.*, p. 339).

What is clear from this analysis is not only the need to see a close relationship between professional and bureaucratic action but a need to recognise that the power of the professional/bureaucrats (giving them the capacity to fulfil their interests) is bound up with the power of those who 'make use of' bureaucratic organisations (which gives them the capacity to meet *their* interests). Therefore we would expect personnel specialists to seek knowledge, information and techniques which would enable them to further both their own interests and those of their employers. One of the aims of this chapter is to examine the extent to which this is the case. But a sociological study of the *ideas* associated with an occupational group has to go further than a consideration of technical knowledge and information. I have revealed a concern with the relationship between knowledge and interests and such a concern necessarily takes us into the realm of *ideology*.

A strong tendency in discussions of ideology has been to demarcate the ideological from the scientific, implying that the former is distortive whilst the latter has the quality of objectivity (see Parsons, 1959, for example). Whilst there is some point in such a distinction, the use of the notion of ideology in this study is somewhat different. An ideological statement is seen here as one which is supportive of an interest of a given social group. The quality of ideology lies in the *use* of certain ideas rather than in the existence of 'ideologies' as complete and systematically related sets of propositions which can be contrasted with scientific thought. It is therefore quite conceivable that a scientifically respectable 'fact' could be used ideologically – in so far as its quotation served to further the interests of a social group which the speaker or writer is in effect representing. The way in which I will therefore approach the knowledge and ideas associated with the occupational group of personnel specialists is to see them as having concurrently both technical and ideological functions. This follows Child's analysis of management thought as having *legitimatory* and *technical* functions:

> The legitimatory function was primarily linked to the securing
> of social recognition and approval for managerial authority
> and the way in which it was used, while the technical function
> was primarily linked to the search for practical means of
> rendering that authority maximally effective (1969a, p. 23).

My approach will be to examine certain of the ideas which are expounded and applied by those doing personnel work and by those writing for or attempting to influence these practitioners. The consonance between group interests and particular ideas or knowledge will be stressed throughout. Towards the end of the chapter I will discuss whether or not any particular notions are sufficiently prevalent within personnel management thinking for us to go as far as detecting a possible *occupational ideology* – an 'ideology' in the sense that various ideas are readily available and are, in practice, exploited by personnel specialists or their spokesmen for legitimatory purposes.

This is not, however, to fail to differentiate between the ideas expressed by writers or professional spokesmen and those accepted or made use of by practitioners. The personnel practitioners are members of social groups such as their employing organisations or the 'management teams' within these as well as members of the occupational group. The writers, academics and professional spokesmen are not constrained by these same factors and we can thus expect a problematic relationship to exist between 'practitioners' and 'thinkers' – very much as Child suggests (1968 and 1969a). I shall therefore look at personnel management thinking by comparing and contrasting ideas operating at both levels. My analysis is very much influenced by a theoretically based expectation for those ideas of the 'thinkers' which are in effect taken up by practitioners to be those which are functional for the practitioners in their coping with the pressures of organisational life. The 'thinkers' will, however, tend to recognise this tendency and adjust their output to fulfil such functions.

The 'presidential philosophy' which was examined in the previous chapter (Lyons, 1972) represents a useful case study here. I attempted to show how that exposition had components which displayed legitimatory functions with regard to the range of interest groups to which personnel specialists, both as individuals and as an occupational grouping, relate. Lyons was looking towards the government, the trade unions and to non-personnel managers. The justificatory import of his message was not only directed towards external groups but was also directed internally, justifying membership of the professional body. Group ideologies are in a sense, then, negotiated between 'spokesmen' and members. Child saw a lack of connection between the 'spokesman'-created British management thought and the ideas of practising managers (Child, 1969a.). But he also saw a demise of that thought. Any gap which might be detected between spokesman-created personnel thinking and the ideas of practitioners might lead to a similar situation.

An alternative possibility, however, and one which we must bear in mind throughout the ensuing discussions, is that any such gap might be understood as a tendency of the thinkers to be *ahead* of the practitioners. Such a possibility is strongly suggested by the fact that an increasingly important channel of knowledge dissemination on the part of the professional body is in a published book form which has to be *marketed* and therefore designed with practitioner consumption in mind.[1] The same possibility is suggested by the trend claimed to be occurring by the institute whereby the increased entry qualifications are attracting occupational entrants of a level of academic ability higher than had previously been the case This might suggest a potentially higher level of acceptance of more theoretical or academically generated material.[2]

But, in the long run, the ideas which gain any wider currency – whether they be relatively abstract matters such as certain conceptions of the nature of personnel management or more concrete practical techniques – will be those where there is an elective affinity between *idea* and *interest*. Such an approach avoids any suggestion that ideas simply follow from interests and do not have what Child calls any 'autonomous influence' (1968, pp. 229–30). Having made this important point, I shall now examine one of the most important sources of recent personnel management thought: the social sciences. I shall attempt to show how social science ideas were taken up by the spokesmen or thinkers of the personnel occupation and how they related these ideas to the problems and interests of members of the occupation, as these were perceived by the thinkers. I shall then turn to some analysis of how the practitioners in my sample view social science thought and how far they appear to be influenced by such ideas.

Personnel management and social science thinking

In looking at the sources of social science thinking which have influenced personnel management thought in Britain it becomes apparent that we need to differentiate between the more academic, often more sociologically inclined, inputs which have largely been mediated by the Institute of Personnel Management and the more American-influenced, psychologically based, inputs from what I would call the *behavioural science entrepreneurs*. I hope that the difference between these two, admittedly overlapping, sources will become apparent in what follows. They are both sources which are more recent than the original social science input which came from the work done in occupational psychology by the armed forces and the Industrial Fatigue Research Board during World War I (Crichton, 1968, p. 22) and which was followed up by other bodies such as the National Institute of Industrial Psychology. The influence here has been mainly on techniques such as selection and appraisal which have been done largely by specialists within the personnel occupation. The importance of this influence should not be underestimated but, for the moment, I will turn to the more recent influence of British social science academics on the personnel management thinking which has developed under the auspices of the I.P.M. The importance of this lies in the influence that it has had on the overall conceptions of personnel management at the professional body level.

Child connects the decline of a distinct body of management thought 'sustained by a distinct management movement' with the increasing influence of ideas deriving from academic sources (1968, p. 223). His suggestion is that these ideas had an impact since they provided 'new knowledge relevant to management's technical functions' (*ibid.*, p. 224). Involved in the turning to these sources was a rejection of the human relations approach associated with Mayo and the Hawthorne experiments. The attractiveness of that approach had been, as Child pointed out in another article (1964), partly related to the coincidence between its tenets and those of the influential Quaker employers (whose influence was particularly great, of course, in the personnel sphere). But that influence decreased with the later emphasis on efficiency, and human relations themes went the same way, as it was recognised that they were 'merely industrial betterment writ large' and not likely to aid the integration of the personnel practitioner into the managerial team (Fox, 1966a, p. 15).

Child's judgment is that the personnel management movement has felt 'quite acutely the uncertainty consequent upon the rejection of its former human relations orthodoxy and the current lack of an equally definitive replacement' (1969a, p. 187). But the 1950s saw not only a decline in the human relations orthodoxy, it also saw the 'discovery' of the importance of structural and technical factors in the organisation of work. This was particularly reflected in the studies of Burns and Stalker (1961) and of Woodward (1958). Significantly, Woodward, whose research undermined current managerial assumptions beyond the human relations ones, was an active thinker within the I.P.M. and was editor of its journal at one stage.[3] It was Lupton, an industrial sociologist and at that time a professor of industrial relations, who most systematically based a conception of the personnel management role on these social science ideas, in a booklet published by the I.P.M. in 1964. In this document we see more than simply a suggestion for specific training policies for personnel specialists. The whole document can be interpreted as an offering to those in the occupation of a new group ideology: as a set of proposals which would help the personnel specialist to play a significant role in the management of organisations together with a rationale and justification for such an authoritative position.

Lupton makes it clear that the contribution which the social sciences can make is something other than in terms of the human relations orthodoxy; what he refers to as 'the once strongly held belief – now often doubted – that increases in human satisfaction are closely related to productive efficiency' (1964, p. 10). He suggests that the 'present aims and ideology of personnel management do not stand up very well to the analyses and findings of sociologists and psychologists' (ibid., p. 53). The alternative is that the personnel specialists should become applied social scientists – 'specialists in the analysis of the social and psychological problems which accompany technical and economic change' (ibid., p. 53). The suggestion is that organisations require expertly trained diagnosticians who can advise the decision makers on how structures and procedures can be adapted to changing social, economic and technological circumstances. The emphasis is less explicitly on integration into the management team as such as on the achieving of a strategic importance within the organisation. Lupton is clearly looking here to a problem of the occupational group which has been shown to be commonly felt: that of establishing credibility in the organisation. He also appears to be striking a familiar chord in an attempt to kill the old 'welfare image'. This is seen as inappropriate, as is the similarly disliked 'admin.' element of the job:

> It is extremely doubtful, in my view, whether the problems which we are facing and will continue to face will yield to the mixture of philanthropic ideology and administrative technique

which are the typical basis of much personnel management at present . . . (*ibid.*, p. 53).

But Lupton goes further than this. So keen is he to recognise the threat to credibility in any suggestion of philanthropy that he is happy to reject the very word 'social' from the collective title of the academic disciplines which hold the key to respectability. He refers throughout the document to 'behavioural science' –

I believe that the American term 'Behavioural Sciences' has a less confusing connotation than the British term 'social sciences', which often conjures up notions of philanthropy and social case work (*ibid.*, p. 3).

In a sense, the proposition which is being put in Lupton's work is one which makes the personnel specialist very much a technocrat rather than a professional. But despite the significant differences between what is being suggested and the traditional symbol of the profession, the value of the notion of professionalism to any new group ideology is clearly recognised. Lupton associates his arguments with those of another industrial relations professor – Fogarty – the man whom Stokes (1971) attacked as a leader of the 'efficiency lobby'. Fogarty's proposal was that the personnel manager should be 'the specialist in the economic use of human beings' (1963). Nevertheless Lupton is able to say in his preface, 'I agree with Professor Fogarty that we ought to be looking to the future development of personnel management as a profession . . .' (1964, p. 3). Crichton comments on this type of argument:

The solution which is recommended by the academics is to rediscover the meaning of 'professional' – learning to put less emphasis on ethics, on values, on professional norms, more on learning about the social sciences (1968, p. 330).

The word 'professional' has too much legitimatory utility to be abandoned, it would seem. But it has to be redefined to mean what it suits the spokesman to mean. This indicates the sensitivity of these particular thinkers to what I saw in the previous chapter as an ambivalent attitude among personnel practitioners to the notion of professionalism.

The arguments of these academics were forcefully reiterated by another industrial sociologist of eminence in the first article of a series entitled 'Trends in Personnel Management' published by *New Society* in 1966. Fox's article, 'From Welfare to Organisation', is almost threatening. Personnel officers who see themselves as repositories of a company's long-term conscience will become 'even more the men-in-the-middle, decreasingly relevant to policy-making'

(1966a, p. 15). The 'structural determinants of behaviour at work' are stressed in the place of personal relationships, welfare and 'leadership'. The implication of this is that there will be

> an important new function in large and medium sized companies of so designing organisational structure, work arrangements, controls, payment systems and personnel policies in general as to evoke the optimum patterns of behaviour most relevant to the company's objectives. Such a task can only be achieved through a partnership between general managers and a specialist in social organisation who can advise on the behavioural consequences of particular methods of organising work, authority and rewards (*ibid.*, p. 15).

And then comes the threat:

> If personnel management does not provide this specialism and equip itself to maintain a constructive dialogue with general management, sharing interests and objectives, then it risks relegating itself permanently to inferior status. There will be other claimants for the new role (*ibid.*, p. 15).

Here is a thinker or 'spokesman' pointing to what I have called an objective interest – a potential way for the occupational group to further its advantage. If mobilisation does not take place on the lines suggested (and a heavy responsibility is seen as resting on the I.P.M.'s shoulders) then the job might be taken on by production engineers or 'organisational analysts' (*ibid.*).[4]

The extent to which these ideas have established themselves as something approaching an orthodoxy at the professional body level is indicated by the content of the syllabuses for the examinations of the I.P.M. which, within the new regulations of the institute, are necessary to qualify for membership. The social sciences of economics, psychology and sociology are taught in a relatively general (i.e. not particularly 'applied') way in preparation for the examinations which allow transition from student to associate member and these are then developed in the higher-level courses which allow members to move up to corporate membership and which include 'Applied Behavioural Sciences', 'Management Systems' and 'Personnel Management Policies'. An early edition of the I.P.M.'s 'learned' journal contained an article by another professorial figure, one very much associated with attempts to utilise social science in organisations, entitled 'Personnel Management and the Social Sciences' (Cherns, 1972). This article argued that 'the main impact of the social sciences on personnel management has been through their interaction with social climates and ideologies, paving the way for, rather than directly initiating, changes in personnel practices' (*ibid.*, p. 11) but he felt that the 'most promising analytical develop-ments' were those of sociologists. The examples given are very much those whose work is relevant to the problem of organisational design – something very much at the structural and strategic level.

The question of the relationship between the social science ideas and the interests of members of the personnel occupation now has to be carefully examined to see if any generalisations can be made. I have suggested that one would seek some elective affinity between ideas and interests, and have mentioned, in particular, the expecta-tion that members of the occupation would tend to be receptive to ideas which could play a part in furthering the interests of the employers as well as those of the personnel workers themselves. The writers whose arguments are reviewed above clearly relate the efforts of their proposed type of personnel specialist to the goals of the controllers of organisations. And the suggestion is there that a particular strategic contribution which can be made is that of organisational adaptation to changing circumstances. Hence the structural emphasis and the leaning towards sociological perspectives. As Cherns puts it, 'It is no accident that sociology is coming to the fore in industry in a period when the relationship between the organisation and its environment is becoming critical' (1972, p. 11).

However, I believe that one can probe more deeply into this social science thinking to detect an underlying theme which has a potenti-ally very relevant legitimatory promise for the personnel occupation. In the light of the analysis of personnel work which I made in chapter 3, where the ambivalence of the position of the personnel specialist was stressed, we might expect there to be some considerable appeal in any set or type of ideas which could to some extent help resolve or rationalise the dual orientations of the occupation. The application of social *science* would imply criteria of formal rationality but, in so far as social thinking can be seen as linking analytical and calculative methods with considerations of human needs, such thinking might offer a way of relating formally rational criteria to materially rational ones.

An earlier, and now discredited, approach was to see the fulfilment of welfare criteria as producing organisational effectiveness. The promise of the new and alternative approach lay in the possibility that a range of structural alternatives could be available to the organisational designer who could choose from this range an approach which would take into account both the goals and purposes of the controllers of the organisation as well as the human and environmental contextual constraints. The 'right' organisational design would provide work for human beings which would enable them to meet their psychological and social as well as their economic needs whilst their performing of that work would fulfil the employers' requirements. The ideological import of such thinking (see Davis and Taylor, 1972, for examples), which implies that individual and organisational needs can be brought together to achieve mutual satisfaction, is considerable for any occupation which adopts such techniques as its technology. The trained diagnostician becomes a key man in the organisation: since there is no 'one best way', he has to be there constantly analysing contingencies and recommending optional strategies.

Underlying this social science thought, then, is a notion of 'optimising', paralleling the notions of the managerial economists who, following the work of Barnard, have in their own way tackled the problems which I described in chapter 3 in terms of a conflict between formal and material rationality (Barnard's 'efficiency' and 'effectiveness'). The promise of this thinking is its suggestion of possible *synthesis*. This idea is brought out in Henstridge's contribution to the I.P.M.'s learned journal where an attempt is made to provide a framework for the analysis of personnel management. This analysis sees as its 'overriding implication . . . the need for very considerable expertise in personnel management; this is most likely to come from the social scientist' (Henstridge, 1975, p. 52). And

one of the most important aspects of the personnel management role is that of *synthesis*. By this we mean the synthesis of the opposing views and interests . . . the union as against management, line manager against total organisation. In this respect the personnel manager can never 'win' – there are few black and white situations, few *right* solutions. The personnel task is to find *acceptable* solutions . . . to achieve working solutions which are compatible with top management's goals and acceptable to the plurality of interests which exists in the organisation (*ibid.*, p. 51).

Any occupation which can make the type of contribution suggested here is likely to further its interests by embracing a technology (with an associated ideology) which has this sort of promise. I suggest that the elective affinity between social science thinking and the interests of personnel specialists, as interpreted by certain 'spokesmen', is to be seen in the notion of *synthesis* which is implicit in that thinking.

I have derived this idea of synthesis as an implicit ideological resource from my analysis of the structural, sociological and relatively academically based social science thinking which appears to be influential in I.P.M. circles. But I believe that the same sort of idea is implicit in the second type of social science thinking which I mentioned earlier – that which has become available to a large extent through the *marketing* efforts of what I call the *behavioural science entrepreneurs*. Here we find a range of usually socio-psychologically based techniques, which often derive from American academic sources but which are implemented very often by commercial consultancies (which may or may not be run by the originating academics themselves). The titles of the packaged techniques here include Job Enrichment, the Managerial Grid, Management by Objectives, 3-D effectiveness, Coverdale training, Organisation Development, sensitivity training, T-groups, APEX, GENCO and Planned Organisational Change.

To talk 'behavioural science' in this world is to talk of 'O.D.', 'system four', 'hygiene factors', 'M. by O.', 'theory Y', 'motivation', 'participation', and, for the novelty of numbers, '9–1'![5] Aspects of these manifestations of social science thinking have been taken up by some British academic and management education institutions but there has been a certain academic distaste for the sort of oversimplification[6] involved in many of these approaches as well as reservations about their claim to some universality of application. Cherns in his article on personnel management and social science rejected the 'behavioural science' title partly because of its identification in the eyes of industry with 'a particular set of packages and devices' (1972, p. 4).[7] Some explanation of the appeal of the material is perhaps given in Sadler's words,

> Managers tend to pay most attention to the sorts of definitive research findings which can be expressed so simply and consistently that they could be printed on a postcard (quoted by Sills, 1975, p. 9).

I would repeat, here, the point which I made earlier, that there is overlap between these two inputs of social science thinking into personnel management ideas and knowledge. The I.P.M. has at one level stressed the importance of the former approach and this is perhaps understandable in that the structural approach can less readily be provided by external consultants and therefore has a greater potential as a special expertise for internal specialists – in the personnel department. But this is not to suggest that the I.P.M. through its publications does not disseminate material of the psychological, neo-human relations type. It most certainly does this and its booklet *The Behavioural Sciences* is a guide to the range of approaches, including those of the 'behaviour science entrepreneurs' (Sills, 1973).

Implicit in all of these approaches, as I said earlier, is the idea of *synthesis*. We see it, for example, in the scheme for designing wage-payment systems developed by Lupton and Gowler (1969) and deriving from research in industrial sociology, in which the aim is to achieve a 'fit' between the reward system and the variety of structural contingencies and we see it in the other tradition in the case of 'management by objectives' – a technique very much of the behavioural science entrepreneurs' stable. Peach attempts to apply the latter approach to personnel management, modifying the consultant's definition to give

> a dynamic system which seeks to maximise the contribution of the human resources of the enterprise to the company's profit and growth goals, through the integration of the personnel function and its objectives with those goals. For the personnel manager it is an even more demanding and rewarding style of contributing to the management of a business and for satisfying his need to be recognised, to contribute and develop himself (Peach, 1975, p. 20).

The synthesis here is, specifically, between the 'organisation's goals' and the goals of the individual manager (as an employee). But, inevitably, given the nature of the managerial task as conceived in this study, the meeting of goals other than those of the organisational controllers are only likely to be encouraged, generally, in so far as their meeting is seen as a successful *means* of achieving 'organisational goals'. To this extent social science techniques are correctly described as 'manipulative'.

The ideological value of the implicit synthesis notion, at the level of general managerial ideology, is that it suggests the possibility of some sort of community of interest between managers and employees. Hence we see the point of the phrase 'mock socialism' used by Nichols in his examination of a case where job enrichment was applied in an industrial plant (1975). Nichols shows how, despite the enlarging of jobs and the giving of a greater say to workers, there was no question of a move in the *locus* of control away from management towards the employees. The trend was for the workers to 'manage themselves for *management*' (Nichols, 1975, p. 257). There was also a tendency for there to be a reduction in the scope of what could be collectively bargained over (*ibid.*, pp. 263–4).

The rhetoric behind a great deal of the applied social science thinking is one of 'give and take'. Organisations can no longer, in the context of social change, expect straightforwardly to 'mould' employees to their purposes, it is suggested. This argument can be found in both British reviews of the relevance of the social sciences for personnel management (Smith and Drake, 1969, for example) and American ones like that of Schlesinger (1965). Instead of a one-way process, there now has to be a two-way one in which the personnel specialist can be the catalyst – the 'change agent'. Schlesinger, who sees the 'one major objective' of a personnel

department as 'increasing the "fit" between employees and organisation', sees the role in this way:

> The personnel specialist, like the human engineer, has to help
> build efficient working systems by adapting man to
> organisational procedures, organisational procedures to man,
> and both to the accelerated pressures for social change
> (Schlesinger, 1965, p. 3).

Thought and practice

Having examined the trends in personnel management thinking at
the 'thinker' and occupational 'spokesmen' level, attention can now
be turned to the extent to which such ideas are reflected in accounts
produced in the course of interviews with *practitioners*. Social science
thought clearly plays a significant role in the ideas and techniques
espoused by those in the professional body. The strategy of the
I.P.M. is to ensure that all future members are well versed in such
thinking. Whilst, as I argued earlier in this chapter, we would expect
the ideas of 'spokesmen' to be in a sense *ahead* of those of members,
it is nevertheless very pertinent to look at the value of these ideas for
practitioners compared with the value for thinkers.

I did not explicitly raise the issue of social science thinking in the
interviews until I had asked more general questions. The responses
to the question *Do you do any reading relevant to your job but beyond
what is formally required?* have to be approached with some reservation. Out of the 100 interviewed 75 said that they did reading of this
type, but I feel that we should note two possibilities here. The first is
that many personnel specialists possibly feel that they would be
expected to read and therefore a certain amount of positive answering
here may be understood as part of a process of reflecting what might
be seen as an appropriate occupational image. Such a tendency might
be reinforced by the fact that this question was asked immediately
after the questions on professionalism (where, as we have seen,
'knowledge' is a pertinent issue). Second, we have to remember that
respondents were being interviewed by someone from an academic
institution, and someone whose very presence was connected with a
presumed relevance of books to managerial life (or vice versa!). My
reservations are supported by the generality of the answers received
to the follow-up question which I put to all those claiming to read:
What sort of thing? Typical types of response here were

'Oh, the odd book, and personnel magazines.'

'Enough to keep me generally up to date.'

'Stuff on national political events and legislation.'

'Whatever I come across in the library.'

'You know, any management stuff, books and magazines.'

Early in the interview programme I pressed respondents who gave general answers to tell me, for example, the title of the last book they read or, in the case of those mentioning the I.P.M. magazines, I tended to ask what they thought of one or two named articles which had appeared shortly before the interview. However, such a questioning policy proved too embarrassing for me to continue: nearly all those to whom I put such questions (about 20 per cent of the total sample) could not name a book and none remembered anything of the magazine articles.[8] Having said this, I have attempted in Table 7.1 to give some indication of the type of material mentioned by respondents in cases where there was any specificity whatsoever in the answer:

TABLE 7.1 *Specific types of reading material mentioned*

I.P.M. Magazines	29	*The Economist*	2
General books on management	12	*Harvard Business Review*	2
Legislation	10	Industrial relations/union material	2
Sociology/psychology	9	C.B.I. material	1
Training/skills/job evaluation	5	Training board material	1
I.P.M. books	5	Industrial Society material	1
Management Today	3		
			82

These 82 items were taken from the 53 accounts which contained any specificity of this type. Only 7 authors were mentioned throughout my one hundred interviews and 4 of these were mentioned by one man. Only 1 of this 7 was not an American behavioural science populariser or a consultant.[9] Whether or not these 'findings' indicate support for a view of the personnel practitioners as applied social scientists is something I shall return to when we have established more of a context in which these responses can be placed.

Another fairly general question was: *Do you feel that personnel management has a basic body of knowledge or an underlying body of theory?* (if 'yes', *in what way?*). The responses fall into three more-or-less equal groupings: those who said 'No', those who said 'Yes' but were unspecific and those who said 'Yes' and who attempted to specify it. Examples of comments made by that third which felt there was no such body are:

'It's more a question of attitudes.'

'There ought to be one.'

'It's more moral than theoretical.'

'All people are different.'

'The field's too wide.'

'It's commonsense really.'

And those who said there was a body but did not specify it gave accounts which were not dissimilar, despite their being preceded by a positive rather than negative:

'But it involves emotion and instinct.'

'It's always changing.'

'But practice is important.'

'It's unexpressed and comes with experience.'

'It's too broad to specify.'

'It's not in books.'

Two-thirds of the sample, then, are not able to *identify* a body of knowledge or theory. The strange fact that half of these people nevertheless said that they thought that such a body existed is probably best understood by reference to the general feelings about professionalism. We saw earlier that some sort of professional image was seen as valuable to personnel practitioners and perhaps here we are seeing an underlying awareness that the notion of a profession must imply the existence of a body of knowledge whatever it might contain. The remaining third, those who attempted to define the body, tended to give accounts which covered three areas: legislation; techniques like job evaluation, interviewing, payment systems; and the social sciences. Of these, only 13 people directly or indirectly mentioned the social sciences, for example:

'A knowledge of people in groups – social science.'

'Sociology and psychology.'

'Behavioural science.'

'The psychology of work.'

'Motivation theory.'

'The study of people and their behaviour.'

To summarise this evidence for the moment then, we can say that, in contrast to the thinking of 'professional' spokesmen and academics on personnel management and the value of social science to it, only 13 per cent of a sample of practitioners spontaneously mentioned the social sciences when asked about a possible body of knowledge or theory associated with personnel work. Such a finding could be analysed in terms of the point made above that thinkers might simply be 'ahead' of practitioners. Such an explanation, straightforwardly interpreted, is weakened, however, by the fact that in the sample of practitioners under examination there are 48 members of I.P.M. These all receive regular literature from the institute (at least twice monthly) and would therefore be expected to be aware of the importance of the social sciences in the eyes of the institute, not least as indicated by the widely publicised content of the examination syllabuses with their very heavy social science emphasis. But even if we recognise that many I.P.M. members may not pay a lot of attention to the literature they receive, we have to take note of the fact that, although only 13 people mentioned social sciences in this content, 22 members of the sample are themselves in some way qualified in the social sciences (having degrees or having taken the I.P.M. exams). And to this number we should perhaps add the 21 student members of the I.P.M. who are either being taught or have been taught social science material. Overall, I suggest that it is reasonable to assume that at least 50 per cent of my sample have more than a passing familiarity with social science thinking. So why do so few mention it in a context where we might expect them to?

The evidence strongly suggests that, at least amongst this 100 practising personnel specialists, Lupton's concept of the personnel manager as the organisational repository of social science expertise has not been taken up. But this need not necessarily be simply a matter of the practitioners not choosing to take on such a role – it may be more a matter, once again, of situational or organisational factors. We may remember the man whom I quoted in the previous chapter who asked, if 'diagnosticians' were available to employers, how many organisations would know 'what the fuck to do with them?' Indeed, as I shall show in the next chapter, something like a half of those in my sample reported that their organisation did not make full or appropriate use of the personnel specialists whom they employed. The suggestion is often made by both practitioners and writers on personnel management that personnel specialists are too often used to solve short-term problems or to 'fire-fight'. Social science thinking would not play a major part in such a role, at least not the structural or the longer-term social change-oriented type of thinking. If social science thinking were to play any part at all we might expect the more psychologically inclined elements, the interpersonal emphasis, to be more pertinent. To see if this is so we can turn to the responses to my question *How do you feel about the relevance of social or behavioural science to personnel management?*

I had to recognise the danger of the inevitable biasing pressure resulting from my own status as a social scientist in asking this question. There was a tendency for people to preface comments with, for example, 'with all due respect for your own profession'. To then recognise that I was being lumped together on occasions with the type of behavioural science entrepreneur whose work might offend any self-respecting academic sociologist, I found most unsettling![10] It may have been my own social science identity or it might equally well be a matter of the professional-image-presentation tendency that explains the pattern whereby 88 of the 100 interviewees said that they felt the social/behavioural sciences to be relevant to personnel management. A number of these denied that they knew much about the subjects but felt they were relevant. Some spoke about the important background value of the disciplines, helping the personnel manager for instance in analysing problems if not in solving them. A third of those seeing relevance in the disciplines were careful to qualify their approval:

'It's essential because you're dealing with people. But it's not the be all and end all.'

'It's very relevant as long as it doesn't get too theoretical.'

'It's directly relevant but it does need to be related to experience.'

Representation of the 8 accounts from those rejecting any relevance were:

'I have met some competent people but a lot of social scientists are do-gooders. They'd be better in the social services but even that would be too tough for them.'

'It's common sense. I'm very critical of it. A lot is merely making systematic what is common sense thought.'

'I hope you don't mind me saying it and don't think I'm being funny. But everybody here laughs at social scientists. We see them as people trying to put the world to rights. You've got to have a lot of practical experience. Our people get amazed when these types come in spouting theory at them. People are not theory – they are facts.'

Analysis of the content of the accounts claiming some relevance for the social/behavioural sciences indicates very strongly the tendency for these disciplines to be thought of more at the individual and interpersonal levels. The discipline of sociology is mentioned explicitly fewer than half-a-dozen times and even fewer accounts

155

make any reference to matters of organisational structure or design and there is no mention whatsoever of the relationship between the organisation and the community or of social change processes. And these are all things strongly emphasised by the writers and thinkers whose work was examined earlier. The psychological content, however, is given strong emphasis, this being explicit in a third of the cases. For example,

'Psychology is more important than sociology. There aren't many social problems in local government.'

'You've got to understand what turns people on and off. You've got to know about the differences in human nature and how to cope with the differences.'

'You need to know how people tick. Herzberg and so on are useful tools.'

But a lot of the time one cannot help feeling that there is less concern with any academic discipline of psychology than a tendency to think in terms of some folk-concept of psychology:

'You use a lot of psychology in industrial relations. It may seem like conning to some. We use psychology to approach people in a manner which is acceptable to them. You have to see the patterns in individual and group behaviour.'

That account was given by a personnel manager whose assistant was a psychology graduate. The assistant thought psychology to be less relevant (he only used his training, he suggested, in applying statistics and in assessment work). The following account is a particularly bold statement of what I felt was implicit in many of the accounts here. The personnel manager giving this response was someone who had started his career on the shop floor and who was currently looking for a seat on the board of the fairly small company in which he did a line management job as well as the personnel one. He said:

'You've got to be able to assess people from a psychological point of view. You stick your neck out every time you employ someone. You need to know whether someone is telling you a load of guff. I've had people come here from Rampton and Broadmoor and, although they didn't let on, I could tell. Professionalism is knowing people. All this can get lost in a white-tile type personnel department. We're too shrewd to be taken in.'

This type of account might amuse or might irritate the academic psychologist. But the type of ability that this man had – and he went on to give examples of his abilities in motivating people – was such as to give him credibility with his fellow managers. What I will suggest

from my overall analysis of these accounts is that there is a clear tendency for personnel managers to work within a *psychologistic* frame of reference. This can partly be understood as reflecting the fact that the majority of practitioners do not at the present time have a training in the more *social* scientific approaches. But the tendency for even those trained in this area to make little or no reference whatsoever to structural or community – let alone societal – factors brings us back to situational exigencies, I would suggest. The personnel practitioners tend not to operate at a strategic level and perhaps to claim an ability to do so at their present level of credibility in their organisations would consign them to the 'too academic' or 'too theoretical' bin, a favourite managerial category for over-thoughtful rejects. The personnel practitioner's job itself and a general pressure towards short-term pragmatism are probably at the basis of these apparent attitudes to social science thinking. Before closer analysis is made of these situational pressures, however, it is necessary to attempt to ascertain whether the reservations about social science thinking which are suggested as prevalent by examination of the accounts given in response to the above questions (which all have academic connotations) are reflected in accounts given in reponse to very general questions on managerial and employment issues. Do statements made about very general issues reveal any influence of the social science thinking which is felt by some to be important for personnel people and to which a significant proportion of the sample have been exposed?

The first of these general questions was *What do you think is the biggest problem facing managements generally today?* In response to this 110 issues were mentioned. The two largest categories (22 mentions each) were *economic* (inflation, keeping costs down, lack of profitability, etc.) and problems relating to the relationship between management and *organised labour*. A close rival to these (19 mentions) was a group of answers which expressed concern about management's authority – or rather lack of it. Typically: 'The basic problem is that people have a take-it or leave-it attitude to their jobs. So management have no control,' or '(The problem is) getting a fair day's work for a fair day's pay.' Probably closely related to this were the 9 responses which referred to a problem of 'getting through to employees' or 'getting some sort of credibility.' Although interviewees were asked, prior to this group of questions, to give a 'fairly quick off-the-cuff' answer, it is nevertheless interesting to note that few answers indicate that the respondents put the difficulties down to the problems of the way work is organised or authority structured. The response, 'The difficulties all arise from mechanisation and the extent of meaningless work,' stands on its own, although 5 respondents did indicate that the problem of management today is

157

that of learning to 'share power' or 'adapt to new types of relationship with employees'. It does seem to be part of a pattern which emerged from my interview data that personnel practitioners tend to work at an analytical level which conceptualises the human problems associated with employment in terms of individuals, attitudes and interpersonal relationships far more frequently than in terms of structural or organisational problems. A recognition of the latter type of factor would be central to the Fox/Lupton diagnostician conception of the personnel specialist. A similar tendency is perhaps seen in the remaining category of answers to this question which is of any significant size. This group of 15 responses suggested that management's biggest problems are the managers themselves; their lack of skills, talents, flexibility or sense of direction.

The above responses do not, then, reveal any great apparent tendency on the part of the personnel practitioners to locate problems in their socio-technical and environmental context (and the responses of those who have been taught sociology at some point in their careers do not fall into a pattern which is any different from the general one). The next issue to be confronted is that of whether the apparent tendency to think in individualistic rather than sociological terms is accompanied by any evidence of absorption of the type of psychologically oriented thought to which there appeared to be some leaning in the accounts considered earlier. These accounts were often psychologistically phrased in terms of 'how people tick' and 'what motivates people'. The few social scientists mentioned were predominantly those often referred to as 'motivation theorists' – Likert, MacGregor and, especially, Herzberg. Sheridan has commented that, together with productivity bargaining, Herzberg's 'theory of motivation' was one of the two major ideas to have caught the imagination of personnel specialists in Britain in recent years (1972, p. 127). I was interested to find what evidence there would be of imaginations having been caught in the answers to the question *Thinking of employees generally – I am thinking more of ordinary workpeople – what do you think their jobs mean to them?* Over three-quarters of the sample here saw jobs as meaning predominantly 'money' or 'security'. Amongst the remainder there were sometimes strongly expressed beliefs in the importance of job satisfaction, or 'pride' amongst employees. But the point to which I would draw attention would be the tendency for the great majority to give the types of answer which they did so readily; that what sociologists call an 'instrumental orientation to work' is apparently *taken for granted* by so many of those in personnel work.

To comment personally on these responses: I was not surprised by them even though I would admit that I felt some apprehension on hearing so large a proportion of interviewees so unhesitatingly or so categorically saying things like 'the money', 'a meal ticket', 'cash for a car or for the bingo'. I would not suggest that these comments are in any sense 'wrong' or even that they are necessarily inconsistent with a belief in the possibilities of job design, job enrichment and the rest altering this situation. But, and perhaps this is the crux of the matter, the implication of the majority of these responses is that these personnel practitioners were not particularly ready to take up a position whereby their role could become one of using the technically useful and legitimatory technology of behavioural science to bring together the meeting of managerial goals and the 'higher level' human needs and fulfilments of employees in some sort of synthesis, so establishing themselves as a key occupational group within management.

The third question of this group on general issues was *What part do you think that trade unions should play in employing organisations?* My primary purpose in asking this was to find out the extent to which the ideas of Fox, particularly those expressed in his research paper for the Royal Commission on trade unions and employers associations (Fox, 1966b), have influenced the thinking of personnel practitioners. Although Fox has more recently been critical of certain aspects of the earlier ideas which he expressed (see Fox, 1973) his analysis has become something of an orthodoxy in the field of industrial relations training and it was most recently advocated in 1972 by the author in the I.P.M.'s *Personnel Management* in what the editor of that journal called its 'leading article' of the month (Fox, 1972). The argument suggests the inappropriateness of what is called the *unitary frame of reference* for analysing and understanding industrial relations. Such an approach is said to be inappropriate in its failure to recognise the fundamental conflicts of interest which exist between employers and employed. To believe in a community of interests in employing organisations is to misunderstand reality and, potentially therefore, to adopt inappropriate policies. By recognising the underlying conflicts which exist, 'Management will gain deeper insight into group grievances, and by understanding them better will be better equipped to make rational decisions about them' (Fox, 1972, p. 21). The nature of the accounts given in response to the above question are not such that they can be simply allocated to a *unitary* or a *pluralistic* frame of reference category. We could, however, say that something like a quarter of the respondents gave accounts which implied some recognition of some basic conflicts of interest. For example.

'They should look after the best interests of their members. They must be a sectional group because the powers they are organised against are more sectional.'

'I've no doubt employers would exploit people if they were not faced by organised labour.'

'They are a service for the workers. They should fight for better conditions.'

But the majority of accounts tended to reveal a general distaste for unions which were anything other than a very *loyal* opposition. Particularly common themes were the calls for unions to be *responsible* or *accountable:*

'They should play an equal part with management. But I would qualify this by saying that they have got to be accountable. With their increasing power they will have to become responsible. They still tend to say about problems "Aha, that's management's problem".'

There seems to be a general acceptance of trade unions, but implicit in this is often a suggestion that the union is almost part of management:

'They should play a leading role in representing the membership and a leading role in supporting the personnel policies of the company.'

'They are a tool to be used by management. They have a potential role in giving management the information it needs.'

'I'm a great believer in trade unions from the point of view of industry generally. A good convenor helps a plant run well.'

'They should have an equal part with management to secure industry's well being.'

'The union should represent the employees but not conflict with the company.'

The value of the union as a communication channel between management and employees is a popular theme. For example,

'My views have changed. I used to be opposed to encouraging unions but our top management said to bring them in. I can now see their purpose. Having met a number of their leaders I can see beyond their façade and realise that many of the extremes that people on the outside see are really just ritual dances. They can be very effective as communicators – better than the company itself in fact. And they can improve group cohesion.'

Several other interviewees commented either that they had been surprised to find how 'reasonable' trade unionists were on first becoming involved with them or how much less militant they were than the public assumed. The few people who gave accounts highly antagonistic to trade unions were, with one exception, people who did not become involved at all in industrial relations work – usually because they were in non-unionised settings.

Despite the extent to which public discussion of issues of industrial democracy and worker control was increasing during the period in which the interview programme took place, only one or two respondents (both senior men) suggested that there should or might be any major changes in the way the work organisations are controlled. There was, however, a tendency for the word 'participation' to be used, but it seemed to me that it was almost always used in such a way as to appear to be adopting the rhetoric of power-sharing whilst remaining firmly attached to a unitary conception of relationships in which the decision makers are the managers. For example: 'Their role should be participative involvement with the actual decisions made by management,' or 'They should be involved in decision-making processes but the managers should make the decisions.'

Ideas, knowledge and situational pressures

It would appear from the above type of evidence that the personnel management thinking of the writers and academics diverges somewhat from that of the practitioners. Strother attempted to compare the two approaches in the American setting and his investigations suggested that 'the bridge between theory and practice in personnel management can clearly stand a lot of repair' (1959, p. 63). But to judge whether this is a matter of the failure of the academics to become involved in the 'real world' or the failure of personnel practitioners to see the importance of academically generated knowledge is not a major concern here. My suggestion is that there is something of a dialectical relationship between the thinking of the two levels. The group spokesmen will tend to offer certain ideas, approaches and legitimatory utterances, some of which will be taken up to some extent by practitioners and some of which will not. Situational pressures on the practitioners – the pressure on them to solve short-term problems rather than strategic ones, for instance – may lead to certain ideas being less well received than others. But the ideas being offered may have utility to the practitioner in that they sometimes provide a means whereby he can alter or reduce certain of the pressures. Before I attempt to illustrate some of the ways in which this two-way process of idea-development might occur, however, it is necessary to look a little more closely at the reasons for the type of thinking which appears to be current among many of the practitioners.

161

The type of psychologistic, individualistic thinking as well as the relatively 'organicist' approach (Nichols, 1969, ch. 17) in which community of purpose and interdependence is stressed has an important history in British management thought. Child's analysis of the assumptions common to Quaker and human relations theorists shows how they stressed the importance of individual and interpersonal relationships:

> Most important of all, the whole framework of industrial relations was placed by both in terms not of the sociological 'power structure' model, but of a psychological one of 'goodwill' or 'social skills' (Child, 1964, p. 308).

But the widespread acceptance of such ideas was not simply a result of the ideas of Quakers and human relations writers being 'influential' – it was as much a matter of such notions having a considerable legitimatory value for practising managers. To be able to persuade one's subordinates that they have a community of interests with one is advantageous to anyone in authority (see Bendix, 1963, on human relations as managerial ideology). And the point is that the bulk of actual practising managers and a large proportion of the personnel specialists *do in practice operate in terms of interpersonal relationships* and in terms of *motivating subordinates* as well as *'persuading' colleagues and rivals* within management.

To the academic observer there are important structural cultural and environmental factors to be taken into account by managers. But for the majority of practitioners, they 'hold down' their jobs by demonstrating much more immediate and practical skills. To operate in terms of the 'structural' is to conceptualise life in terms which tend to be more theoretical than practical. And this is problematic for the practitioner. Some of the reasons for this are indicated by Freidson's analysis of an occupation where one might expect theoretical knowledge to be recognised as important and indeed intrinsic to practice. However, Freidson detects a significant gap between the theorist and the practitioner in the medical field:

> By and large, I think it can be said that the practitioner has a different view of his work than the theoretician or investigator. In fact, he has a different way of looking at the world. First, the aim of the practitioner is not knowledge but *action*. Successful action is preferred, but action with very little chance for success is to be preferred over no action at all (Freidson, 1970, p. 168).

He goes on to distinguish the mind of the practitioner from that of the thinker in terms of a *faith* that what he is doing is right; a *pragmatic* approach whereby he is 'prone to rely on apparent "results" rather than on theory, and he is prone to tinker if he does not seem to be getting "results" '; a *subjectivism* whereby he is prone to 'trust his own accumulation of personal, *first hand experience* in preference to abstract principles or "book knowledge" ', an emphasis on *indeterminancy or uncertainty* and 'not on the idea of regularity or of lawful, scientific behaviour' (*ibid.*, p. 169). The fact that Freidson, who has studied the medical profession as closely as any sociologist has studied any occupation, should make these generalisations about an occupation in which there is a very powerful emphasis on education and a long period of training makes them very worthy of attention. What it would lead us to suggest in the case of the relationship between the social-science-oriented thinkers and the practising personnel workers is that there will always be a contrast or even a conflict of emphasis between the two, this resulting from the contrasting situational exigencies to which they are exposed in their respective organisational bases. Thus, where the academic sees severe limitations in human relations ideas, for example, the practising line or personnel manager may find them of great utility in his day-to-day management work. My own close involvement with foremen in the engineering industry taught me this: those supervisors who paid close attention to the personal and social needs of their workers and those who 'counselled' employees with personal problems were often among the most *effective* – within managerial criteria. The great importance of the social skills to the personnel specialists will become apparent in the next chapter. The fact that human relations ideas produce little more than palliatives is not particularly important to many of the personnel practitioners: it is palliatives that they are looking for.

Having argued that there is an inevitably contrasting emphasis between the thinkers on the one hand and the practitioners on the other, I shall return to my earlier point about a two-way processual relationship between the two. The tensions between the two types of thinking may produce the dynamic behind the generation-modification-adoption process whereby personnel management thinking develops. To illustrate the type of process I have in mind I will take the example of Lupton's work. His I.P.M. booklet and the arguments contained within it, stressing underlying patterns and structural issues, has been influential at the thinker level. It does not appear, however, to have strongly influenced the practitioners' conception of their role. A later publication of Lupton's may receive wider acceptance. The writing of Lupton and Gowler (1969) on designing wage-payment systems incorporates a lot of contemporary industrial sociology thinking of the 'contingency theory' type, but it presents it in such a way that the *practical* man can apply it. The

163

achievement of the Lupton and Gowler approach is that it has converted theoretical ideas into a manageable *technique*.

Despite the sophisticated theoretical knowledge behind the scheme, my own experience of utilising it when I was employed in industry was that it was welcomed by managers particularly because it was not 'too theoretical'. The 'marketed package' approach of the behavioural science entrepreneurs has probably been relatively well received for this type of reason. One suspects Lupton and his colleagues have worked on the basis of such an insight – maintaining the appeal of the *practical* and the not too theoretical, whilst recognising that as Bowey, a former colleague of Lupton, argues 'too many managers are still on the look-out for the marketed package, the simple solution to all their problems' (Lawrence, 1976, p. 17). The recognition that social science thinking will have to be adapted to the pragmatism of the practitioners if it is to become the technology of the personnel specialist is implicit in part of the conclusion to Sills's book on behavioural science techniques published by I.P.M.:

> The techniques contain and offer enough to suggest that their use could and probably should, benefit organisations. Their payoffs are likely to be higher (and meet managerial expectations more readily), the more they are used to promote changes which are short-term, small-scale and, most importantly, seen as experimental (1973, p. 43).

The suggestion is that if you learn to walk first, later you may be able to run: the author continues,

> This is not to devalue the techniques; technical developments in the natural sciences have generally advanced one step at a time; so, too, will personnel and organisational developments based on the behavioural sciences (*ibid.*, p. 43).

Towards an occupational ideology?

My judgment, based on the above analysis, is that social and behavioural science thinking, modified by the dialectical diffusion process which I have described, will be increasingly important in an occupation in which increasing emphasis is being placed upon education and training. As long as that thinking is converted to a significant extent into practicable techniques and identifiable programmes, it has too much technical and legitimatory utility for the occupational spokesmen to abandon it. Its implicit notion of *synthesis* can give to it ideological power, whether ideology is seen in terms of supporting interests (Nichols, 1969; Rogers and Berg, 1961) or in reducing 'role-strain' (Sutton *et al.*, 1956). The synthesising promise of social science ideas, in their suggestion of the possibility of bringing together individual and organisational goals, can be attractive to the controllers of organisation and hence assist the improved status of the personnel specialists who apply that thinking. The implicit synthesis idea can also function ideologically for the personnel occupation in that it can justify the *integration* of those doing the various sub-specialisms into a single grouping – thus increasing the coherence of the occupation. Henstridge argues for such an integration as part of his emphasis on the synthesising role of personnel management (1975), and Smith and Drake argue similarly for the integration of the different aspects of 'human resources management' (1969).

One of the central problems for the personnel occupation is, I have argued continually, that of being involved with conflicting criteria: those commonly referred to as welfare and efficiency. If social-science-based techniques are to provide the personnel occupation with both a technology and the basis for an occupational ideology they would need to be linked with some ideological device which would help cope with the strains resulting from this dual orientation. I would suggest that such a device is available and that it is one which also helps resolve what might be seen as something of a contradiction: the more frequent bringing to bear of calculative 'scientific' (formally rational) techniques to deal with the problematic implications of utilising human beings as units of labour (the limitations of the wider application of formal rationality). This is the device of claiming that human beings are the 'most valuable asset' that an organisation possesses and that, therefore, its importance should be recognised by its being carefully studied, measured, planned for and rewarded. To do this is to *care for* employees, but caring not as matter of philanthropy but a matter of sound *investment*. And worthwhile investment must mean the use of expertise whilst, at the same time, the importance of human resources to the organisation must be reflected in the presence of the human resources – personnel – expert on the board.

This 'ideological device', in various forms, is one which I have noticed arising throughout my interviewing programme and it is increasingly appearing in personnel textbooks and technique manuals, often in a justificatory preface. A typical example appears in an I.P.M. book on manpower planning:

> It is gradually becoming accepted that manpower is a resource like capital and materials; but the effective deployment of human resources is as difficult to master as the effective deployment of physical and financial resources (I.P.M., 1967, p. 18).

Like a more recent book on the same topic also published by I.P.M. (Bramham, 1975, p. 15), these authors see a general tendency to neglect this resource. They then go on,

> Yet by ensuring that employees are at all times contributing to the firm's future viability not only is the best use made of the resource by the firm but individuals can receive the maximum amount of job satisfaction for themselves (*ibid.*, p. 18).

The way that the resources are to be utilised (and here a company's internal publication – the *BP Shield* is quoted) – is 'by employing the most sophisticated techniques of organisation and management that are available' (*ibid.*). Another good example of this type of attempt to synthesise welfare and efficiency criteria is provided by a book partly sponsored by the I.P.M. on manpower training and development, where the authors go to great length to establish that '*systematic* training' is a sound business 'investment' (Kenney and Donnelly, 1972, p. 16). To a long list of advantages to the organisation of such training is added 'the social and private benefits. . . . The advantages to society of having a well-trained national workforce are very real' (*ibid.*, p. 17). In America, where behavioural sciences techniques are already widely advocated, taught and written about, the fusing of the technical and legitimatory aspects of personnel management is further advanced. This is illustrated in the entry on personnel administration in the *Encyclopedia of Management* in which three elements of personnel administration are detected. It is, first, a 'specialised body of knowledge'; second, a 'viewpoint', philosophy or 'value set' and, third, 'it consists of specialised methods, tools and techniques through which its viewpoint is implemented' (Bedrosian, 1973). The entry refers to the profitability of 'good' personnel policies, denies that personnel administration is 'a series of human relations gimmicks' and claims that 'a central principle is that people are an organisation's most important asset' (*ibid.*).

Social science thinking, developed in particular forms, together with various related techniques, does appear to have within it a strong technical and ideological base for the personnel occupation. It can help it contribute to formally rational criteria whilst at the same time looking towards the human needs which, if not carefully manipulated, might threaten the materially rational goals of the organisational controllers, whose servants the personnel specialists are. As was argued in the *Personnel Review* article by Sills: 'The behavioural sciences are able to offer a lot; and they hold out the promise of a lot more. They generate knowledge, which in turn represents power' (1975, p. 11).

8 Organisational power and influence

One of the ultimate purposes of this study is to provide an analysis of the part that the personnel occupation plays in maintaining the 'mode of integration' of modern capitalist industrial society. Such a concern inevitably takes us into issues of power. But modern capitalist industrial society is very much *organisational society*, with bureaucratic organisations of all types playing a major part in the power structures of such a society. Personnel specialists, by the nature of their work, operate within such organisations and therefore, before we can talk about the contribution that the occupation makes at the societal level, we have to consider the extent to which the members of the occupation have or might potentially have power or influence in the ways that organisations are run. Katz has commented that 'power is one of the most disagreed about topics' and it is true that 'few people, including scholars, are able to agree on the nature and substance of power' (1968, p. 66). Rather than reviewing the extensive debates which have occurred within sociology over this issue, I shall simply put forward my own conception of power – this being something that is implicit in the general theoretical scheme which has been utilised throughout this study.

Power is the capacity that any group or individual possesses whereby the outcome of any situation can be affected in such a way that access is achieved or maintained to whatever resources are scarce and valued within a society or a part of that society. To have power is to have advantage relative to other competing or potentially competing groups or individuals.[1] Since, within my theoretical perspective, the relationship between the individual and the organisation is one in which the individual makes contributions to the organisation's functioning in return for which certain rewards are received, the power of a member of the organisation would be reflected in the extent of the rewards to which he has access (those being scarce and

167

valued resources such as money, prestige, and autonomy[2]). But, since the controllers of organisations will only tend to give rewards in proportion to the extent to which the individual contributes to their achieving of their goals ('organisational goals'), we can see that the power of an organisational member derives from his behaviour as an agent of the organisational controllers or dominant coalition. Thus the power or influence of any given manager or department of an organisation is, in the long run, the capacity to affect events only in so far as this is congruent with the interests of the organisational controllers. And, given the scarcity of those things which are 're-wards', we would expect to find competition occurring between managers.

The classic study of the competition and conflicts which occur between managers in organisations over the available scarce resources is that of Dalton (1951, 1959). He particularly stresses the 'career' reward. Landsberger has criticised Dalton, however, for laying too much stress on the influence of criteria such as religion and age which are 'irrelevant from the organisation's point of view' and suggests that, whereas these 'informal' factors should be recognised as important, more attention needs to be given to the extent to which the conflicts may be seen as aspects of interdepartmental relation-ships (1961, p. 302). These conflictful horizontal relationships should be seen not only as frequent and inevitable, Landsberger suggests, but also as *useful* for the organisation which 'may benefit from having all sides of a problem clearly argued by some group within it' (*ibid.*, p. 300).[3] Burns has also stressed the structural consequences of competition between organisational members, arguing that the conflicts and competition of 'micropolitics' are both mechanisms of *change* and intrinsic parts of the *control* aspect of the organisation. Co-operation and conflict are two sides of the same coin:

> In fact, members of a corporation are at one and the same
> time cooperators in a common enterprise and rivals for the
> material and intangible rewards of successful competition with
> each other. The hierarchic order of rank and power that
> prevails in them is at the same time a single control system and
> a career ladder (Burns, 1961, p. 261).

Competition and conflicts of interest between managers can be seen as built into the very structures of employing organisations. But, as Landsberger suggests and as Perrow argues, care has to be taken to avoid becoming preoccupied with *interpersonal* power at the expense of considering the major departments or sub-units of the organisation and the ways in which 'all of these sub-units are not likely to be equally powerful' (Perrow, 1970a, p. 59). Perrow's own researches in this area led him to the conclusion that in eleven of the twelve industrial firms which he studied, managers considered the sales departments to be the most powerful. Perrow explains this in terms of the 'strategic position with respect to the environment' of the sales departments (*ibid.*, p. 82). The suggestion here that some departments may be strategically more important than others and hence more powerful is an interesting one in the light of the arguments put forward in chapter 3 where the personnel specialists were seen to be increasing their importance as pressures are being put on organisations by government and by employee organisations, and as personnel specialists increasingly become seen as the appropriate ones to cope with these pressures. The more problematic labour becomes as a resource for the organisation so may the personnel department potentially acquire strategic importance. But it can only achieve this as long as it demonstrates a special competence in the handling of the labour resources. And this takes us back to the strategies considered in the previous two chapters. Cherns is particularly concerned to stress the acquisition of social science knowledge as a strategy which may enable personnel specialists to achieve central importance. Following the arguments of Thompson (1967) he suggests that 'leadership in an organisation passes to the sector which is attempting to cope with an organisation's area of maximum uncertainty' (Cherns, 1972, p. 10). Cherns argues that during various phases in Britain since the war, engineers have given such leadership, followed by accountants and then by marketing experts. He goes on to ask: 'What next? We are already seeing that the interface between the organisation and society is becoming turbulent. Personnel managers, fasten your seat belts!' (*ibid.*, p. 11). Although the implications of the idea of 'leadership' have to be treated with reservation, the relationship between power and the coping with uncertainty is well worth following up.

Both Crozier (1964) and Thompson (1967) make use of the idea of *uncertainty* in their analyses of power within organisations but perhaps the most systematic use has been made of it by Hickson *et al.* in their 'strategic contingency' theory of organisational power (1971). In this theory the power of a sub-unit of an organisation is seen as resulting from the extent to which it is *not contingent* (i.e. dependent) on other sub-units, together with its not being *substitutable* by any other sub-units and its *centrality* to the organisational system. Its centrality derives from its coping with a high degree of uncertainty. Power relations between sub-units are the result of imbalances in the interdependency between departments, this interdependence resulting from a division of labour in which an overall organisational task is to cope with uncertainties arising in the environment. The organisation as a system has a *need* for certainty since, as Thompson puts it, it is 'indeterminate and faced with

169

uncertainty, but subject to criteria of rationality' (1967, p. 13). This theory, I suggest, contains insights which can be valuable in the understanding of the issues which are central to my present analysis. But the theory cannot be utilised as it stands since its underlying assumptions are very much at odds with the 'social action' ones basic to this study. Not only is there a tendency to reify the organisation as a system which reacts in terms of 'system needs' but the assumption of unitary sub-units is also questionable. As Clegg says 'if one hypothesizes that a sub-unit is a unitary and harmonious collective, speaking and acting with one voice, one is on a sticky wicket' (1975, p. 46). The more crucial criticism which Clegg makes of the 'strategic contingency' theory, however, is to be found in his argument that Hickson *et al.* are not in fact *explaining* power at all. They convert 'less dependency' of organisational sub-units to 'power' (p. 49) and end up mistaking the surface aspects of power for something which needs to be analysed more as a 'deep structure' – the form of domination and control at the societal level (*ibid.*). This coincides with my own position: any explanation of power must be in terms of the overall structure of advantages at the societal level. Any power wielded by members of organisational sub-units must be seen as derived from its contribution to that 'deeper' structure. As long as this is borne in mind, then, advantage can be taken of the insights in the Hickson *et al.* theory.

If the insights of the 'strategic contingency' theory are to be utilised within the social-action frame of reference we have to replace the emphasis on the almost deterministic role of the 'environment' with an emphasis on the ways that individuals and social groups are themselves actively involved in creating and defining contingencies, in terms of which they can then act. The importance of recognising 'the part played by individuals in the structuring of social action over time' is convincingly illustrated by Pettigrew's very useful study of the 'politics of organisational decision-making' where he shows how 'by their ability to exert power over others, individuals can change or maintain structures as well as the norms and expectations upon which these structures rest' (1973, p. 31). Goldner indicates some of the ways in which this can happen. He points out how, within organisations, there are strong pressures towards rationalisation: 'No activities of the organisation – at least none of those that "make a difference" – are left to chance' (1970, p. 97). And this provides the individual with an opportunity to further his interests: 'In fact, it is advantageous to an individual's career to find such activities if they are not already apparent' (*ibid.*, p. 97). Thus specialisation and differentiation occur, to 'reduce all areas of uncertainty', partly as a result of individuals' career-oriented efforts, but such increasing division of labour creates 'overlaps' and more uncertainties (*ibid.*).

The dynamics of the structuring of organisations thus involve the dialectic of individual effort and structural constraint. The increasingly successful efforts of personnel specialists in augmenting their organisational power is thus to be seen partly in terms of the ways in which they have located and defined uncertainties and then made a successful claim to the requisite expertise to cope with them. If we then take note of one of the basic insights of the Hickson *et al.* theory, we can see that one of the services which the I.P.M. can provide to the personnel practitioner is the knowledge and expertise (and certification of these) to help him establish *unsubstitutibility*. His *power* within the organisation is thus enhanced as this unsubstitutibility, combined with *centrality*, contributes to his department's becoming less contingent on other departments.

The type of analysis to which I am moving can be simply illustrated by an autobiographical example. Shortly after joining the company in which I was employed as a new graduate I created a job for myself by persuading the management of the factory of the existence of an area of uncertainty which needed to be covered – the employee aspects of the proposed new factory. As I was looking to further my career, I tried to establish that I had the requisite distinctive competence as a trained 'industrial sociologist' and, once I was in the post, I made myself 'unsubstitutible' by claiming to be the only person with the necessary contacts and knowledge gained by experience. The example is useful, I suggest, because I feel my personal experience is very much what Dawe (1973) terms 'representative experience' (see above p. 3). I have repeatedly seen similar strategies followed whilst I watched various personnel departments expand ('empire build') as career advantages and structural 'uncertainties' are brought together by individual personnel specialists who see the need for a 'job evaluation manager' today and a 'remunerations manager' the next. But what my personal example can be used to illustrate particularly well is the bounded nature of the power that results from these factors. Whilst it is true that, compared to other employees of my age, I can be seen as having had quite considerable 'power' in terms of influencing day-to-day outcomes, whatever power or influence I had was almost entirely dependent on the extent to which I was part of the overall 'structure of domination' – an agent of those ultimately benefiting most from the organisation's performance.

The above analysis is intended to achieve two things. First, it is present to locate the earlier analyses of the development of personnel management and the occupational strategies of personnel specialists within the important theoretical issue of the nature of organisational power and the relationship of the latter to the issue of societal power. And, second, it is meant to provide a framework for the more empirically based discussion of the relationships between personnel specialists and other managerial groups within organisations which is to follow.

Organisational relationships – the problems

The conflicts and ambivalences underlying the job of the personnel worker were described in some detail in chapter 3 where it was also shown how, as personnel specialists become better established within managements, they may, paradoxically, find themselves experiencing even greater problems in their relationships with others in management. This basically arises as a result of the requirement to operate more in terms of criteria related to materially rational considerations – criteria such as longer-term organisational survival and organisation-wide policies as opposed to sectional goal achievement – rather than in more straightforward formally rational criteria which are, more typically, applied to many managers whose responsibilities cover a more specific or restricted area or function. Such problems are intrinsic to the personnel function, it is suggested. This means that if personnel practitioners are going to be wielding power – in the sense in which I have suggested we can see power within organisations – then we would expect them to be indulging in organisational tactics and strategies to cope with these problems. These would match the occupational ones which were considered earlier. Before these accommodative moves are considered, however, we have to look more closely at the nature of the problems within organisations as they are generally structured.

The principle upon which the structural position of the personnel department officially depends is traditionally that of the 'line-staff' doctrine. On this principle, departments are demarcated into *line* ones which are directly responsible for achieving the goals of the organisation and which have the power to make and implement all decisions and *staff* departments which are those which provide services to the line and which counsel and advise the line. As Rhenman *et al.* point out, the principle is 'not only a pattern for classifying tasks and organisational units. It also contains normative rules for the behaviour of both line and staff units' (1970, p. 12). Despite the wide acceptance of this principle of formal organisation, it has been subjected to considerable criticism by writers on management. McGregor, in a well-known epithet, called it 'psychologically absurd and in practice unworkable' (1948, p. 7) and Drucker saw attempts to differentiate between line and staff authority as meaningless and suggested that they should be dropped (1954, pp. 241–3). The nature of the tasks of the personnel function – particularly those of implementing and 'policing' trade union agreements and those of ensuring that higher-level organisational policies or legislative requirements

are complied with – tends to mean that the so-called 'advice' which
line management is given by personnel is, as one interviewee put it,
'advice which has to be followed'. It seems to be something of a
rhetorical device to call what are in effect executive commands
'advice'. The ambiguity of the personnel function in terms of the
line-staff doctrine thus creates tensions in what Landsberger called
the horizontal dimension of the organisation. But it is also problematic in terms of the relationship with the top management of the
organisation. Whether the personnel specialist is officially 'advisory'
or 'executive', the authority which he commands must clearly be
influenced, in a bureaucracy, by his relationship with people in these
senior positions.

To gain some overall impression of how the people in my sample
evaluated the role which their own personnel function was given in
the organisations, I asked the general question *How well do you feel
that your organisation uses the resources that it has in its personnel
specialists?* Answers have ranged from 'fully' to 'bloody badly' and,
significantly, something like a half of the respondents were unhappy
about the extent which the function was being used or about the way
it was being used. A common complaint was that, as one put it, 'We
are very fully stretched. But we are being used for the wrong things
– patching things up and putting out fires.' Or 'We are used too often
to simply "oil the works" when we should really be far more
involved in making policies and in planning.'

However, another theme of these responses was that things were
'improving'. A lot of stress was put on 'proving our usefulness' or
being successful in 'selling the service'. Once again we see the
emphasis on the efforts of the occupational members themselves in
establishing themselves and achieving credibility. The situation which
we can see them as combating becomes very apparent on examining
the literature of recent years on the organisational position of
Personnel. The P.E.P. survey of industrial management published in
the mid-sixties argued that, in the seeking of productivity, 'the value
of a good personnel manager can scarcely be overrated' yet, to
achieve anything, his voice had to be heard at a 'high enough level of
management' – something which was frequently not occurring (1965,
pp. 97–8). The report of the Royal Commission on Trade Unions
and Employers' Associations noted the increase in the number of
personnel managers and the scope of their job but asked, 'If companies have their own personnel specialists, why have they not
introduced effective personnel policies to control methods of
negotiation and pay structures within their firms?' (Donovan, 1968,
p. 25).

The more recent C.I.R. report on the role of management in
industrial relations again found insufficient integration of industrial

relations policy making into the running of businesses at the higher levels (C.I.R., 1973) but the report was not felt in I.P.M. circles to be as specific as it might have been on the place of 'the personnel/ industrial relations specialist' (I.P.M., 1973, p. 7). The Department of Employment's paper on the reform of collective bargaining had, however, argued for the appointment of directors solely responsible for personnel (1971). Winkler in his study of company directors saw directors as very much isolated from personnel and industrial relations problems. This he saw as partly suiting them:

> Psychologically, isolation functions as a defence mechanism. If labour problems arise, the director has a double repository for blame: not just the recalcitrant workers, but the subordinates to whom he delegated the task of keeping them quiet (Winkler, 1974, pp. 211–12).

This might be seen as offering some explanation of the situation described in the 'Comment' feature of the I.P.M.'s *Personnel Management* where it was argued that the Industrial Relations Act in particular would seem to have 'assured (personnel managers) of a place at the heart of the policy-making procedure' but it was also felt that 'recent events . . . might well have caused many personnel managers to wonder whether somebody up there is not trying to rob them of that vital role' (Lawrence, 1971, p. 3).

Further light is shed on the matter by an article by a trade union leader who observed that 'in the majority of companies, one gets the impression that the personnel manager is a sort of buffer or conduit between the trade union side and those with the real power to authorise settlements' (Jenkins, 1973, p. 34). This may well, again, suit top management in that 'the constant need to refer back to higher authority can be a most effective delaying tactic' (*ibid.*, p. 35). This, Jenkins feels, may be counter-productive for the organisation, not least because a 'vicious circle has been created whereby the brighter managers steer clear of the personnel function because of its lack of status, and in consequence the personnel function remains in low regard because of its relative lack of talent . . .' (*ibid.*, p. 35). Poole, on the basis of academic research, sees a similar vicious circle whereby,

> unless personnel departments are vested with the necessary authority to handle industrial relations problems they will inevitably remain unattractive avenues for settling disputes from both the management's and the worker's point of view. This in turn lowers their status and authority in the workplace still further with the result that it becomes difficult to attract and retain first rate staff and, not surprisingly, to establish general industrial relations policies at plant level (1973, p. 38).

A personnel officer employed in an organisation with a large and well-developed personnel department said, at an I.P.M. branch meeting which I attended, that he felt that very often 'Personnel is a dustbin for misfits.' All these problems are often brought together in discussions of the personnel function in terms of its being 'in the middle'.

Man in the middle

Very often the 'man in the middle' problem [4] is used to refer to the negative and frustrating aspects of the personnel role, this at times being compared to that of the foreman (see Crichton, 1963, p. 164, for example). The frustrations of the personnel specialist here are emphasised by a Vice-President of the I.P.M.:

> Nearly always he is the 'man in the middle'. For management, who pay his salary, he must argue the company case; from the union viewpoint he is expected to negotiate acceptable terms and conditions for the staff. If the personnel man adopts a progressive policy, management says 'slow down'. If he goes at the pace of many employers associations, he is accused by the unions of 'lagging behind' (Dryburgh, 1972, p. 3).

The frustrations derive from various aspects of this situation. The knowledge and expertise that the new 'personnel "professional" ' is acquiring is 'frequently not recognised or used by his company'; the 'measures of success are hard to quantify' and, often, advice has to be given which is 'in conflict with our own personal viewpoint' (ibid.). Frustration may also derive, it is suggested, from lack of personnel representation on the board and from what I would call the *ambiguity* of the situation, which Dryburgh neatly states: 'In many ways line managers are the practitioners of our skill' (ibid.).

Yet there is the problem that 'frequently the personnel man has a bigger struggle with the attitudes of his own management to change than he does with the attitudes of those on the shop floor' (ibid.). To test my own interviewees' positions on this issue I put to them the question: *Some argue that the personnel manager is 'in between' – between, that is, the management generally and the employees. Do you agree with this idea of the job?* The particular way in which this question was worded inevitably influenced the type of response which it received, but what is interesting is that two-thirds of the respondents gave accounts which suggested that the function was 'in between' and that they did not disapprove of this fact or suggested that the function *ought* to be in between in this way. A personnel manager in the textiles industry said:

175

'Yes. One gets accused by employees of being a bosses' man and by the bosses of being the most militant shop-steward. But this does mean that you can put over the shop-floor view to management and vice versa.'

A divisional training man commented:

'Yes. Because of his peculiar role he appears to be sitting on the fence. The fence is perhaps most apparent in I.R. There is a fence in training though; you see a need for training but the managers are reluctant because they see it as unproductive.'

But a common theme of this account was to the effect that, although the personnel specialist is in the middle, he is nevertheless in the final resort accountable to management:

'He has a mediating role but he is on the management side. He is a go between but always needs management's approval for anything he wishes to do.'

'He's on the fence between the two. He's there to help both sides. But when the chips are down he thinks about who butters the bread. In any dispute he'll always side with management in the end.'

In this willingness of a majority of a sample of personnel specialists to see themselves somehow 'in the middle' – and this willingness was as great amongst more senior as among junior people and as popular with the younger respondents as the older – we may see something of a contradiction in that it has been claimed that a central aspiration of those in the personnel occupation has been to achieve credibility as members of the 'management team'. Examination of the following account can help resolve the apparent contradiction. It was given by a 'personnel and industrial relations manager' of an engineering company.

'He has to appear as an in-between – as a linkman to the shop floor. But management must see him as part of their team. It's a matter of a neutral *appearance*.'

It may not be, then, as Fox suggested (1966a, p. 16), that the personnel specialist is doomed if he is seen as the 'man in the middle'. Although he does have to establish his usefulness and effectiveness with the rest of management, he nevertheless has to retain some element of neutrality, objectivity or whatever as a *means* towards making his contribution to management goals. In so far as management require someone within their number to act as a specialist link or communication channel with employees and their representatives – and I suggest, industrial relations being as they generally are, that this is likely to be a common necessity – then they have to allow that person some opportunity to claim sufficient 'objectivity' to gain the trust of employees over certain issues. A particular approach which I learned and personally applied as an industrial relations officer was to make it clear to employee representatives that one was part of management but that on *specific issues* one was, in some cases, willing to oppose the general management position and, in other cases, willing to act as a 'neutral' mediator. But one always stressed that in the long run one was bound by management's decisions. To gain trust one had to establish that it would always be made clear which position or role one was taking up on any particular issue. This, however, is merely one person's way of handling the type of ambiguous situation in which the personnel specialists find themselves. But I would suggest that it is not just the more junior type of personnel worker who contemplates siding with employees on issues. It was, for example, a director of a very large manufacturing concern who said,

'There is sometimes an in-between role to play. We do have to protect employees from the worst excesses of capitalist-oriented managers. We must represent to management the effect of decisions on people and defend those people.'

Despite this argument that maintaining an element of being 'in the middle' is necessary to personnel specialists, we have to recognise that the personnel role is complicated by so much ambiguity and so much concern for credibility that some individuals are likely to reject any such image of their job. Noting that 6 of my respondents were equivocal on this issue, we are left with a total of 27 people who were concerned to reject the 'in between' notion. This was done sometimes quite strongly:

'This often happens, but it shouldn't. He's not some sort of half-baked Dr Kissinger.'

'Bloody rubbish. I used to believe this and found myself ending up a bloody message boy.'

'No. He's 99·9 per cent a manager. Once he ceases to be, he loses power.'

Intra-organisational conflicts

However well the personnel specialist may have become accepted as part of the management of an organisation, whether or not he retains any element of an in-between, the theoretical analysis produced earlier makes it quite clear that we cannot expect to find managers belonging to one unitary all-agreeing non-competing 'team'. Managers and specialists are in competition between themselves for scarce resources and the rewards which the organisation offers. Power itself is both a means and an end in the struggles which occur in the world of organisational micropolitics. Conflicts and competition inevitably occurs between individuals, as Dalton's work shows particularly well (1950, 1951, 1959), and individuals get together in informal cliques and cabals to protect and further shared interests (Burns, 1955). I was not in a position in this piece of research to investigate these issues systematically and therefore kept my questioning to the type of sub-unit or departmental conflicts stressed by Landsberger (1961) and to which I referred earlier. The question which I asked in my interviews was *How do you get on with people in other departments or functions?* and the vast majority of the responses were on the lines of 'O.K.' or 'very well generally'. Evidence of intra-organisational conflicts did emerge, however, in response to the subsequent question: *Are there any major conflicts or areas where such conflicts most readily occur?*

Something over a third of the respondents answered this in terms of the 'line departments' or cited departments such as 'production' or, in a public administration context, 'office managers' which would generally be regarded as parts of the line structure. This type of conflict is what we would expect, given the conflicting criteria of the line manager and the personnel manager which I have frequently stressed. Crichton sees such conflicts arising from the issue of 'a different time-span from most other managers' and the fact that 'he is obliged by his frame of reference to get other managers to consider people's feelings' (1963, pp. 162–3). But if we accept that, as suggested earlier, the power of members of organisational sub-units is likely to be related to the strategic importance of that sub-unit and if we also recognise that the so-called line departments may not always be as strategically central as other sub-units, then we can expect to see personnel specialists in some organisations reporting conflicts with other than line departments. This is to be expected in such cases since, as was emphasised earlier, the 'power' of a sub-unit is very much involved with a low degree of *dependence* on other sub-units. Thus there are good grounds to expect a department or function with this type of *relative autonomy* to tend to resist interference by another department in its relationship with its own employees – this leading to potential conflicts with the personnel department.

Such evidence does in fact emerge. In advanced technology situations, for instance, we find responses typified by these three from personnel specialists all employed in the same advanced engineering company.

'Engineering management. There are some eccentric people in key positions.'

'The engineering managers. They see us as delaying them and always cramping their ground. We're regarded as restricting their flexibility.'

'The engineers always get just what they want and in their wake come some of the biggest problems that we've got.'

In organisations producing consumer goods there was a clear tendency for interviewees to mention the departments most closely involved with the market. To take the responses of three respondents employed in such a company, for instance:

'I get trouble with the whizz-kid type departments like marketing.'

'Yes there are areas where people discreetly go their own way. Marketing is a good example. There isn't a mass of staff and what there is is generally of a higher grade.'

'The marketing and merchandising areas. It's the nature of the beast – they are self-confident, extrovert and articulate. They want the run of the company.'

The value of being able to look at several individuals from the same organisation is that any underlying pattern that might be disguised by individuals' own explanations – things like eccentricity or articulateness – can become more apparent. These accounts do suggest some validity of the type of suggeston made above. A suggestion that the fairly superficial type of explanation of independence may cover up some more political reason is implicit in the account of a manager in another sales-oriented organisation:

'Yes, it's the marketing people here. They're more chiefs than Indians and they see their personnel requirements in a different way. They say "we're marketing so we need people with flair – a different sort of people from other departments" and things like that. Yet when you look at the jobs in that area, they're no different from those in any other department.'

The particular function which is mentioned most frequently, however, after the line departments, is the financial one. We thus get accounts such as

'Finance – because of political considerations.' [a retailing firm]

'Finance tend to think they are all-important. They believe that once you've got some good financial men you're alright. Cost and Works accountants are very much in demand and so they are very sensitive.' [engineering]

'It's the Treasurers that make the problems for us.' [Health Service]

'I get on well with the costs people here – I've taken some of the load off them since I came here. But in my previous company there was often conflict with them. Everybody used to say "accountants are in charge here".'

'We're coming to a crisis with the accountants over manpower and planning. We see the need for manpower but accountants tend not to see them as a legitimate drain on resources.' [public administration]

The structurally based problem of conflicting criteria in which personnel people are involved would lead us to expect tensions between personnel and finance. Accountants would be expected to operate in terms of formally rational criteria probably even more prevalently than line managers. Problems of conflicting criteria are suggested by the following account of a remunerations manager in a large manufacturing organisation:

'Oh yes. The finance function look on us warily. They tend not to believe us. They often look askance at us because, although we are developing professionally and developing a precise science, you still can't put a tape measure around everything.'

However, I would not wish to imply any form of structural or environmental determinism in looking at these intra-organisational conflicts. Structural and environmental contingencies are of importance, but we have to see them as mediated by competing individuals or occupational groups. The occupational background of the accountants mentioned above may be important on the lines suggested by the following account given by a local government personnel officer with reference to a professional type occupational group:

'It's the architects in my experience. They are very bad on co-operation. They see others as below them. They tend to act on their own and they have their own systems.'

Autonomy is an important element of the professionalism concept which suggests that any professionally conscious group might well create problems for personnel. But, having indicated factors relevant to occupational groupings, we also have to take account of the power which may be negotiated by a particular individual and his own sub-unit. The possibilities here are indicated by the account of a personnel officer in the headquarters of a retailing organisation:

'The computer department – it has a lot of power in our organisation. They pulled us out of a bad position when they were brought in. The boss of the computer department holds the reins here – by reminding the rest that it was them who got the firm out of the shit. When power like that exists with one bloke and his department, it's bound to make things more difficult for us.'

To conclude this section, I think it is worthwhile to point out that if there is any tendency towards a bias in these responses, it will be towards playing down conflict. This is suggested by the responses to the first and more open of the two questions asked in this part of the interview, where the impression is given, quite understandably, that the individual 'gets on well' with everybody. Such a tendency is also suggested by the case of a personnel manager who went to some length at this point in the interview to emphasise how successful he was in keeping good relationships with management and supervision generally. Yet the same man in his earlier answer to the question on the way in which the organisation makes use of its personnel specialists suggested that personnel in that company were 'abused rather than used' – 'When we make policy, as we do on the people side, the line managers say "Fucking hell – Personnel has done it again".'[5]

Perceptions of power

To find out how the personnel specialists in my sample saw the power of the personnel function I asked the two questions. The first was *What power or influence do you think that the personnel specialist generally has in organisations?* and the second was simply *What about here?* Pointing out, as usual, the dangers of arbitrariness in classifying individuals' accounts, I put forward Table 8.1 to indicate an overall pattern which is apparent in the responses to these questions.

TABLE 8.1 *Perceived power or influence of personnel specialists both generally and in respondents' own organisation*

	Generally	In respondents' own organisation
A lot	9	47
Medium or variable	59	33
Little	32	20
	100	100

The tendency to give answers which can be put in a middle category is probably a natural one, particularly when the respondent is asked to generalise about something on which he may not have a great deal of knowledge. Nevertheless, there does appear to be a significant tendency for respondents to see the personnel people being more influential in their own organisations than generally. This apparent pattern might be a reflection of some psychological mechanism relating to the specificity of one question and the non-specificity of the other. Closer examination of the accounts does, however, suggest something else as well. It is quite striking how much respondents appear to see the power or influence of any personnel department as very much dependent on the personal qualities of the head of that department or function. Typically responses are: 'Personnel has a considerable influence here. The Director of Personnel is held in high regard,' and 'Yes, I have a lot of influence. But it is ME and not my title or position which gives me this.' The fact that there is, overall, less of a tendency to see influence among personnel people generally reflects in large part, I suggest, the emergent nature of the occupation. There is an awareness that personnel is generally fighting a battle to remove its traditional welfare or marginal image and success is seen as largely dependent on the efforts of particular individuals. But it is only in the case of the respondent's own organisation that the efforts of such individuals are likely to be perceived.

I have in the previous chapter pointed to the way in which my respondents tend to think in individualistic or interpersonal terms and the accounts here may reflect this. On the other hand it is as likely, if not more so, that it is the dependence of the personal specialist on interpersonal relationships that influences the general indication to think in such a way. The importance of relationships is emphasised by a number of respondents:

'Your relationship with the Managing Director makes a big difference to the amount of influence that you have. I do deal directly with the M.D. and it helps a lot.'

'I have general influence because I am able to influence the General Manager.'

But this is not to suggest that the interviewees do not see the more structural or environmentally contingent factors influencing the power of the personnel function:

'Personnel is getting a more and more substantial amount of power as organisations increasingly find that labour is the make or break resource. Legislation is a big factor here.'

'The amount of leverage you have is often down to how
unionised the firm is.'

And although the mention of such factors is far less prevalent than
the mention of personal qualities, an awareness of the more structural
factors affecting departmental power is implicit in the fairly frequently made assertion that there is a trend towards increased influence:
'Things are improving for us as people slowly become aware of just
how much we are needed – how necessary our services are becoming.'

Tactics and stratagems

The importance of individual qualities and interpersonal skills becomes even more central as we turn to the methods of operation of
our personnel practitioners. In asking the question *In what ways do
you get your way in your relationships with managers outside the
personnel department, either in policy matters or in day-to-day
managing?* I had in mind more than just the ways in which power or
influence is used. I was also interested to see how the practitioners
see themselves coping with what has been shown throughout this
study to be highly problematic: the relationships of personnel
specialists and other members of management. How are the tensions,
ambiguities and conflicts intrinsic to the relationships handled in
practice? The first clue to this comes from the way in which, despite
my own use of both of the words *power* and *influence*, the interviewees only rarely made reference to power or authority, frequently
indicating that it was *influence* that was appropriate to them.[6] A
whole range of approaches to the problem of getting things done
were described and they cannot all be put into categories to reveal

TABLE 8.2 *How respondents report they get their own way (no. of
approaches mentioned)*

Persuasion/argument/convincing people, etc.	49
Cultivating contacts/working on relationships/winning people's confidence, etc.	23
Authority/direct orders/telling/pulling rank/getting authority from the top, etc.	19
Planting ideas in the minds of others, etc.	15
Threats/bullying/blackmailing/cajoling, etc.	12
Use of expertise/knowledge	8
Name dropping	8
Miscellaneous	24
Total	158

any pattern. Thus in Table 8.2 I have grouped approaches as best I can, leaving a category of 'miscellaneous' techniques to cover the wide range of tactics cited by individual respondents.

This table, with its inevitable limitations, does suggest the relatively minor part which formal authority plays in the lives of the personnel specialists, although I would suggest that it may well be a general trait of people in management to play down somewhat the extent to which they utilise formal authority and play up the use of persuasion. The table does suggest, however, that personal and highly pragmatic skills do play a major part, vastly outweighing any dependence on claimed expertise or knowledge. This usefully puts into context the occupational or professional strategies considered earlier and throws some light on the emphasis on practicality and pragmatism at the expense of theory or book-learning which was discussed above in the previous chapter. To claim knowledge and expertise might well be counter-productive in the practice of managing, as Crichton suggested with reference to social science knowledge:

> It might be argued that training in the social sciences may enable the personnel manager to cope better with his job because his professional advice should then become more reliable. On the other hand, training in such a non-exact discipline may intensify the difference in outlook between him and other managers (1963, p. 166).[7]

The position that the personnel specialist is often in is one where to carry out the tasks required of his function he has to get people in other departments – often more senior than himself – to do things they might not otherwise do or may well not wish to do at all. Yet the personnel specialist is generally in the official position where he is 'staff' and can therefore only advise. It is not surprising, therefore, that to do his job he is dependent on the range of stratagems and covert techniques described in my collection of accounts. A favourite approach is that typified in the following:

> 'People always look suspiciously at change – they are always against it to start with. Therefore the best way to manoeuvre is to talk round the thing until the other bloke thinks that it's his own idea.'

The subtleties of this operation seem to be considerable:

> 'In the main you work towards getting them to give you the answer you want. You have to work subtly because you are often dealing with people who don't see things rationally. You come a cropper if you try to use logic with reference to the emotional aspects of the guy you are dealing with.'

A personnel manager illustrated this approach by describing a case where he wished to see a certain manager moved from an office on the shop floor for which he was responsible and where he was adjacent to the supervisor. He tackled the problem over a two-year period, gently indicating the problems which were being created – 'It was a process of attrition. Eventually the bloke moved out – thinking it was his own idea.'

Somewhat more sinister-sounding than the above tactic are those referred to variously as 'threats', 'bullying' and 'blackmailing':

'Sometimes I let them stew a bit. It's effective but cruel – you tend to say "let the bugger stew in his own juice and he'll then come crawling".'

This compares with:

'You get a manager who doesn't see things the way you do – he doesn't want to fall in line. So you just quietly say to them "carry on and do it your way but don't come to me when the shit begins to fly".'

But all this has to be done with care:

'I bully and cajole, to be honest. But I always make sure that I am backed up by established policies and precedents. I can't afford to mess about and I certainly can't afford to make mistakes.'

The stress which was frequently put on the avoidance of mistakes is probably connected with the perennial problem of credibility. It was a typical component of those accounts which referred to establishing the right relationships and the winning of people's confidence. An example of the dangers was given by a personnel manager who had established a personnel function in a plant:

'I just dare not make a mistake. For instance, shortly after I got the job here I recruited someone who had just been discharged from prison. And then we had a robbery. His criminal record then came out when the police investigated. I had been given false information, but instantly the jokes started coming at me.'

Where organisations are unionised we find that this 'structural' factor can be made use of by the individual actor:

'I can always say "this is the way its going to be because we've got a union agreement". It can be useful to be able to threaten managers with the union.'

185

Or more subtly:

> 'You can't say to people that they can't do this or they can't do that because it would spark off a claim or a grievance somewhere else.'

Goldner, in his analysis of industrial relations specialists, points out how the unions, their 'nominal antagonists', provide their 'source of internal power' (1970, p. 105). They can frequently point to the danger of 'whipsawing' which would threaten the very necessary 'uniform industrial relations policy' (*ibid.*, p. 105). Their own source of power lay in their claim to possessing the 'bigger picture' (*ibid.*, p. 106). A particularly interesting argument of Goldner's is that the marginality of the industrial relations men enabled them 'to enjoy a good deal of organisational freedom and power along with the anxieties which accompany uncertainty' (*ibid.*, p. 126) and this corresponds precisely with the argument which I put forward in my discussion of orientations to work, where I suggested that the same things which created difficulties and 'costs' for personnel people could also provide the rewards. The sources which Goldner mentions here are ones which also appear in the accounts given to me: being in a position to 'interpret' clauses of agreements; acting as an intermediary for senior managers; and constructing the measurement systems by which their own performance is evaluated. Another important source of influence derives from the fact that the personnel or industrial relations practitioner is often outside the normal channels of authority and may therefore be approached by employees with problems which they fear taking to their superior (Goldner, 1970, p. 127).

As an industrial relations officer I personally found this an invaluable source of information and hence power. Information as a source of power is emphasised by many writers (see Burns and Stalker (1961), for example). Pettigrew's case study (1973) is an excellent illustration of its importance and he makes particular use of the idea of *gatekeepers* within communication structures.[8] These are people whose role 'contains the possibility not only of opening and closing communication channels but also of collecting and reformulating information' (*ibid.*, p. 233). I gained the impression that several of the senior personnel people in my sample had gained their organisational influence in ways not dissimilar to those used by the head of management services in Pettigrew's case. He was a gatekeeper:

> His strategic placement as the communications link between the technical specialists and the . . . board, together with his degree of political access, constituted his greatest advantages. With control over the information flow in the decision process,

he was able to focus attention successfully on his demands and, at the same time, to hinder others from generating support for theirs (*ibid.*, p. 233).

And if an individual manager is able to manipulate information and knowledge in this way we must recognise that he may be in a position to 'negotiate realities' to his own and possibly his department's advantage. 'Uncertainties', to use the language of the contingency theories, do not simply arise out of the environment, unmediated. They will be interpreted, defined or even created by sectional interests.

This latter argument takes us away from more pragmatic stratagems and tactics towards a more strategic possibility. An important strategic significance of the personnel specialist may be his part in the process of selecting employees. Perrow sees a role for the personnel specialist here 'to limit uncertainty and increase predictability' in selecting the 'organisation's staff' (1970b, p. 53). And Gouldner, in the course of his famous case study, demonstrates the importance of the personnel function here:

> The personnel manager occupies a crucial position through his influence on the recruiting process. It is within his person that complex social forces crystallize, expressing themselves as 'criteria of personnel selection'. These criteria of selection are never purely technical but always include certain unofficial values concerning the applicant's social and psychological make up. Both the formal and informal criteria can, by virtue of their sifting effects, profoundly influence the social characteristics of the plant personnel and their subsequent functioning (Gouldner, 1964, pp. 63–4).

Whyte, in his equally famous book *The Organisation Man*, reports a study which he did which indicated the personnel executives' predilection for 'administrators' rather than 'individualists' (1960, pp. 127–8). Although I see little evidence in the British situation for the personnel specialists playing quite the same role as Whyte suggests, there is some clear scope for influence to be gained through participation in selecting, training ('socialising') and so on. This is indicated by the case of one of my personnel directors, who started his response to my question on how he 'got his way' by referring to persuasion and rational argument. He then went on:

> 'But I keep the department powerful in various ways. I have the training department under my control and I therefore have patronage. And I've also got industrial relations, appointments and recruitment. Over a period of time I can develop a situation where a number of people aspiring to and reaching

influential positions will have been assisted by me. You need carrots to wield power. As people go up the ladder in the organisation they'll say to others "don't cross him". In fact I am god almighty to the graduate trainees. I impress them from the start. When they come here I say "I will knock you into management material".'

It is perhaps necessary here to remind ourselves that we are still referring to an occupation which, officially, generally only fills an advisory capacity. The fact that the personnel executive is far more influential than he might seem leads Henning and French to refer to the 'mythical personnel manager': 'Though he may manipulate men and policies with the velvet glove of persuasion, the iron hand of authority is there . . .' (1961, p. 33). These authors wish to relegate the 'mythical personnel manager to the realm of folklore' (*ibid.*, p. 44) but I suspect that in this they are underestimating the extent to which it may suit personnel practitioners (if not theorists) to keep their power relatively covert. That this is what happens in effect, if not in intent, is suggested by an empirical study done by the same authors, who find that personnel executives are seen to have less authority by other executive groups than the personnel executives see themselves as possessing (French and Henning, 1966, p. 199). I would suggest that, given the intrinsic and structurally based conflicts which exist between the personnel function and other groups, the rhetoric of being 'advisory' is a useful one. In practice that which is 'advisory' and that which is 'executive' become the same thing. This becomes quite apparent if we look at an argument put forward by one of the occupation's leading group-ideologists or 'spokesmen', in comments reproduced on the editorial page of *Personnel Management* on his becoming I.P.M. president:

Furthermore, said Mr Lyons, 'there is nothing incompatible about the personnel role being an advisory one and having a senior personnel man on the board of directors'. There was plenty of work in advising colleagues on the board as to policy, and the fact that the role was advisory had no bearing on the level at which the man might operate. Moreover, Mr Lyons thought that the personnel manager *should* be in at the start of policy-making because of the effect of policy on employees. The working out of advice of the sort that is likely to be taken is in itself very much an executive job. So it would seem that the path to the boardroom remains unimpeded (Lawrence, 1971, p. 3).

Overall it appears that impression-management or image-creation is very important to members of the personnel occupation. They need power to do the tasks required of them by their employers, but they also have tensions and conflictual relationships to which they have to accommodate. McFarland describes a range of 'accommodative mechanisms' which he located in his American study, these covering some of the tactics which I have described as well as 'administrative', 'socio-psychological' and other adaptations, including professionalisation (McFarland, 1962). Goldner refers to 'salesmanship as an accommodative mechanism' (1970, p. 121), an emphasis I have seen throughout the accounts collected in my own study. Not only do the personnel practitioners themselves frequently refer to 'selling themselves' but, in a presentation to an I.P.M. branch meeting on the topic of the relationship between personnel and line managers, a visiting line manager explained that it was only in preparing for the meeting that he discovered just what his own personnel department covered. He criticised the members of his audience in general:

> 'There's a lot in Personnel that line people don't know about. Personnel people are not selling themselves. Listening to your problems here tonight I suggest that you are not doing enough to offer a service.'

A number of heads were wisely nodded in response to this![9]

Image, credibility and women

On the issue of establishing credibility, one of my women interviewees said:

> 'I've had to fight a double battle . . . showing that I can contribute to the managing of this firm despite being a woman and despite being called the personnel officer.'

One respondent was clearly doing a job which would normally have been given the title personnel *manager*. However she was only called personnel *officer*, partly on the grounds that as a woman she would need to be called *manageress* which would carry unfortunate connotations connected with canteens and the like! Such minor discriminations – like in another case where a new personnel director was introduced by a chief executive in a negotiating situation as 'this delightful young lady' – may seem typical of the superficial manifestations of the very major career discrimination against women which generally exists (see Hunt, 1975). But there is something more than this in the case of the personnel occupation, as Miller and Coghill (1964) have suggested. Personnel management finds itself in a particular dilemma with regard to its women members at its present stage of development. This is largely connected with the desire to kill the welfare image of the occupation. And the welfare image is a 'feminine' one both in that our culture relates femininity to 'caring' and as a result of the fact that the precursors of the modern personnel specialists were largely women industrial social workers. Thus, to achieve credibility, senior personnel executives may find themselves discriminating against women in recruiting to the function. We therefore get career advisers recommending women to apply for personnel jobs, which they often see as particularly appropriate for women, whilst those jobs in practice (or at least the ones with a managerial element of potential) are seen by the recruiters as inappropriate for women. There was a clear tendency amongst those men interviewees responsible for recruitment to personnel departments to lump together women with 'social work types' and 'churchy people'. Such recruits were to be avoided.

It is ironic that the personnel occupation, which finds it necessary to indulge in a discriminatory occupational strategy, contains the very people who are often to be charged in organisations with implementing equal opportunity and equal pay legislation.[10] Sociological study of race relations has shown the value of analysing discriminatory behaviour in terms of *interests* and *structural* issues rather than in terms of *prejudice*. Although prejudice against women is probably as common among personnel men as among any others, I suggest that we can recognise a deeper pressure towards discrimination here. It is probably the case that it is more in the interests of the personnel manager to discriminate against women's career advancement in his occupation than it is for the male members of many other occupations. Yet again we see an example of the ambiguities so much associated with the personnel role – ambiguities which arise in part from the individual personnel specialist's requirement to act as an agent of his employing organisation's controllers and his or her need to fulfil personal wants and aspirations. Power and influence are both means and ends for the personnel practitioner.

9 Social integration, personnel management and social change

According to French, personnel management is

the recruitment, selection, development, utilisation of, and accommodation to, human resources by organisations. The human resources of an organisation consist of all individuals, regardless of their role, who are engaged in any of the organisation's activities. An organisation may be a manufacturing firm, an insurance company, a government agency, a hospital, a university, a social club, a ski resort, a public school system, or a church. It may be small or large, simple or complex (1970, p. 3).

The personnel management task has to be carried out in any organisation which employs human beings as resources. And as such organisations have increased in size and as the resource of labour has, for a variety of reasons, become an increasingly significant source of uncertainty for the controllers of organisations, so we have seen an increasing number of specialists engaged in various aspects of the personnel management task. The twentieth century has seen the steady emergence of a recognisable occupation: an increasingly self-aware group of people undertaking work careers which involve full-time attention to the labour resources of advanced industrial capitalist society. Since work and employment in organisations is central to the lives of a large proportion of the population of such societies as well as to their economies, the part that this occupation plays in the maintenance of such social orders must be a matter of keen interest for the sociologist – whether he be a sociologist whose primary interest is in work and employment or one who is simply interested in how these societies hold together. My purpose here is to bring together the arguments deployed in previous chapters in the hope of indicating the value of thinking of the personnel occupation in terms of a 'societal contribution' and, at the same time, to make some concluding generalisations on the sociology of work.

Before conclusions can be drawn about the nature of the personnel occupation's contribution to social integration, it has to be made clear what is meant by such a notion of integration. I am claiming that the particular type of society in which this study was carried out is, notwithstanding the arguments of some thinkers about *post-industrialism* and *post-capitalism*,[1] an industrial capitalist one. The industrial capitalist mode of social integration which developed in Western societies with the industrial revolution is one which, despite considerable modification, still prevails in societies such as modern Britain. My developmental account saw it arising as a result of the efforts of particular individuals and newly emerging social groups (with the later alliance of older social groupings). The interests of these groups were furthered by the utilisation of certain calculatively rational ideas and techniques and, particularly, by the development of a work-based social order in which labour power is bought and sold on a market basis. The groups' interests are met in that they have achieved overall advantage in terms of access to and use of the resources or goods which are scarce and valued in the society. The resulting social structure can be seen as *structure of advantage*. Social integration, whereby the pattern of advantage is stabilised to create a 'mode of integration', is achieved by a range of means including those by which the hegemonic groups allocate various rewards to those who contribute to the maintenance of the structure of advantage (in which the dominant groups are the most advantaged). But, since there are basic contradictions in this social structure, resulting from the constant tendency in social life for chosen means to subvert higher level goals (i.e., for *formally rational* techniques, for instance, to subvert *materially rationally* conceived ends), the mode of integration has to be continually modified to cope with challenges and crises which result from the underlying conflicts and tensions. Hence we see a range of institutional changes in the educational, state welfare and other spheres as well as in the polity, and we see social groups and, more typically, individuals who might present a challenge to the structure of advantage being incorporated into that structure – whether by the awarding of relatively higher salaries or share options to managers or the awarding of peerages and places in the decision-making processes to labour leaders.

The industrial capitalist mode of integration is maintained, however much modification may occur, as long as a structure of advantage is maintained in which the dominant social groups by and large remain the most advantaged in terms of the goods available in the society, and that this position of advantage remains dependent on the utilisation of labour power on a basis where property, profit and market criteria are central. Academic research has indicated the ways in which advantages have been maintained by minorities with regard to wealth, property and power – although such issues are by no means settled.[2] But, as Giddens has pointed out, there are 'differentiations of market capacity which do not directly derive from the factor of property ownership' (1973, p. 103). He follows Weber in recognising the importance of certain skills, including educational qualifications, as a major factor influencing market capacity. He goes on to suggest that we might view these capacities as a form of 'property' which is itself exchanged on the market for goods. This closely corresponds to the arguments which I put forward in introducing my implicit-contract scheme which related these capacities or resources back to the family and class position of the person entering employment. Giddens faces the problem in which the Weberian scheme seems to suggest the existence of as many classes as there are different market positions. He does this by retaining Marx's simpler notion of two major interest groups (owners and non-owners of property or, in effect, buyers and sellers of labour power) whilst suggesting the existence of *three* social classes, the members of which possess three types of market capacity: 'ownership of property in the means of production; possession of educational or technical qualifications; and possession of manual labour-power' (*ibid.*, p. 107). As long as the second type of capacity is seen as including certain skills which may not necessarily be accompanied by a formal qualification we can see that this model of class *structuration* usefully formalises in class terms the assumptions made throughout this study. We can thus locate the personnel specialists within a structure which is based on two conflicting objective interests: they are, strictly speaking, propertyless proletarians yet they clearly occupy a class position distinct from that of manual workers. They occupy the middle-class position by virtue of their selling their skills to those holding the capital – skills in the acquisition and administration of labour resources on the behalf (in effect) of those in the 'upper'-class position.

The above analysis sees managers as *agents* of the most advantaged groups in industrial capitalist society, working in the ultimate interests of those groups. In this way they contribute to social integration. But the argument cannot be left there. Recognition has to be given to a particularly powerful and widely accepted thesis which contradicts analyses of this type: the thesis of the separation of the ownership and control of business. This widely accepted thesis (Zeitlin, 1974) takes a variety of forms but, put simply, suggests that the 'control' of enterprises is no longer effectively in the hands of property owners but is in the hands of the 'managers' who have taken the place of the old entrepreneurs in running businesses. This allows them to operate in terms of criteria other than profit maximisation – whether these be altruistic or self-interest-oriented criteria. Recent surveys of the evidence severely undermine the validity of this thesis (Nicholls, 1969; Child, 1969b; Zeitlin, 1974). The evidence suggests, as Child puts it, that there are in modern capitalist society 'wider economic, social and technological constraints operating on the business enterprise which tend to minimise the behavioural differences between owner-managers and non-propertied managers' (1969b, p. 51). All enterprises face similar market constraints, as Child points out and as Blackburn forcefully argues, indicating the centrality of the finance function in business – a centrality arising from its relationship with the market environment (Blackburn, 1972). Blackburn claims that the 'sphere of competence of the specialist is very strictly defined by his own particular skill' – his specialisation thus limiting his power (*ibid.*, p. 178). Thus, 'to imagine that the personnel manager, production manager or supervisor has any choice other than to extract surplus value as efficiently as possible from his labour force is quite absurd' (*ibid.*, p. 108). The market analyst, take-over specialist and asset-strippers are on constant watch.

The argument that 'managers still operate in a capitalist market and hence must be just as oriented to the traditional capitalist goal, profit, as owners' is looked at in an important empirical study of company directors (Pahl and Winkler, 1974) in which the authors say that this argument 'was completely confirmed by our observations' (p. 118). They frequently encountered 'professional managers':

> Their idea of professionalism is not that usually employed by sociologists, but more like that of actors, the ability to produce a competent performance in any circumstances, no matter how unpromising. The indicators of successful performance are profits, growth and return on investment. The essence of the professional manager is his rigorousness and exclusive dedication to financial values . . . [The professional managers observed who had taken over from family managements] not only were . . . more oriented to profit, they were more capable of obtaining it (*ibid.*, p. 118).

And management's rewards are likely to be tied to success in such performances (Westergaard and Resler, 1975, p. 162). As Rex comments,

> He does his job for the firm because he receives precisely those rewards which Kingsley Davis and Wilbert Moore have suggested are functional to social systems. . . . Given these, why should he not be recruited to the business of using labour

efficiently as a resource? Surely this is the main point about our cadre of industrial managers. Their ideology is, above all, the ideology of using their men's labour efficiently, and it is through achievements in this sphere that they achieve self-esteem (1974a, pp. 122–3).

If we accept that the managers within the business world are ultimately forced to operate within market and profitability criteria, the question must still be faced of what criteria are pertinent for managers in the non-commercial sector. This study has looked at personnel specialists in public administration and nationalised industries, where profitability might not seem so important as a constraint on performance. To some extent, the operating constraints on those managing in these spheres are undoubtedly different but, in the long run, they are bound by the same pressures. As Westergaard and Resler point out,

> it would be impracticable for public sector industry as a minority element to pursue investment, pricing and pay policies which would put it widely outside the general market conditions set by the predominance of private enterprise. Publicly owned industry would still, as now, have to recruit all levels of its personnel – including board members, executives and managers at high premiums – in the same hierarchically divided labour markets as private industry. It would still have to sell its products in markets the effective demand of which reflects the skew distribution of income and wealth. It would have to raise its capital, if not from the same immediate sources, then on much the same terms as private enterprise (1975, p. 215).

Any student of current affairs in contemporary Britain would be well aware of the extent of pressures on nationalised industries, at least to avoid or reduce deficits if not make surpluses. And this means the 'efficient' utilisation of labour and its deployment on a basis little different from that in any commercial business. However much British Steel or British Rail, for example, may pursue advanced and enlightened personnel policies, both industries are constantly under examination for potential 'rationalisation'. A major area in which both of these industries have been seen as pursuing 'enlightened' personnel policies has been that of redundancy. The point here is that the labour resource cannot be any less tractable in a public than in a private enterprise. And the same student of current affairs who would note these pressures would also observe those being exerted on public administrators to use labour efficiently, as a squeeze is put upon public expenditure – to a large extent as a result of pressures from international money *markets*.

What I am saying here is that, in the type of society under consideration, all managers who are involved in employing people, in whatever kind of organisation, are, in the long run, bound to deal with that labour in terms of the return that can be obtained from it. Given the nature of the environment of these organisations, any manager who deviated markedly from these criteria, putting employee welfare before (longer-term) organisational advantage, would be *failing to do his job*. An illustration of the argument that employing organisations tend not to give higher rewards than they *need* to in market terms is given in the recent evidence of highly 'respectable' British employers paying wages in South Africa which can be described in the British press as scandalous yet which are simply geared to the prevailing conditions in that particular market.[3] The point is that any personnel executive suggesting paying African labour at European rates would be suggesting his own incompetence – given what his job is.[4]

The above analysis may appear to be verging on a determinism which belies the intent of this study to recognise the ability of people to make their own world as well as to cope with its constraints. If managers in employing organisations do not have ultimate control of those organisations or, in fact, anything like it, may they not still have some scope for modifying practices so that some criteria other than 'organisational effectiveness' might be met? Is it necessarily true that the manager cannot be interested in a practical sense in welfare or social justice *per se*, but only looks to such matters as means of furthering the interests of those who benefit primarily from the fulfilment of 'organisational goals'? It is in proposing some answers to these questions that this study can contribute to the debate about the role of managements in advanced capitalist society. This is the case because, in looking at the personnel occupation, we are looking at a sector of management which has in its history a strong interest in 'betterment' and employee welfare. In addition to this, it is an area to which we might expect managers with values less consonant with the treating of people as exploitable resources to be attracted. If there is an area of management, then, to which we might look for a leaning towards alternative employment orientations to those traditionally typical of industrial capitalist society, it is the personnel management area. And, furthermore, this is an occupation where there is strong evidence of an interest in professionalisation – an interest which would, at least on first sight, suggest some adherence to non-profit or some altruistic criteria of performance. Thomason, in the concluding chapter of his I.P.M. textbook where he valuates and looks at the future of the personnel function, suggests that there is some choice here for members of the personnel occupation. They can debate the question about the occupation:

does it comprise managerial persons who occupy a role of agent to some enterprise principal which will expect a local orientation in their work, or is there any meaningful sense in which these persons are professionals able to provide a service to clients (whether enterprises or persons) from a cosmopolitan basis of orientation which is itself protected by the occupational association? (Thomason, 1975, p. 425).

And it is here that we must return to the issue of professionalisation and look at its meaning at a societal level. This means looking at the thesis which Halmos has put forward in *The Personal Service Society* (1970) about the rise of a new ethic in society – one which is more altruistic and humane than that of traditional capitalist society and one which is mediated by the increasing influence of social science thinking and notions of professionalism.

Halmos sees professionalisation as a key process in society, one which, together with the influence of certain aspects of social science thinking on professional education, is bringing a new *service ethic* to bear on the running of society. One of the spheres in which the effect of this is beginning to be felt, it is claimed, is that of the business world and, here, Halmos puts forward the following:

My hypothesis is that mainly as a result of the multiplication of instances in which business is influenced by professional expertise, a certain discolouring of the banners of 'Profit First' is noticeable. On the one hand, patriotic slogans such as 'Efficiency First' or 'Productivity First', especially at a time when these are national objectives, exert some influence. On the other hand, the businessman is learning to look up to the professional expert whom he employs in ever-growing numbers, and whilst trying to preserve his tough-minded entrepreneurial approach to the things of this world he is slanting this approach so that some, by no means unimportant, accommodation takes place between his tough-mindedness and the relative tender-mindedness of the professional man (1970, p. 115).

Halmos supports his hypothesis with evidence from management writers and thinkers and, unfortunately, in the place of what would be much more pertinent evidence, he puts forward such unsupported contentions as:

nowadays, a growing number of high-level decisions in business, reached in the headquarters of the enterprise, follow haruspication by human relations consultants, and socio-psychological experts of various kinds (*ibid.*, p. 123).

197

The most relevant evidence available here, that of Winkler (1974), suggests anything but this in practice. The thesis is not supported by that piece of research on leaders of business, and I must now bring in my own findings with regard to professionalisation. Nichols, in his study of businessmen, observed that 'if one must talk about professionalism at all, those in personnel probably approximate most closely to the notions of the "professional manager" ' (1969, p. 198).[5] Does my evidence of the interest in professionalisation support Halmos' thesis? He says,

> I agree with Bernard Barber that professionalism in business remains more an ideological aspiration than a social fact, but I must stress that the widespread hankering after the dignity and honour of a professional status among Western management leaders and businessmen is itself also a socio-cultural fact, which clearly signifies a profound discontent with an exclusively mercenary role definition in the world of business, and a nostalgic longing to amend the role definition (*ibid.*, p. 122).

My evidence in chapter 6 on the personnel practitioners' interest in professionalisation does indicate the strength of such an interest. The early members of the occupation who first spoke in professional terms were, it is true, very concerned with welfare and the betterment of those in employment. But we see, with development of the occupation, a growing aspiration towards acceptance and member-ship of the management 'team' and an increasingly strong concern with 'industry's needs'. What the notion of professionalism symbo-lises for the contemporary personnel specialist is *competence* and this, I argue, is competence in the meeting of general managerial goals. Criteria of service do not appear to be particularly salient in the personnel practitioner's definitions of professionalism, and the major support for the professionalisation *strategy* appears to be in terms of personal career advancement and an opportunity to obtain information and advice to aid them in their contribution to the overall management of the enterprise. To *be professional* is to be competent in the efficient running of the organisation – even if this 'efficiency' is conceived in a longer-term sense than that of many non-personnel managers. Not only is the notion of professionalism which is adhered to here not particularly inclined towards a welfare or service ethic, it is to an extent dependent on a rejection of such ideas. The type of professionalism advocated by one of the leading 'spokesmen' involves an explicit rejection of any 'philanthropic ideology' (Lupton, 1964).

Not only are the personnel specialists the group to which we look on the professionalisation issue, they are also the group with the strongest potential interest in applying social-science-type knowledge in the world of work. Does my evidence of its influence on practitioners (as opposed to the thinkers and writers) indicate any trend in the direction indicated by Halmos? His arguments are sufficiently subtle here for my evidence not to contradict them, but there is little positive support for them in my analysis in chapter 7. Although we see good evidence of a significant input of social science thought in the education and training of personnel specialists, its influence appears, to say the least, to stay in the background. I have suggested that the level of analysis on which they operate is an *individualistic* one, which might suggest some personal-service orientation, but it is also a *psychologistic* leaning with an interest in 'what makes people tick' which has as many manipulative overtones as personal welfare or liberating ones. The type of social or behavioural science described in the personnel literature has a strong positivistic flavour.[6] It is very much knowledge of the type which Habermas sees as contributing to *instrumental action* rather than to anything *emancipatory* (Habermas, 1971; and see also Schroyer, 1970). This is knowledge of a type which has ideological and political implications at the societal level as both Habermas (1971) and Fay (1975) have argued. In the implicit promise of the social science thinking put forward as relevant to personnel management to help achieve a *synthesis* between individuals' needs and 'organisational goals' we see a way in which it goes beyond a purely formally rational instrumentalism, however. But, in so far as these ideas suggest that attention needs to be paid to matters other than short-term calculations of efficiency, output, profit or whatever, attention is brought to issues which look to materially rational criteria of longer-term *organisational* 'effectiveness' rather than to the interests of employees or the 'community' in themselves. The promise of social science to personnel practitioners is both a *technical* one and a *legitimatory* one: it suggests both techniques and rationales through which the personnel function can further the rationalisation of human resources and, at the same time, cope with the conflict between this type of formal rationality and the material rationality of the organisational controllers. Human beings become an 'asset' or an 'investment' whose importance is recognised by the attention paid to them by the manpower planners, job analysts, industrial relations specialists, training officers and the rest of the personnel practitioners whose own importance is established by the general recognition of the value of the labour resource. As one personnel manager said to me, 'the people here are our most valuable asset – we owe it to them to make efficient use of their efforts'. And to talk of 'efficiency' is ideologically convenient, of course; it begs the question of the values in terms of which it is conceived as a criterion of action (cf. Fay, 1975, pp. 50–1).

The potentially central role of the personnel specialists in both furthering formally rational use of human effort and in dealing with the general conflicts between formal and material rationalities was illustrated in chapter 5 with the case of redundancies. At the time of a redundancy people are relatively explicitly examined as units of labour – as tractable and disposable resources. And in collecting accounts of how my respondents would expect to handle certain aspects of redundancies I hope that I have managed to provide some insight into facets of managerial decision making. Because decision making in redundancy situations is among the more overt situations in which people are considered in formally calculative terms, it was a particularly pertinent situation in which to analyse the accounts of those who, on the basis of what I was able to gather about personal values and political leanings, might have been expected to have spoken of acting differently from the bulk of the interviewees. In fact, what we saw was that the 'left'-inclined individuals spoke of acting, overall, in terms of criteria generally little different from those of the other personnel specialists. The individual practitioner did have some scope but he can be understood as largely constrained by the need to act so as to compromise between the conflicting criteria inherent in the situation in which he finds himself. Situational exigencies were seen as more important than social values in certain ways. What was illustrated here, I suggest, is that Becker's point about the greater salience of the specificity of actual situations in informing action, compared with the individual's personal values and long-term perspectives (1961, p. 442) can give insight into the wider issue of social integration. Individual challenges to any particular order may be reduced in effectiveness by the pressures of the moment: the pressures to solve an immediate problem. Hence, Freidson's extension of this notion, discussed above in chapter 7, which, among other things, indicates the primacy of pragmatism and practicality over theoretical thought and book-knowledge, suggests a possible pressure reducing the effects of social science thinking and its connected ethos on actual behaviour. And, for example, academically outmoded human relations ideas may still be embraced, I suggested, because they are *useful*. They may be mere palliatives but the organisational position of the practising manager is such that palliatives are very relevant. Similarly, the apparent attachment of many personnel specialists to a unitary frame of reference in looking at industrial relations may appear to be short-sighted and perhaps ingenuous to the academic, but the truth of the situation is that, where the idea of management and unions 'working together' may seem naïve to the sociological realist, the way in which the personnel man and woman gets through his or her working day is often, in practice, precisely by working in harmony with those with whom he or she is theoretically acting in conflict. Assumptions of consensus in social relations, taboo for the sociologist, may be psychologically helpful to the situation-bound personnel manager.

The argument put forward in chapter 8 was that the power or influence which the personnel manager has is to be understood in terms of his autonomy or lack of dependence on other managerial functions *within the organisation*. The influence of the personnel specialist is dependent on the help he can provide to the dominant coalition of the organisation in its achieving of its objectives, and this is illustrated by the tendency of interviewees to stress the importance of the relationships between the chief executive and the head of the personnel function. The changes which do come about at the hands of the personnel function are typically the result of reacting to certain, particularly longer-term, business or other contextual pressures or the accommodating to legislative or trade union initiatives. There is little evidence of any mainspring of initiative within the personnel occupation. The organisation of work is primarily on the formally rational principles of 'scientific management' with the personnel function having to cope with some of the inherent 'dysfunctions'. As Braverman stresses:

> Work itself is organised according to Taylorian principles,
> while personnel departments and academics have busied
> themselves with the selection, training, manipulation, pacification,
> and adjustment of 'manpower' to suit the work processes so
> organised. Taylorism dominates the world of production; the
> practitioners of 'human relations' and 'industrial psychology'
> are the maintenance crew for the human machinery (1974,
> p. 87).

Braverman quotes the influential management writer Drucker to support his contention that the apparent disappearance of Taylorism as a separate school is largely because 'it is no longer the property of a faction, since its fundamental teachings have become the bedrock of all work design' (*ibid.*, p. 87).[7] The role for the personnel function which is advocated by certain of the writers and spokesmen for the personnel occupation is one in which the personnel expert can influence work design from the start, but there is no support in my evidence for any belief that such a role is being played in practice. One management writer has commented to me on the findings of my research that in many of the organisations falling into my sample

> there is a limited and old-fashioned conception of the personnel
> function, and it is rather depressing that such a small
> percentage of your respondents are concerned with problems
> of organisational design and its role in the community.

If it is true, however, that, as Rex has put it, 'the proof of the power is in the pay-off and comes in a currency other than power' (1974b, p. 210) then the increase in salary levels mentioned in chapter 3 would indicate the personnel specialist's increased relative power within organisations. And salary is part of the reward which the organisational controllers give in return for a *contribution*, this being a contribution towards the goals of those who are the prime beneficiaries of the way in which the organisations are run. Formal organisations, as I have conceptualised them, are themselves devices created by historically specific social groups to establish and maintain their material advantage in a type of society which resulted to a large extent from their initiatives. The 'power' of any management group is the power of an agent, it is a strictly bounded and situationally specific power.

The labour resources upon which employing organisations depend are essentially problematic for those running organisations. The development of large-scale bureaucracies, the development of a mobile and tractable labour force and the underlying principle of a division of labour all have their counterproductive elements, as I argued in chapters 2 and 3. The personnel specialists find themselves coping with problems arising from this on a day-to-day basis and other, perhaps more significant, initiatives in countering the self-defeating aspects of overall work organisation have come from government and, often connected, trade union pressures. The personnel department is often the mediator here. But members of the personnel occupation are also aware of the increasing and less formal pressures from below and we see the personnel literature, particularly that of the I.P.M., producing ideas for coping with such phenomena as sit-ins and factory occupations (e.g. Thomas, 1976; I.P.M., 1976b). The need for reaction here was mentioned by a senior personnel man in a talk to an I.P.M. branch meeting at which I observed. The way he spoke is, I suggest, quite revealing in terms of the way the personnel function generally develops and copes. After describing the organisation of personnel management in his own company, a large and important employer in the area, he went on:

'all this can be seen as an expression of the enlightened conscience of the senior management of the company. Yet, it is in fact the only way senior management could cope with personnel problems – because of the growth of trade unions and, especially, legislation. And now we have the problems to which we will have to react with some form of co-determination. Industrial democracy in some form simply has to come. It is all part of the flow of circumstances to which personnel management has had and will have to respond'.

The Institute of Personnel Management increasingly attempts to take initiatives and to influence policies at a national level. The president of the institute said, in 1975, in commenting on the increase in 'government intervention and control':

> In the face of this the I.P.M. has not remained passive. Often at short notice . . . our national committees have voiced the professional personnel manager's feeling and concern by commenting on the series of White Papers and Bills produced by the Department of Employment. How much effect our advice has had on departmental or ministerial determination is difficult to say (Roff, 1975, p. 3).

A few months later we find *Personnel Management* commenting on the setting up of the Committee of Inquiry on Industrial Democracy under Sir Alan Bullock: 'Practising personnel people are conspicuous by their absence' (I.P.M., 1976c).

Whatever the influence of personnel people nationally, the individual personnel specialist operates primarily within the confines of his own employing organisation and under the command of its dominant coalition. If the type of changed style of leadership of which Halmos writes is coming about at all here it is as a result of politically mediated pressures and practical problems rather than any process of professionalisation or any autonomous influence of the social sciences. If jobs are enlarged or 'participation' encouraged it will be because that is the only way that the job will go on getting done.[8] But to say this is not to move away from my contention that the personnel occupation does act as a social institution contributing to the maintenance of a given social order. If the managements of organisations were to fail in some general way to meet their goals through the failure to cope with the type of unintended consequences of their policies, techniques and structures with which the personnel function tends to cope, then each organisation would disintegrate, so leading to the collapse of the societal mode of integration.[9] The social integrative role of personnel management can be seen in the United States by the recognition at one stage of its role in countering communism[10] and, in Britain, the benefit of royal patronage has been sought and found by the I.P.M.[11] The Duke of Edinburgh wrote in the foreword to the institute's annual report for 1973:

> Perhaps the most important challenge to the profession in the future will be the whole problem of the quality of life at work. This will mean achieving a careful balance between the economic requirements of industry and the social requirements of the people who work in it.

I am delighted to be Patron of the Institute during its Jubilee Year. I admire what has been achieved and I have great hopes for the future (H.R.H. The Duke of Edinburgh, 1973).

And in considering matters of integration, some mention has to be made here of religion – something which has been important in many sociologists' analyses of social integration. The Non-conformist conscience clearly played a part in the foundations of the personnel occupation, something which I illustrated with the cases of Rowntree and Boot. Where there was an elective affinity between the religious ideas and the material interests of these entrepreneurs, I would suggest that the mention of Non-conformist beliefs by a proportion of my interviewees is perhaps an indicator of some corresponding relationship between the 'ghost of dead religious beliefs' (as Weber called the lingering influence of *The Protestant Ethic*, 1965, p. 181) and the individualistic and pragmatic ideas of a large proportion of the respondents. Moore has shown, in a case study of a particular area of County Durham, the ways in which Methodism influenced the growth of a type of reformist 'leftish' thought which stood as an alternative to the more revolutionary implications of socialism proper (1974). Such an influence may, in some residual sense, be relevant to the ways in which those personnel people with nominally 'left' views accommodate to a career in the management of labour.[12]

These latter points are part of a less direct way in which I hope that this study in the sociology of work may contribute to the analysis of the integration of the type of society studied: that is in its coverage of a hundred people who are not only personnel specialists and members of managements but who are also themselves employees. The chapters on occupational entry and on orientation to work in particular do, I hope, give some insight into the way that people are constrained by and come to terms with the society in which they find themselves and actively adapt both themselves and their situations in the process of fulfilling what Dawe called 'self-integrative purposes' (1973, p. 32). We have seen the constraints of family background, educational opportunity and social class on the one hand and efforts to achieve social mobility, career advancement and the conversion of occupational frustrations to sources of work satisfaction, on the other. The intention here has been to demonstrate some of the potentialities of a sociology of work expanded beyond the traditional subdivisions and based on a social-action framework which does justice to both individual human effort and social constraint. In going deeper than the surface 'realities' of social life, albeit from the personal, but I hope relatively explicit, viewpoint of just one sociologist, I trust that I have produced something of the type of critical insight which was among the criteria set out in chapter 1.

Human beings are creative agents – they are constructors of realities and creators of structures and are not the puppets of 'society' nor the creatures of social systems. Yet people are highly constrained by what the sociologist can most conveniently conceptualise as social, economic and political *structures*. In pointing to conflicts, tensions and contradictions underlying modern industrial capitalist society, I am not working from some assumption of any immanent tendency towards a socialist millennium. Because of what Weber called *ethical irrationalities* and the *paradox of consequences* in the social world, we would find contradictions arising in any alternative form of society. This is in no way to argue against the pursuit of radical change but, whatever type of society is created and, as long as goods are to be produced on any large scale, that society would require its functional equivalent to a personnel management occupation. For the present, however, we can expect industrial capitalism to go on being adapted, with members of the personnel occupation adapting along with it, both as agents and as acted upon. They will continue to be involved in conflicts and tensions and will find both the costs and rewards of their employment within the ambiguity of their occupational and organisational positions. A personnel manager, commenting to me on the ambiguities of the positions of personnel workers wrote,

'There is a passage in Virgil's *Georgics* which suggests that the young tree which bends with the current of flood-water will survive and flourish, whereas the stiff, thick-stemmed tree will snap off and be swept away. I always knew deep down that a classical education had direct relevance to personnel work. . . .'

Appendix 1
The interview sample—composition

The sample was not chosen on the basis of any statistically acceptable random method, nor were the various categories intended statistically to match either the national or local population of personnel specialists. The main procedure used was to telephone or write to personnel people in a range of employing organisations asking to interview one or more of the personnel staff. The willingness of people to co-operate and indeed the keenness of the great majority of people approached to be interviewed was far greater than anticipated. As I built up the sample I attempted to ensure that I was giving coverage to a 'reasonable' range of industries, job levels, subspecialisms, ages, qualifications and so on. Given that the notion of a 'reasonable' spread is somewhat arbitrary and personal, my intention is to allow my readers to judge for themselves what biasing factors may be present in the sample by considering the following breakdowns.

Job level

I have utilised the increasingly popular distinction between personnel manager and personnel officer to indicate level of seniority within the organisation. On the basis of inevitably somewhat arbitrary criteria, I have divided the sample into 60 personnel managers (the most senior of whom I designate director or senior executive) and 40 personnel officers.

In practice, there is a vast range of titles for personnel practitioners and this type of simplification was very necessary. To illustrate the point: the head of the personnel function in a local authority (like in industry, although to a lesser extent) might either be called personnel officer or personnel director. In line with the trend of usage, such a person would be referred to in this study as a personnel director.

Whether the respondent is a generalist personnel practitioner or a training or industrial relations specialist, he is here referred to as a personnel manager/officer/director.

Sex

Male: 81   Female: 19
Of the 19 women, 6 are managers and one of these is a director.

Age

30 and under:	31	5 (*No. of whom are managers*)
31 to 40:	26	21 (*No. of whom are managers*)
41 to 50:	26	19 (*No. of whom are managers*)
51 and over:	17	15 (*No. of whom are managers*)
	100	60

Industry

The apparent 'over-representation' of certain areas of employment is less than it might appear, in that the personnel function is generally more highly developed in areas like engineering compared with, say, textiles.

Miscellaneous manufacturing	6
Heavy manufacturing	6
Textiles	6
Engineering	27
Food, drink and tobacco	8
Electrical engineering, telecommunications, etc.	7
Chemicals and allied industries	7
Printing, paper and publishing	5
Retail, distribution and transport	13
Commerce	3
Public administration	14
	100

N.B. I have not attempted to analyse organisations by *size* because many organisations were part of larger organisations, some were more autonomous than others and, in many cases, it was very difficult to decide exactly what the *boundary* of any given unit was, especially with regard to personnel policies.

Institute of Personnel Management membership

Student membership	21
Affiliate membership	1
Associate membership	1
Member	18
Fellow	7
	—
	48

Social class of origin

This is derived from father's occupation.

Middle class I (including professional, managerial, administrative, business)	42
Middle class II (including routine clerical, junior non-manual, shopworkers, salesmen)	20
	—
	62
	—
Intermediate (where fathers have moved from manual into supervisory work or are self-employed manual workers)	13
Working class (manual workers)	24
	—
	37
	—
Not known	1
	—
	100

Graduates

36

Those with large industrial relations components to their jobs

35

208

Those who are training specialists

13 (most of these have responsibilities beyond simply training)

Those who more or less started their careers in personnel work

24

Appendix 2
The interview

Job (title and brief description)
Job Level: reporting to
        subordinates
Age
Sex
Place of Birth
Father's Job(s)
Mother's Job(s)
Education
Qualifications
Previous Jobs (and duration)
Main interests outside work

Thinking back as far as you can into childhood, what jobs did you think you might like to do? And how did your ideas change over time?

How did you come into the personnel field?

How did you think of personnel work before you became involved in it? What image did it have?

Can you see any connection between your parents' influence (or your general family background) and the fact that you are in personnel work?

Are there any religious, political or moral influences or interests which you feel may be relevant to your being in this work?

What most appeals to you about personnel work?

What do you most dislike about personnel work?

If you can imagine it, what would your ideal job be?

Is there anything generally different or distinctive about people who work in personnel management – are they a type in any way?

Does personnel work require any special abilities?

How do you see the role of the personnel department in the organisation – what role does it play?

What is the biggest difficulty faced by the personnel manager?

Some people argue that there is an inevitable conflict between an organisation being efficient on the one hand and socially just or fair on the other. How do you feel about this?

Some argue that the personnel manager is 'in between' – between, that is, the management generally and the employees. Do you agree with this idea of the job?

How well do you think your organisation uses the resources that it has in its personnel specialists?

What does the idea of a profession mean to you?

Do you see personnel management as a profession – is it one or ought it to become one?

Are you a member of the Institute of Personnel Management? Why (not)?

The I.P.M. appears to be attempting to make entry into personnel management more difficult. What do you think about this? (Briefly explain current entry policy where necessary.)

Do you attend meetings, conferences, etc. connected with but outside your actual job? If yes, what sort of thing?

Do you do any reading relevant to your job but beyond what is formally required? If yes, what sort of thing?

Do you feel that personnel management has a basic body of knowledge or an underlying body of theory? If yes, in what way?

What do you feel about the relevance of social or behavioural science to personnel management?

What do you think is the biggest problem facing managements generally today?

Thinking of employees generally – and I am thinking more of ordinary workpeople – what do you think that their jobs mean to them?

211

What part do you think that trade unions should play in employing organisations?

Are there situations where redundancy is inevitable?

In a situation where a redundancy is inevitable, what principles do you personally feel should be applied when it is carried out? (Explain that by 'inevitable' is meant a situation where the redundancy decision has been made 'at the top' and when other strategies such as early retirement, wastage etc., would not be sufficient. 'Principles' refers to the criteria for selecting who goes.)

What power or influence do you think the personnel specialist generally has in organisations?

What about here?

In what ways do you manage to get your way in your relationships with other departments, either in policy matters or in day-to-day managing?

How do you get on with people in other departments or functions?

Are there any major conflicts or areas where such conflicts most readily occur?

What kind of know-how is of most relevance
for (i) your own work
(ii) personnel specialists in general.

What kind of post-experience courses would be
of most benefit to (i) personnel specialists

What fields (areas) of personnel might have you
worked in   are you
currently working in?

212   What are the moral/ethical dilemmas
that face you as a P.S.

Notes

Chapter 1 The sociological framework

1 Bottomore has characterised Gouldner's reflexive sociology as 'the sociologist contemplating his own navel' (1975, p. 44).

2 For a useful critique see Attewell (1974).

3 Dawe in his version of reflexive sociology calls for a return to an interest in 'active social relationships' – a phrase which he takes from Raymond Williams who uses it to refer to the problem of 'who controls and who is controlled, by what specific institutions and means' (Dawe, 1973, p. 52). Such a concern is the proposed alternative to the arguments and counter-arguments about materialism and idealism in social theory. My involvement in a work organisation, in that area of the organisation where various aspects of power and control become most visible, gave me the type of experience which I hope enables me to contribute to social theory in the way that I take Dawe to be advocating.

4 The paper from which this quotation is taken is one which rehearsed a number of ideas basic to this chapter and the theoretical infrastructure of the whole study. It illustrates my approach to theorising with an analysis of aspects of a process of organisational change in which divergent orientations and structurally based conflicts between groups manifested themselves in grievances and differences over various minor details of the change.

5 See Albrow (1970, ch. 3) on the misconstructions based on a misreading of Weber's work here.

6 Best known here are Hughes and Becker, see chapter 5 below.

7 Silverman (1970) is one of the few writers on organisational theory to stress the importance of the Chicago school.

8 On the idea of action research, see Clark (1972) and Brown (1967).

9 A particularly interesting discussion of the dangers of social scientists supporting the status quo is that of Argyris (1972, p. 82).

10 To make certain points I found myself bringing together findings and insights from Human Relations writers, sociological conflict theorists, the sociotechnical-systems thinkers and so on.

213

11 Douglas explains the reasoning behind this criticism and also offers an unusual and interesting alternative interpretation: that functionalism's stress on the interdependence of the parts of a social system indicates the futility of anything but *radical* if not violent, attempts to change the system (1970a, pp. 192–3). On this reading, structural functionalism is radical in import.

12 This point can well be illustrated by the concept of *community*. Nisbet (1970) sees this as a 'conservative' concept in its role within the sociological tradition. But the concept can equally well be used in a radical context as it is, for instance, in certain varieties of socialist thought.

13 An excellent illustration of what I am calling the practicalities of concept use is Fox's theorising in *Beyond Contract* (1974) which provides a highly coherent analysis which utilises concepts from the work of Blau and Jacques whilst incorporating little or nothing of the structure of sentiments underlying the work of either of these writers.

14 See, especially, Goldthorpe and Lockwood *et al.* (1968) and Silverman (1970).

15 I am thinking here of the human relations tradition. See Roethlisberger and Dickson (1939).

16 Wertheim (1974, p. 91). He points out that in 'Weber's view, all kinds of social institutions – including the family, the church, the state – do not exist except inasmuch as those concerned subjectively accept their uniting function' (*ibid.*, p. 91).

17 For a detailed discussion and sources on Weber's thinking here, see Bruun (1972).

18 In the first generation of any society it will be a matter of individuals choosing to ally with others. With the second generation, people will find themselves to an extent born or otherwise put into 'coalitions'.

19 See Stolzman on Runciman's point that 'the delineation of advantages in a given society can normally be accomplished by reference to its own collective standards' (Stolzman, 1975, p. 111).

20 I am making use here of Dahrendorf's phrase (1959).

21 A similar point is made by Prandy (1965).

22 In a sense, these correspond to some aspects of the role of 'opinion leaders' in American mass communications social psychology. See Lazarsfeld, Berelson and Gaudet (1944).

23 See Mills (1970, p. 50).

24 See, for instance, Cicourel (1964); Douglas (1971); Filmer *et al.* (1972); Hindess (1973).

25 See Scott and Lyman (1968).

26 See Mills (1967).

27 See reference given in note 24.

28 I am, however, concerned to communicate with more than just 'sociologists'. Throughout my research work I have attempted to follow some of the guidelines set down by Schutz: the 'principle of relevance' and the postulates of 'subjective interpretation' and 'adequacy' (Schutz, 1943, pp. 145–7). It was partly with these in mind that I sent to each of the people whom I interviewed (as well as to a considerable number of others) a paper which indicated the general

'findings' of my interview programme and some of my tentative interpretations. The conversations, letters and discussions which followed from this have been invaluable and give me confidence that my arguments are not over 'sociologistic' and that even though there are disagreements over interpretations, that at least the thoughts and actions of the actors in my study are in the 'life world' reasonable and understandable for the actor himself as well as for his fellow men' (Schutz, 1943, p. 147).

Chapter 2 Industrialisation, rationalisation and the emergence of the personnel occupation

1 See Bendix (1963, p. 64) and Winter (1974, pp. 1134–5) on the notion of *elective affinity*.
2 See Weber (1965). Particularly useful in clarifying the issues and dealing with some of the controversies over the 'Weber thesis' is Moore (1971).
3 To reify ideas in this way – to adopt something like the Durkheimian notion of a social current – would be to contradict the basically methodologically individualist stance taken here. Although my overall position is not a Popperian one, it is useful here to point to the way in which Popper indicates the compatibility of methodological individualism with a recognition of 'ideas in the objective sense' in his 'third world' – his third 'ontological category' (Popper, 1973). Another way of looking at the influence of an abstract is that of Berger and Luckmann who write of the creation of social institutions through the process of objectivation of human activity. They stress the 'sheer force of (institutions') facticity' (1971, p. 28).
4 Particularly Blumer (1960). For a wider discussion of the arguments about the 'effects' of the industrial revolution on the working classes, see Thompson (1968, ch. 6).
5 O'Neill goes on: 'Measured by the standard of its ability to produce such basic ingredients of humane society as a universal "minimum" standard of health, housing, education and public safety, the performance of monopoly capitalism is glaringly lop-sided' (1973, p. 25).
6 Perhaps the best-known critique of Weber's position here is that of Marcuse (1965). I believe Marcuse to be wrong in his analysis. For criticisms of Marcuse, see Stammer (ed.) (1971). Habermas is useful on balancing Marcuse, and both Mommsen (1974) and Beetham (1974) are helpful in clarifying Weber's position on capitalism. As Mommsen says, 'Weber was anything but a blind partisan of modern capitalism' (1974, p. xv).
7 Ellul's assault is on *technique*. He sees modern civilisation, as Merton puts it in his introduction to Ellul's *The Technological Society*, as 'committed to the quest for continually improved means to carelessly examined ends. Indeed, technique transforms ends into means . . . "know-how" takes on an ultimate value' (Ellul, 1964, p. vi).
8 Merton's contribution was one of the earliest of what became a series of works on the 'dysfunctions of bureaucracy', as Merton termed them. Ironically, these writers often considered themselves to be contributing

215

to a critique of Weber. A great deal of the error here is to be accounted for by the frequent confusing of 'formal rationality' with 'efficiency'. It is often supposed that Weber saw bureaucracy as 'efficient' whereas he, in fact, argued nothing of the kind. For an invaluable clarification of the issues here, see Albrow (1970, ch. 3).

9 Particularly useful here are Eilbirt (1959); Hagerdorn (1958) and Wood (1960).

10 One feels that he would have provided Weber with a very interesting case study of the 'protestant ethic' in operation. The significance of this point is that Boot was a very late entrepreneur of the religiously motivated type, in Weber's terms. He thought the religious ethic less important after the turn of the nineteenth century (see Weber, 1927, p. 369).

11 It is interesting to note, however, that Rowntree opens the introduction to his 1921 book by pointing out how the labour unrest which was 'one of the most serious problems confronting the country' in prewar years 'has now broken out again with redoubled force' (1921, p. v). His book was written in response to a situation where 'the whole basis of industry is challenged' (p. vii). The conditions which 'have not been adequately secured under the capitalistic system' (p. viii) would have to be provided by 'evolutionary changes' of three types: 'legislation, negotiation and the initiatives of employers' (p. viii).

12 Niven says: 'by the end of the war personnel management's essential place in the [sic] industry had been beyond the boundaries of individual factories as it had never been before; for the second time, it had gained the recognition of the Government; but even more important it was now accepted to a great extent by the unions' (Niven, 1967, p. 102). Niven cites a trade union resolution actually calling for the extension of the employment of welfare and personnel officers (p. 102). The importance of this change cannot, I suggest, be underestimated. The relationship between trade unions and personnel management will emerge as a relevant issue in the later chapters of this study.

13 The faster growth of personnel management in America may be partly explained by a lower reluctance on the part of the American propagandists to show a money value in welfare than was felt by British propagandists like Proud and Kelly. See McGivering on this (1970, pp. 181–2).

Chapter 3 Personnel management: conflicts and ambiguities

1 As Child says, the notion of a dominant coalition is useful but it is 'an abstraction and could be misleading if not used cautiously'. He stresses that the term does not 'necessarily identify the formally designated holders of authority in an organisation; rather it refers to those who collectively happen to hold most power over a particular period of time'. He also stresses that the notion does not imply that other groups do not have power to modify or constrain plans. Indeed, such power can be substantial (1972, p. 13). I would add to this that the idea does not imply complete autonomy: the dominant coalition in a commercial

organisation is constrained by markets among other things, and the coalition in a local government organisation operate within the constraints laid down by, among other things, their elected council.

2 The 'stereotype' figure portrayed here could do for personnel officers and managers what the character on the film 'I'm Alright Jack' did for shop stewards. I doubt whether this accolade is one welcomed within the 'profession'!

3 My analysis of responses given to each question in my interview has involved looking for patterns in terms of the following criteria: level, sex, qualification, I.P.M. membership, social class of origin, age, subspecialism, type of employment. Other criteria are applied when relevant to specific issues, e.g. those having taken exams in personnel management, those with social science degrees, and so on.

Wherever I find a pattern in the responses this is reported as below, where I point out that those personnel managers who lean more towards an interventionist conception of their work tend to come from those with a large industrial relations component in their work.

The main problem in looking for patterns is that one is using qualitative data – 'accounts' which cannot often be forced into categories which can then be analysed in terms of specific variables. Whenever I have done this, it is only for the indicative value. It is done more easily with more specific or 'harder' data, as will be apparent in the next chapter where certain 'demographic' features are considered.

4 The argument here is supported by my own observations, but is also justifiable in terms of the sociological literature in such administrative areas. See, for example, the section on the 'new middle class' in Dahrendorf (1959).

5 Richard Stokes is described in a profile of him in *Personnel Management* (September, 1972, pp. 18–19) as 'reputed to be something of a maverick in the personnel field'. He is quoted as saying, 'We must soon begin to see the time when companies question their social responsibilities and people in personnel ought to be taking a lead in this direction.' He has stood as a parliamentary Labour candidate.

6 See Parker (1969). It is interesting that Peter Parker, who at the time of writing is the Chairman of British Rail has, like Stokes, been a parliamentary candidate for the Labour party. A profile of him appeared in *Personnel Management* in December, 1972.

7 At a seminar which I held to discuss the preliminary findings of my interview programme, involving both sociologists and personnel managers, and at which I put this point, the personnel men emphatically supported this view. A sociologist, however, suggested that I was naïve here and that my respondents did not stress conflict with unions because this was so obvious to them that they did not need to mention it. This, I suggest, is to misunderstand the problem. My 'participant' experience strongly indicates a situation where, in practical day-to-day matters, managers present many more problems than do unions – in terms of *getting one's job done*.

8 An interesting discussion on these lines is that of Legge and Exley (1974).

217

Chapter 4 Occupational entry

1 Cf. Dahrendorf (1959). Weber's analysis of bureaucracy was, of course, in this context: he looked at bureaucracy in the setting of his political sociology and his analysis of different types of *domination*.

2 See Behrend (1957) on the *effort bargain*, one part of the implicit contract. The term *implicit contract* is used by Mumford (1972) but in a sense somewhat different from that suggested here.

3 In using the idea of *contract*, I am taking it outside the ideological use suggested by Fox's characterisation of the concept as a master symbol of capitalism, accepting, with Fox, that it is a good deal less than contract (1974, p. 173). This is because the inequalities of power between employer and employee negate the possible acceptance of the contract as based on a totally voluntary exchange of 'freely bargained promises' (*ibid.*, p. 173). I retain the concept of contract by building into it assumptions of potential inequalities, inequalities which result in what Macpherson calls a 'net transfer of some of the powers of one man to another' (1962). This is done by adding to the idea of the effort bargain as developed by Behrend (1957) and Baldamus (1961) the recognition that this must be combined with a surrender of autonomy on the part of the individual in any employment situation.

Although I have accepted that the implicit contract is less than contract, I would claim that, paradoxically, it is at the same time more than contract. This is in so far as it is part of what Hyman and Brough call the 'negotiated order of workplace relationships' which relates back to Durkheim's notion of the non-contractual elements of contract (1975, p. 67) and the existence of an 'area of common normative understandings and assumptions' (*ibid.*, p. 25).

4 This analysis corresponds with Baldamus's notion of wage parity but does, I suggest, go further in that it can be used to analyse a wider spectrum of organisational positions and a wider range of situations than does Baldamus's scheme (1961). A worker may well accept an increasing degree of wage disparity for instance in order to retain his job in a deteriorating labour market (security) and a graduate management trainee might well sacrifice immediate earnings for the perceived opportunity to gain promotion at a later date (career).

5 On the two types of effort see Baldamus (1951).

6 This is particularly the case with the unionised employees where the shop steward or union representative may articulate such interests. Examples of this and an equivalent process within a management group are given in Watson (1976a). As that paper indicates, I have found the implicit contract model of great utility in analysing industrial relations situations.

7 This case illustrates the arbitrariness of putting cases into categories. This woman had initially chosen to be a teacher, one might argue. But, on the other hand, she had never been employed as a teacher and personnel work is her first job. The point is, however, she could well have been put into category IIIa.

Chapter 5 Orientations, values and adjustments

1 In suggesting a state of *balance* in one's definition of the situation in terms of an *implicit contract* I do not wish to imply too much stability or a notion of necessary 'contentment'. One may be highly dissatisfied with some aspect of one's job whilst maintaining *balance* through the compensation of an expected future improvement.

2 I am agreeing with this in so far as Freidson is commenting on the work done in what is normally seen as the sociology of occupations. In the sociology of *industry* it was the overemphasis on work-settings to which Goldthorpe, Lockwood *et al.* (1968) were reacting, ironically, – and perhaps over-reacting.

Freidson goes on to say about the failure to look at work settings that it 'is particularly the case for the professions':

> On the whole, students of the professions . . . have adopted the same individualistic value position of the men they study. They have been inclined to postulate and search for personal qualities that are distinctly 'professional'. . . . Deficient behaviour on the part of a professional tends to be explained as the result of being a deficient kind of person, or at least of having been inadequately or improperly 'socialized'. . . . (Freidson, 1970, p. 88).

3 Since commencing this research project I have had constantly to reiterate to both managers and some academics that I am not studying the '*attitudes* of personnel managers'!

4 For example, when people gave what might at first appear to be a 'neutral' account such as 'welfare work', we have to *situate* this description in the context of the wider concerns of the typical personnel specialist. Doing this reminds us that for the typical personnel specialist the 'welfare image' is a problem, something of the past that has to be killed. Something similar is the case with the description 'a hiring and firing department'. This is not the image that even recruitment specialists favour!

5 And indeed the organisation. Two of these more 'reserved' respondents were employed in the same large company, for example. Some of their reserve might have been related to their personalities I felt, but some was clearly related to certain political moves going on in that organisation. It appeared that there was a competitive situation in existence and interviewees were very interested to find out which of their colleagues I was interviewing.

6 Just how unrewarding a lot of managerial work is is indicated by Campanis (1970) and Fletcher (1973).

7 Ritzer cites Solomon's arguments about occupational sociology being subsumed under the heading of role theory (1972, p. 116). Solomon's article appears in a book of essays presented to E. C. Hughes by others of the Chicago School (Solomon, 1968). Hughes, whose work is not weighed down with the trappings of role theory, is nevertheless seen as a role theorist by Solomon.

8 For example, in the organisation in which I was employed, a straight LIFO policy would have denuded the computer departments and left

the drawing offices virtually untouched. The level of occupational specialism was such that retraining and redeployment possibilities were restricted – which they might not be in a less technologically advanced industry.

9 This is a written account commenting on my earlier working paper which saw 'compromise' as important in the responses.

Chapter 6   Professionalism: symbol and strategy

1 The issue of whether an occupational group will be interested in professional-type action or trade union-type action is dealt with by Prandy (1965).

2 Timperley and Osbaldeston stress the idea of a professionalisation process. For a critique of their work see Watson (1976b).

3 Nichols (1969) found that among his sample of businessmen in a Northern City it was the personnel specialists who were more interested in professionalism within management. Nichols comments: 'if one must talk about professionalism at all, those in personnel probably approximate most closely to the notion of "the professional manager" ' (p. 168).

Chapter 7   Ideas, knowledge and ideology

1 The I.P.M.'s annual report for 1975 states: 'It is the aim of the publishing department to enhance the I.P.M.'s reputation as a professional body and as a force in management publishing, to provide a useful specialist service to members, to attract an outside readership and to increase sales turnover' (p. 15). Niven stresses the importance of publications to the I.P.M.'s policies (1967, p. 157).

2 The I.P.M.'s Vice-President (Examinations) suggested at a branch meeting which I attended in 1975 that the new regulations were tending to attract a higher standard of recruit to the student member grade.

3 Child quotes the preamble to the I.P.M.'s 1963 'Golden Jubilee Statement':

> in personnel management different methods may be right in different circumstances. What is appropriate will differ according to current social values and custom, the size and traditions of an undertaking, its product or service, and its state of technical development (quoted in Child, 1969a).

This not only conflicts with human relations assumptions but questions the 'one best way' notion implicit in scientific management and the 'classical' school of thinking on principles of organisation (on these see Mouzelis, 1967).

4 It is interesting to note that an article on job design appearing in *Personnel Management* (Edwards, 1974) and seeming to derive from social science thinking in this area makes no reference to social science sources and is described as written from the point of view of 'the production engineer'.

5 For some clarification here see Sills (1973).
6 It may seem paradoxical to talk of over-simplification in reference to such jargon-ridden material but, such is the prevalence of jargon in these packages which consultants offer, that I take its use to be part of a marketing strategy.
7 For an indication of the attitude towards 'packaged' material of one social scientist, see the profile on Bowey (Lawrence, 1976).
8 I stopped asking such questions because I feared that the embarrassment caused might prejudice the interview relationship and lead to a reluctance of respondents to make themselves vulnerable in answering the remaining questions.
9 The exception was Fox. The manager here was in the process of reading *Beyond Contract*. I understand, from another source, that the group of which this man's company was a part had given an award for this book.
10 Cf. Nichols' comment on how his interviewees perceived him:

> because [the interviewer] was a social scientist he seemed to be regarded as some sort of a mongrel efficiency engineer-cum-moral crusader. In the minds of those interviewed a sociologist would appear to be depicted either as a man preoccupied with increasing productivity and/or being more than usually nice to nasty people (Nichols, 1969, p. 250).

Chapter 8 Organisational power and influence

1 This covers the fact that non-action has important power implications. See Bachrach and Baratz (1962) and Lukes (1974).
2 It may seem strange to describe autonomy as a resource. But to indicate my reasoning I will explain how I go as far as saying that even power itself is a 'resource'. This may look like a tautology since power is defined in terms of access to resources. Resources are means by which human wants can be satisfied. Since power is a means to such means, it too is a resource. And power and autonomy are closely related: autonomy is one's freedom from the power of another.
3 Cf. Crozier's (1964, p. 166) criticisms of Dalton.
4 Any sexually discriminatory connotations in my use of this phrase derive from the context in which it is generally used rather than from any attitude of my own.
5 The inconsistency between this individual's accounts are perhaps not quite as great as it might seem. In the earlier account he was referring to 'this company' and in the second he was referring to the part of that company for which he held personnel responsibilities. In one account he was talking about personnel as a generality in the organisation and in the other he was talking about himself. My point is still made, however.
6 I do not wish to enter the terminological debate over the relationship between power and influence. For present purposes we can follow the usage which is implicit in the interview material. Influence is seen simply as a less overt form of power.

221

7 See also on the problems here, Gross (1964).

8 See Easton (1965).

9 For what is practically a salesman's checklist or manifesto see Honey (1976).

10 See the letters pages of *Personnel Management* for November, December, 1975, and January, 1976, for correspondence on sexual discrimination and job advertising.

Chapter 9 Social integration, personnel management and social change

1 See especially Bell (1974).

2 On the problems of investigating these issues and for data, see Urry and Wakeford (1973); Stanworth and Giddens (1974); Noble (1975); Bottomore (1964) and Westergaard and Resler (1975).

3 See, for instance the *Sunday Times*, 16 May 1976, 'Apartheid, the Workers Britain Betrayed', p. 9.

4 See Habermas on the relationship between systems of purposive-rational action and incompetent behaviour (1971, pp. 92–3).

5 Personnel managers are seen as more 'professional' in that they show a greater tendency to hold professional memberships, to be more knowledgeable about management literature and to participate in the affairs of management bodies (1969, p. 198).

6 See, for example, Sills (1975, especially pp. 5–6).

7 Cf. *ibid.*, pp. 139–41.

8 The innovations in work organisation which have occurred in the Swedish car industry have good *practical* reasons behind their introduction. On the *pragmatism* of Swedish management in this area, see Wedderburn (1974, p. 34).

9 Such an analysis is implicit in an article written by the executives of I.B.M. (UK) appearing in *Personnel Management:* 'Social Responsibility: the Investment that Pays Off'.

> To say that business must be involved in public and social affairs does not mean that it ceases to carry out the legitimate tasks it has always done. It simply means that in the light of new variables affecting its activities, it must review its investment mix so that a portion of its resources can be invested in building and maintaining the national fabric on which it, and all other sections of society must depend. Investment in this way can be equated with money spent in research and management development: money spent today to protect the future (Peach and Hargreaves, 1976, p. 21).

And if we see members of management explicitly recognising the need for business to protect its interests through a contribution to social integration, in sociological terms we can see, in Kerr *et al.*'s recent postscript to their *Industrialism and Industrial Man*, famous academic apologists for industrialism talking in terms of *contradictions*:

> Thus technological society might carry the 'seeds of its own destruction' – not in class versus class, but in the discipline that

the technology requires versus the spontaneity of the labour
force that it helps to create. Some of the requirements of the
new society run into conflict with the new man it spawns (1973,
pp. 303–4).

The authors believe, however, that 'pluralistic industrialism will adjust
to this new theme and not be destroyed by it' (*ibid.*, p. 304).

10 Thomas G. Spates (Vice President of General Foods) is reported as
saying in the 1940s that the means of winning the 'hot and cold running
war against totalitarian communism' is to apply 'the American code
of personnel administration' which treats people 'so that they will
achieve and give the best that is in them, while getting the highest
possible degree of individual satisfaction' and 'eliminating the disillusionment and frustrations, the emotional and mental illnesses from
which are formed the subversive attitudes that influence the destinies
of nations' (*New York Times*, 29 June 1948, quoted in Sutton *et al.*,
1956 p. 132).

11 Niven reports that the Duke of Kent was guest of honour at the
Institute's 21st birthday celebrations in 1934. Lord Trent (Jesse Boot)
was the chairman (1967, p. 86).

12 Interestingly, two of the personnel practitioners whom I interviewed
and whom I have characterised as having 'left' views were brought up
in the very area of Durham which Moore studied.

223

Bibliography

ALBROW, M. (1968), 'The study of organisations', in Gould, J. (1968).

ALBROW, M. (1970), *Bureaucracy*, London: Macmillan.

ANTHONY, P. and CRICHTON, A. (1969), *Industrial Relations and the Personnel Specialists*, London: Batsford.

ARGYRIS, C. (1972), *The Applicability of Organisational Sociology*, Cambridge University Press.

ARMSTRONG, Sir W. (1971), *Personnel Management in the Civil Service*, London: H.M.S.O.

ATTEWELL, P. (1974), 'Ethnomethodology since Garfinkel', *Theory and Society*, vol. 1, pp. 139–210.

BACHRACH, P. and BARATZ, M. S. (1962), 'Two faces of power', *American Political Science Review*, vol. 56, pp. 947–52.

BALBUS, I. D. (1975), 'The concept of interest in pluralist and Marxist analysis', *Politics and Society*, vol. 1, pp. 151–77.

BALDAMUS, W. (1951), 'Types of work and motivation', *British Journal of Sociology*, vol. 2, pp. 44–58.

BALDAMUS, W. (1961), *Efficiency and Effort*, London: Tavistock.

BANKS, J. A. (1970), *Marxist Sociology in Action*, London: Faber.

BARITZ, L. (1965), *The Servants of Power*, New York: Wiley.

BARNARD, C. I. (1938), *The Functions of the Executive*, Cambridge, Mass.: Harvard University Press.

BECHHOFER, F. (1974), 'Current approaches to empirical research', in Rex, J. (ed.) (1974).

BECKER, H. S. (1971), *Sociological Work: Method and Substance*, London: Allen Lane.

BECKER, H. S., GEER, B., HUGHES, E. C. and STRAUSS, A. L. (1961), *Boys in White*, University of Chicago Press.

BECKER, H. S., GEER, B., REISMAN, D. and WEISS, R. (eds) (1968), *Institutions and the Person*, Chicago: Aldine.

BEDROSIAN, H. (1973), 'Personnel administration' in *The Encyclopedia of Management*, 2nd edition, ed. Heyel, C., New York: Van Nostrand Reinhold.

224

BEETHAM, D. (1974), *Max Weber and the Theory of Modern Politics*, London: Allen & Unwin.

BEHREND, H. (1957), 'The effort bargain', *Industrial and Labor Relations Review*, vol. 10, pp. 503–15.

BELL, D. (1974), *The Coming of Post Industrial Society*, London: Heinemann.

BENDIX, R. (1961), 'The lower classes and the "democratic revolution" ', *Industrial Relations*, October 1961, pp. 91–116.

BENDIX, R. (1963), *Work and Authority in Industry*, New York: Harper.

BENDIX, R. (1965), 'Max Weber's sociology today', *International Social Science Journal*, vol. 17, pp. 9–22.

BENDIX, R. (1966), *Max Weber: An Intellectual Portrait*, London: Methuen.

BERGER, P. L. and LUCKMANN, T. (1971), *The Social Construction of Reality*, Harmondsworth: Penguin.

BEYNON, H. and BLACKBURN, R. M. (1972), *Perceptions of Work*, Cambridge University Press.

BLACKBURN, R. (1972), 'The new capitalism', in Blackburn, R. (ed.) (1972).

BLACKBURN, R. (ed.) (1972), *Ideology and Social Science*, London: Fontana.

BLUM, A. F. (1971), 'Theorizing', in Douglas, J. D. (ed.) (1971).

BLUMER, H. (1960), 'Early industrialisation and the laboring class', *Sociological Quarterly*, vol. 1, pp. 5–14.

BOTTOMORE, T. B. (1964), *Elites and Society*, London, C. A. Watts.

BOTTOMORE, T. B. (1975), *Sociology as Social Criticism*, London: Allen & Unwin.

BRAMHAM, J. (1975), *Practical Manpower Planning*, London: I.P.M.

BRAVERMAN, H. (1974), *Labor and Monopoly Capital*, New York: Monthly Review Press.

BRIGGS, A. (1961), *A Study of the Work of Seebohm Rowntree*, London: Longmans.

BROWN, R. K. (1967), 'Research and consultancy in industrial enterprises', *Sociology*, vol. 1, pp. 33–60.

BROWN, R. K. (1973), 'Sources of objectives in work and employment', in Child, J. (ed.) (1973).

BRUUN, H. H. (1972), *Science, Values and Politics in Max Weber's Methodology*, Munksgaard, Copenhagen.

BURNS, T. (1955), 'The reference of conduct in small groups', *Human Relations*, vol. 8, pp. 467–86.

BURNS, T. (1961), 'Micropolitics: mechanisms of social change', *Administrative Science Quarterly*, vol. 6, pp. 257–81.

BURNS, T. (1962), 'The sociology of industry', in Welford *et al.* (eds) (1962).

BURNS, T. (1969), 'On the plurality of social systems', in Burns, T. (ed.) (1969).

BURNS, T. (ed.) (1969), *Industrial Man*, Harmondsworth: Penguin.

BURNS, T. and STALKER, G. M. (1961), *The Management of Innovation*, London: Tavistock.

BUTTERISS, M. (1971), *Job Enrichment and Employee Participation in Industry*, London: I.P.M.

CADBURY, E. (1912), *Experiments in Industrial Organisation*, London: Longmans.

CAMPANIS, P. (1970), 'Normlessness in management', in Douglas, J. D. (ed.) (1970b).

CANNON, J. A. (1974), 'Human asset accounting', *Personnel Review*, vol. 3, pp. 14–20.

CHAPMAN, D. (1970), 'Seebohm Rowntree and factory welfare', in Tillett *et al.* (eds) (1970).

CHAPMAN, S. D. (1974), *Jesse Boot of Boots the Chemist*, London: Hodder & Stoughton.

– CHERNS, A. B. (1972), 'Personnel management and the social sciences', *Personnel Review*, vol. 1, pp. 4–11.

CHILD, J. (1964), 'Quaker employers and industrial relations', *Sociological Review*, vol. 12, pp. 293–315.

X CHILD, J. (1968), 'British management thought as a case study within the sociology of knowledge', *Sociological Review*, vol. 16, pp. 217–39.

CHILD, J. (1969a), *British Management Thought*, London: Allen & Unwin.

CHILD, J. (1969b), *The Business Enterprise in Modern Industrial Society*, London: Collier–Macmillan.

CHILD, J. (1972), 'Organisational structure, environment and performance: the role of strategic choice', *Sociology*, vol. 6, pp. 1–22.

CHILD, J. (ed.) (1973), *Man and Organisation*, London: Allen & Unwin.

CICOUREL, A. V. (1964), *Method and Measurement in Sociology*, New York: Free Press.

CLARK, P. A. (1972), *Action Research and Organisational Change*, London: Harper & Row.

CLEGG, S. R. (1975), *Power, Rule and Domination*, London: Routledge & Kegan Paul.

COMMISSION ON INDUSTRIAL RELATIONS (1973), Report No. 34: *The Role of Management in Industrial Relations*, London: H.M.S.O.

X COULSON, M. A. (1972), 'Role – a redundant concept in sociology', in Jackson, J. A. (ed.) (1972).

COULSON, M. A., KEIL, E. T., RIDDELL, C. and STRUTHERS, J. S. (1967), 'Towards a sociological theory of occupational choice: a critique', *Sociological Review*, vol. 15, pp. 301–9.

COULSON, M. A. and RIDDELL, D. S. (1970), *Approaching Sociology*, London: Routledge & Kegan Paul.

COURT, W. H. B. (1967), review of S. Pollard, *The Genesis of Modern Management*, in *History*, vol. 52.

COUSINS, J. M. and DAVIS, R. L. (1974), 'Working class incorporation – a historical approach,' in Parkin, F. (ed.) (1974).

– CRICHTON, A. (1963), 'A persistent stereotype? the personnel manager: the outsider', *Personnel Management*, December, pp. 160–7.

– CRICHTON, A. (1968), *Personnel Management in Context*, London: Batsford.

CROZIER, M. (1964), *The Bureaucratic Phenomenon*, London: Tavistock.

DAHRENDORF, R. (1959), *Class and Class Conflict in Industrial Society*, London: Routledge & Kegan Paul.

DAHRENDORF, R. (1968), *Essays in the Theory of Society*, London: Routledge & Kegan Paul.

DALTON, M. (1950), 'Conflicts between line and staff managerial officers', *American Journal of Sociology*, vol. 15, pp. 342–51.

DALTON, M. (1951), 'Informal factors in career achievement', *American Journal of Sociology*, vol. 56, pp. 407–15.

DALTON, M. (1959), *Men Who Manage*, New York: Wiley.

DANIEL, W. W. (1973), 'Understanding employee behaviour in its context', in Child, J. (ed.) (1973).

DANIELS, A. K. (1975), 'Professionalism in formal organisations', in McKinlay, J. B. (ed.) (1975).

DAVIS, K. and MOORE, W. E. (1945), 'Some principles of stratification', *American Sociological Review*, vol. 10, pp. 242–9.

DAVIS, L. E. and TAYLOR, J. C. (eds) (1972), *Design of Jobs*, Harmondsworth: Penguin.

DAWE, A. (1973), 'The role of experience in the construction of social theory: an essay in reflexive sociology', *Sociological Review*, vol. 21, pp. 25–55.

DEPARTMENT OF EMPLOYMENT (1971), *Manpower Papers No. 5: The Reform of Collective Bargaining at Plant and Company Level*, London: H.M.S.O.

DONOVAN, LORD (1968), *Report of Royal Commission on Trade Unions and Employers' Associations*, London: H.M.S.O.

DOUGLAS, J. D. (1970a), *The Relevance of Sociology*, New York: Appleton-Century-Crofts.

DOUGLAS, J. D. (ed.) (1970b), *Deviance and Respectability*, New York: Basic Books.

DOUGLAS, J. D. (ed.) (1971), *Understanding Everyday Life*, London: Routledge & Kegan Paul.

DREITZEL, H. P. (ed.) (1970), *Recent Sociology* No. 2, London: Collier-Macmillan.

DRONBERGER, I. (1971), *The Political Thought of Max Weber*, New York: Appleton-Century-Crofts.

DRUCKER, P. (1954), *The Practice of Management*, New York: Harper & Row.

DRYBURGH, G. D. M. (1972), 'The man in the middle', *Personnel Management*, May 1972.

DUNKERLEY, D. (1975), *Occupations and Society*, London: Routledge & Kegan Paul.

DURKHEIM, E. (1933), *The Division of Labour in Society*, Chicago: Free Press.

EASTON, D. A. (1965), *A Systems Analysis of Political Life*, New York: Wiley.

EDWARDS, G. A. B. (1974), 'Group technology', *Personnel Management*, May, pp. 35–9.

EILBIRT, H. (1959), 'The development of personnel management in the US', *Business History Review*, vol. 33, pp. 345–64.

EKEH, P. P. (1974), *Social Exchange Theory: the Two Traditions*, London: Heinemann.

ELDRIDGE, J. E. T. (1968), 'Redundancy conflict in an isolated steel community', in Eldridge (1968).

227

ELDRIDGE, J. E. T. (1968), *Industrial Disputes*, London: Routledge & Kegan Paul.

 ELGER, A. J. (1975), 'Industrial organisations: a processual approach', in McKinlay, J. B. (ed.) (1975).

ELLIOT, P. (1972), *The Sociology of the Professions*, London: Macmillan.

ELLUL, J. (1964), *The Technological Society*, New York: Vintage Books.

FAY, B. (1975), *Social Theory and Political Practice*, London: Allen & Unwin.

FILMER, P., PHILLIPSON, M. SILVERMAN, D. and WALSH, D. (1972), *New Directions in Sociological Theory*, London: Collier-Macmillan.

FLETCHER, C. (1973), 'The end of management', in Child, J. (ed.) (1973).

FOGARTY, M. P. (1963), 'An independent comment', *Personnel Management*, March.

FORBES, R. P. (1975), 'The problem of laissez faire bias in Weber's concept of "formal rationality" ', *Sociological Analysis and Theory*, vol. 5, pp. 219-36.

FORD, J. and BOX, S. (1967), 'Sociological theory and occupational choice', *Sociological Review*, vol. 15, pp. 287-99.

FOWLER, A. (1976), *Personnel Management in Local Government*, London: I.P.M.

FOX, A. (1966a), 'From welfare to organisation', *New Society*, vol. 17, pp. 14-16.

FOX, A. (1966b), *Industrial Sociology and Industrial Relations*, Research Paper No. 3, Royal Commission on Trade Unions and Employers' Associations, London: H.M.S.O.

FOX, A. (1971), *A Sociology of Work in Industry*, London: Collier-Macmillan.

FOX, A. (1972), 'Coming to terms with conflict', *Personnel Management*, June, pp. 20-3.

FOX, A. (1973), 'Industrial relations: a critique of pluralist ideology', in Child, J. (ed.) (1973).

FOX, A. (1974), *Beyond Contract: Work, Power and Trust Relations*, London: Faber.

FREEDMAN, M. (1969), *The Process of Work Establishment*, New York: Columbia University Press.

FREIDSON, E. (1970), *Profession of Medicine*, New York: Dodd Mead.

FREIDSON, E. (1973), 'Professions and the occupational principle', in Freidson, E. (ed.) (1973).

FREIDSON, E. (ed.) (1973), *The Professions and their Prospects*, London: Sage.

FRENCH, W. (1970), *The Personnel Process*, 2nd ed, Boston: Houghton Mifflin.

FRENCH, W. and HENNING, D. (1966), 'The authority-influence role of the functional specialist in management', *Academy of Management Journal*, vol. 9, pp. 187-203.

FREUND, J. (1972), *The Sociology of Max Weber*, Harmondsworth: Penguin.

FRIEDMANN, G. (1961), *The anatomy of work: the implications of specialisation*, London: Heinemann.

FRYER, R. H. (1973), 'Redundancy and public policy', printed as Appendix II to Martin, R. and Fryer, R. H. (1973).

GIDDENS, A. (1971), *Capitalism and Modern Social Theory*, Cambridge University Press.

GIDDENS, A. (1973), *The Class Structure of the Advanced Societies*, London: Hutchinson.

GILES, W. J. and ROBINSON, D. F. (1972), *Human Asset Accounting*, London: I.P.M./I.C.M.A.

GILL, H. S. (1975), 'Handling redundancy and how to maintain morale', *Personnel Management*, May.

GINZBERG, E. J., GINZBERG, J. W., AXELRAD, S. and HERMA, J. L. (1951), *Occupational Choice*, New York: Columbia University Press.

GLASER, B. G. (1968), *Organisational Careers*, Chicago: Aldine.

GLASER, B. G. and STRAUSS, A. L. (1964), 'Awareness contexts and social interaction', *American Sociological Review*, vol. 29, pp. 669–79.

GLASER, B. G. and STRAUSS, A. L. (1967), *The Discovery of Grounded Theory*, Chicago: Aldine.

GOFFMAN, E. (1968), *Asylums*, Harmondsworth: Penguin.

GOLDNER, F. H. (1970), 'The division of labor: process and power', in Zald, M. N. (ed.) (1970).

GOLDNER, F. H. and RITTI, R. R. (1970), 'Professionalisation as career immobility', *American Journal of Sociology*, vol. 72, pp. 491–4, 1967; reprinted in Grusky and Miller (eds) (1970).

GOLDTHORPE, J. H. (1969), 'Social inequality and social integration in modern Britain', *Advancement of Science*, December, pp. 190–202.

GOLDTHORPE, J. H., LOCKWOOD, D., BECHHOFER, F. and PLATT, J. (1968), *The Affluent Worker: Industrial Attitudes and Behaviour*, Cambridge University Press.

GOLDTHORPE, J. H. et al. (1969), *The Affluent Worker in the Class Structure*, Cambridge University Press.

GOUGH, J. W. (1969), *The Rise of the Entrepreneur*, London: Batsford.

GOULD, J. (ed.) (1968), *Penguin Social Sciences Survey*, Harmondsworth: Penguin.

GOULDNER, A. W. (1964), *Patterns of Industrial Bureaucracy*, New York: Free Press.

GOULDNER, A. W. (1971), *The Coming Crisis of Western Sociology*, London: Heinemann.

GOULDNER, A. W. (1975), *For Sociology*, Harmondsworth: Penguin.

GROSS, E. (1959), 'The occupational variable as a research category', *American Sociological Review*, vol. 24, pp. 640–9.

GROSS, E. (1964), 'Sources of lateral authority in personnel departments', *Industrial Relations*, vol. 3, pp. 121–33.

GROSS, N., MASON, W. and MCEACHERN, A. (1958), *Explorations in Role Analysis*, New York: Wiley.

GRUSKY, O. and MILLER, G. A. (eds) (1970), *The Sociology of Organisations*, New York: Free Press.

HABERMAS, J. (1971), *Towards a Rational Society*, London: Heinemann.

— HAGERDORN, H. J. (1958), 'A note on the motivation of personnel management: industrial welfare 1885–1910', *Exploration in Entrepreneurial History*, vol. 10, pp. 134–9.

HALL, R. H. (1969), *Occupations and the Social Structure*, Englewood Cliffs: Prentice Hall.

HALL, R. H. and ENGEL, G. V. (1974), 'Autonomy and expertise: threats and barriers to occupational autonomy', in Stewart and Cantor (eds) (1974).

HALMOS, P. (1970), *The Personal Service Society*, London: Constable.

HALMOS, P. (ed.) (1973), *Professionalisation and Social Change:* Introduction, Sociological Review Monograph, No. 20, Keele University.

HAMMOND, J. L. and B. (1966a), *The Town Labourer, 1760–1832*, London: Methuen.

HAMMOND, J. L. and B. (1966b), *The Rise of Modern Industry*, London: Methuen.

HAYSTEAD, J. (1974), 'Social structure, awareness contexts and processes of choice', in Williams, W. M. (ed.) (1974).

— HENNING, D. and FRENCH, W. (1961), 'The mythical personnel manager', *California Management Review*, vol. 3, pp. 33–46.

— HENSTRIDGE, J. (1975), 'Personnel management – a framework for analysis', *Personnel Review*, vol. 4.

HICKSON, D. J., HININGS, C. R., LEE, C. A., SCHNECK, R. E. and PENNINGS, J. M. (1971), 'A strategic contingencies theory of intraorganisational power', *Administrative Science Quarterly*, vol. 16, pp. 216–29.

HINDESS, B. (1973), *The Use of Official Statistics*, London: Macmillan.

H.M.S.O. (1968), *The Civil Service*: Report of the Committee chaired by Lord Fulton.

H.M.S.O. (1972), *Report of a Study Group on Local Authority Management Structures* chaired by M. A. Bains.

⋊ HOBSBAWM, E. J. (1968), *Industry and Empire*, Harmondsworth: Penguin.

HONEY, P. (1976), 'On the trail of the personnel professional', *Personnel Management*, April.

HUGHES, E. C. (1970), 'The humble and the proud', *Sociological Quarterly*, Spring, p. 148.

HUNT, A. (1975), *Management Attitudes and Practices towards Women at Work*, London: H.M.S.O.

HYMAN, R. and BROUGH, I. (1975), *Social Values and Industrial Relations*, Oxford: Blackwell.

I.P.M. (1955), *Techniques or Men?*, London: I.P.M.

— I.P.M. (1963), 'Statement on personnel management and personnel policies', *Personnel Management*, March 1963.

I.P.M. (1967), 'The Edinburgh group', *Perspectives in Manpower Planning*, London: I.P.M.

I.P.M. (1973), 'News and notes', *Personnel Management*, February, p. 7.

I.P.M. (1974a), *A career in personnel management: what it is and how to train for it*, London: I.P.M.

I.P.M. (1974b), 'Harrogate 1974', *I.P.M. Digest*, December.

I.P.M. (1974c), 'All change warns I.P.M. survey', *I.P.M. Digest*, 1974.

I.P.M. (1975a), 'Report on membership survey', *I.P.M. Digest*, January.

I.P.M. (1975b), 'Profits must justify personnel decisions', *I.P.M. Digest*, January.

I.P.M. (1975c), 'Personnel Men on the up and up', *Personnel Management*, December.

I.P.M. (1975d), 'Hard work behind your membership grades', *I.P.M. Digest*, February.

I.P.M. (1976a), 'Personnel – a public service phoenix', *I.P.M. Digest*, February.

I.P.M. (1976b), *Sit-ins and work-ins*, Employee Relations Committee Report.

I.P.M. (1976c), 'No hope for unanimity on participation', *Personnel Management*, November.

ISRAEL, H. (1966), 'Some religious factors in the emergence of industrial society in England', *American Sociological Review*, vol. 31, pp. 589–99.

JACKSON, J. A. (ed.) (1970), *Professions and Professionalisation*, Cambridge University Press.

JACKSON, J. A. (ed.) (1972), *Role*, Cambridge University Press.

JENKINS, C. (1973), 'Is personnel still underpowered?', *Personnel Management*, June, pp. 34–5.

JOHNSON, T. J. (1972), *Professions and Power*, London: Macmillan.

KAHN, R. L. *et al.* (1964), *Organisational Stress: Studies in Role Conflict and Ambiguity*, New York: Wiley.

KATZ, F. E. (1968), *Autonomy and Organisation: the limits of social control*, New York: Random House.

KATZ, F. E. and MARTIN, H. W. (1962), 'Career choice processes', *Social Forces*, vol. 41, pp. 149–54.

KELLY, E. T. (ed.) (1925), *Welfare Work in Industry*, London: Pitman.

KENNEY, J. P. J. and DONNELLY, E. L. (1972), *Manpower Training and Development*, London: I.P.M./Harrap.

KENNY, T. P. (1975), 'Stating the case for welfare', *Personnel Management*, September, pp. 19–21.

KERR, C., DUNLOP, J. T., HARBISON, F., MYERS, C. A. (1973), *Industrialism and Industrial Man*, Harmondsworth: Penguin.

KRAUSE, E. A. (1971), *The Sociology of Occupations*, Boston: Little, Brown.

LANDSBERGER, H. A. (1961), 'The horizontal dimension in bureaucracy', *Administrative Science Quarterly*, vol. 6, pp. 299–332.

LAWRENCE, S. (1971), 'Back seat for personnel managers?', *Personnel Management*, December, p. 3.

LAWRENCE, S. (1976), 'Woman of the moment: Angela Bowey', *Personnel Management*, March.

LAZARSFELD, P. F., BERELSON, B. and GAUDET, H. (1944), *The People's Choice*, New York: Duell, Sloan & Pearce.

LEE, J. (1924), *The Principles of Industrial Welfare*, London: Pitman.

LEGGE, K. and EXLEY, M. (1974), 'Authority, ambiguity and adaptation: the personnel specialists dilemma', *Industrial Relations*, Autumn.

LOCKWOOD, D. (1958), *The Blackcoated Worker*, London: Allen & Unwin.

LOEWITH, K. (1970), 'Weber's interpretation of the bourgeois-capitalistic world in terms of the guiding principles of "rationalisation"', in Wrong, D. (ed.) (1970).

LUKES, S. (1970), 'Some problems about rationality', in Wilson, B. (ed.) (1970).

LUKES, S. (1974), *Power: A Radical View*, London: Macmillan.

LUPTON, T. (1964), *Industrial Behaviour and Personnel Management*, London: I.P.M.

LUPTON, T. and GOWLER, D. (1969), *Selecting a Wage Payment System*, London: Kogan Page.

LYONS, T. P. (1972), 'Presidential Philosophy', *Personnel Management*, October.

LYONS, T. P. (1973), 'Comment', *Personnel Management*, October.

MANN, M. (1973), *Consciousness and Action among the Western Working Class*, London: Macmillan.

MARCUSE, H. (1965), 'Industrialisation and capitalism', *New Left Review*, No. 30, pp. 3–17.

MARGLIN, S. (1971), *What do Bosses Do? The Origins and Functions of Hierarchy in Capitalist Production*, Harvard Institute of Economic Research Discussion Paper no. 222.

MARSHALL, T. H. (1963), *Sociology at the Crossroads*, London: Heinemann.

MARTIN, R. and FRYER, R. H. (1973), *Redundancy and Paternalist Capitalism*, London: Heinemann.

MENNELL, S. (1974), *Sociological Theory: Uses and Unities*, London: Nelson.

MERTON, R. K. (1957), *Social Theory and Social Structure*, Chicago: Free Press.

MERTON, R. K. and BARBER, E. (1963), 'Sociological ambivalence', in Tiryakian, E. A. (ed.) (1963).

MIEWALD, R. D. (1970), 'The greatly exaggerated death of bureaucracy', *California Management Review*, vol. 13, pp. 65–9.

MILLER, D. C. and FORM, W. H. (1951), *Industrial Sociology*, New York: Harper & Row.

MILLER, F. B. (1959a), 'The personnel dilemma: profession or not', *Personnel Journal*, vol. 38, pp. 53–6.

MILLER, F. B. (1959b), 'Why I'm for professionalising', *Personnel Journal*, vol. 38.

MILLER, F. B. and COGHILL, M. A. (1964), 'Sex and the personnel manager', *Industrial and Labor Relations Review*, vol. 18, pp. 32–44.

MILLERSON, G. (1964), *The Qualifying Associations*, London: Routledge & Kegan Paul.

MILLS, C. WRIGHT (1967), *Power, People and Politics*, London: Oxford University Press.

MILLS, C. WRIGHT (1970), *The Sociological Imagination*, Harmondsworth: Penguin.

MISHRA, R. (1973), 'Welfare and Industrial Man', *Sociological Review*, vol. 21, pp. 535–60.

MOMMSEN, W. J. (1974), *The Age of Bureaucracy*, Oxford: Blackwell.

MOORE, R. (1971), 'History, economics and religion: a review of the Max Weber thesis', in Sahay (ed.) (1971).

MOORE, R. (1974), *Pitmen, Preachers and Politics*, Cambridge University Press.

MOORE, W. E. (1951), *Industrial Relations and the Social Order*, New York: Macmillan.

232

MOORE, W. E. (1965), *Industrialisation and Labor*, New York: Russell & Russell.

MOUZELIS, N. (1967), *Organisation and Bureaucracy*, London: Routledge & Kegan Paul.

MUMFORD, E. (1972), *Job Satisfaction: a Study of Computer Specialists*, London: Longmans.

MUSGRAVE, P. W. (1967), 'Towards a sociological theory of occupational choice', *Sociological Review*, vol. 15, pp. 33–46.

MYERS, C. A. (1971), 'The changing role of the personnel manager', *Personnel Review*, vol. 1, pp. 6–11.

MCFARLAND, D. E. (1962), *Cooperation and Conflict in Personnel Administration*, New York: American Foundation for Management Research.

MCGREGOR, D. C. (1948), 'The staff function in human relations', *The Journal of Social Issues*, Summer.

MCGIVERING, I. (1960), 'Personnel Management in Large Manufacturing Firms in Liverpool', M.A. Thesis, Liverpool.

MCGIVERING, I. (1970), 'The development of personnel management', in Tillett *et al.* (eds) (1970).

MACKENZIE, G. (1974), 'The "affluent worker study": an evaluation and critique', in Parkin, F. (ed.) (1974).

MCKINLEY, J. B. (1975), *Processing People*, London: Holt, Rinehart & Winston.

MACPHERSON, C. B. (1970), 'Models of society', in Burns, T. (ed.) (1970).

NICHOLS, T. (1969), *Ownership, Control and Ideology*, London: Allen & Unwin.

NICHOLS, T. (1975), 'The "socialism" of management', *Sociological Review*, vol. 23, pp. 245–65.

NISBET, R. A. (1970), *The Sociological Tradition*, London: Heinemann.

NIVEN, M. M. (1967), *Personnel Management 1913–63*, London: I.P.M.

NOBLE, T. (1975), *Modern Britain: Structure and Change*, London: Batsford.

O'DONNELL, L. A. (1973), 'Rationalism, capitalism and the entrepreneur', *History and Political Economy*, vol. 5, pp. 199–214.

O'NEILL, J. (ed.) (1973), *Modes of Individualism and Collectivism*, London: Heinemann.

OUTHWAITE, W. (1975), *Understanding Social Life*, London: Allen & Unwin.

PAHL, J. M. and PAHL, R. E. (1972), *Managers and their Wives*, Harmondsworth: Penguin.

PAHL, R. E. and WINKLER, J. T. (1974), 'The economic elite: theory and practice', in Stanworth and Giddens (1974).

PARKER, P. (1969), 'Coordinating two cultures', *Personnel Management*, October.

PARKIN, F. (1972), *Class, Inequality and Political Order*, London: Paladin.

PARKIN, F. (ed.) (1974), *The Social Analysis of Class Structure*, London: Tavistock.

PARSONS, T. (1959), 'An approach to the sociology of knowledge', *Transactions of the 4th World Congress of Sociology*.

PATTEN, T. H. Jr. (1968), 'Is personnel administration a profession?', *Personnel Administration*, vol. 31, pp. 39–48.

PAVALKO, R. M. (ed.) (1972), *Sociological Perspectives on Occupations*, Ithaca, Illinois: Peacock.

PEACH, L. H. (1975), 'Personnel management by objectives', *Personnel Management*, March.

PEACH, L. H. and HARGREAVES, B. J. A. (1976), 'Social responsibility: the investment that pays off', *Personnel Management*, June.

P.E.P. (1965), *Thrusters and Sleepers*, London: Allen & Unwin.

PERROW, C. (1970a), 'Departmental power' in Zald, M. N. (ed.) (1970).

PERROW, C. (1970b), *Organisational Analysis*, London: Tavistock.

PETRIE, D. J. (1965), 'The personnel professional – who needs them?', *Personnel*, vol. 42.

PETTIGREW, A. (1973), *The Politics of Organisational Decision-Making*, London: Tavistock.

POCOCK, P. (1971), 'Are manpower planners human?' *Personnel Management*, November, p. 3.

POLLARD, S. (1968), *The Genesis of Modern Management*, Harmondsworth: Penguin.

POOLE, M. (1973), 'A back seat for personnel', *Personnel Management*, May, pp. 38–41.

POPPER, K. (1973), *Objective Knowledge*, Oxford University Press.

POULANTZAS, N. (1973), 'The problem of the capitalist state', in Blackburn, R. (1972).

PRANDY, K. (1965), *Professional Employees*, London: Faber.

PRICE, D. E. C. (1962), 'Personnel management – a service, not a profession', *Personnel Management*, June.

PROUD, E. D. (1916), *Welfare Work*, London: Bell.

REX, J. (1973), *Discovering Sociology*, London: Routledge & Kegan Paul.

REX, J. (1974a), *Sociology and the Demystification of the Modern World*, London: Routledge & Kegan Paul.

REX, J. (1974b), 'Capitalism, elites and the ruling class', in Stanworth and Giddens (1974).

REX, J. (ed.) (1974), *Approaches to Sociology*, London: Routledge & Kegan Paul.

RHENMAN, E., STROMBERG, L. and WESTERLUND, G. (1970), *Conflict and Cooperation in Business Organisations*, London: Wiley.

RIMLINGER, G. V. (1971), *Welfare Policy and Industrialisation in Europe, America and Russia*, New York: Wiley.

RITZER, G. (1972), *Man and his Work: Conflict and Change*, New York: Appleton-Century-Crofts.

RITZER, G. and TRICE, H. M. (1969), *An Occupation in Conflict: A Study of the Personnel Manager*, Ithaca: Cornell University Press.

ROBERTS, J. and STONE, M. (1975), 'Cost effectiveness: the training officers lifeline', *Personnel Management*, September, pp. 27–30.

ROBERTS, K. (1968), 'The entry into employment', *Sociological Review*, vol. 16, pp. 165–84.

ROBERTS, K. (1975), 'The developmental theory of occupational choice' in Esland, C., Salaman, G. and Speakman, M. (1975), *People and Work*, Edinburgh: Holmes McDougall.

ROBINSON, D. (1973), 'Progress in human asset accounting', *Personnel Management*, March, pp. 31–3, 43.

ROE, A. (1964), 'Factors influencing occupational decisions: a pilot study', *Harvard Studies in Career Development, No. 32*, Cambridge, Mass.

ROETHLISBERGER, F. L. and DICKSON, W. J. (1939), *Management and the Worker*, Cambridge, Mass.: Harvard University Press.

ROFF, H. E. (1975), 'Bearing the cross and facing the challenge', *Personnel Management*, October.

ROGERS, D. and BERG, I. E. Jr (1961), 'Occupation and ideology: the case of the small businessman', *Human Organisation*, vol. 20, pp. 103–11.

ROGERS, R. (1974), 'What price people?', *Personnel Management*, December, pp. 40–2.

ROLL, Sir E. (1930), *An Early Experiment in Industrial Organisation*, London: Cass.

ROSE, M. (1975), *Industrial Behaviour*, London: Allen Lane.

ROWNTREE, B. S. (1921), *The Human Factor in Business*, London: Longmans.

SAHAY, A. (1971), *Max Weber and Modern Sociology*, London: Routledge & Kegan Paul.

SCHLESINGER, L. E. (1965), 'Personnel managers and change: monks or missionaries', *Personnel Administration*, August, pp. 3–5, 12–16.

SCHROYER, T. (1970), 'Towards a critical theory for advanced industrial society', in Dreitzel, H. P. (ed.) (1970).

SCHUTZ, A. (1943), 'The problem of rationality in the social world', *Economica*, vol. 10, pp. 130–49.

SCHUTZ, A. (1964/67), *Collected Papers*, 3 vols, The Hague: Nijhoff.

SCOTT, M. and LYMAN, M. (1968), 'Accounts', *American Sociological Review*, vol. 36, pp. 46–62.

SCOTT, W. R. (1966), 'Professionals in bureaucracies', in Vollmer and Mills (1966).

SHERIDAN, P. R. (1972), 'Implications for the personnel and training functions' in Towers *et al.* (eds) (1972).

SHERLOCK, B. and COHEN, A. (1966), 'The strategy of occupational choice: recruitment to dentistry', *Social Forces*, vol. 44, pp. 303–13.

SILLS, P. (1973), *The Behavioural Sciences*, London: I.P.M.

SILLS, P. (1975), 'The behavioural sciences: their potential and limitations', *Personnel Review*, vol. 4, pp. 5–11.

SILVERMAN, D. (1970), *The Theory of Organisations*, London: Heinemann.

SLOCUM, W. L. (1959), 'Some sociological aspects of occupational choice', *American Journal of Economics and Sociology*, vol. 18, pp. 139–47.

SMELSER, N. J. (1959), *Social Change in the Industrial Revolution*, London: Routledge & Kegan Paul.

SMITH, A. (1970), *The Wealth of Nations*, Harmondsworth: Penguin.

SMITH, P. J. and DRAKE, R. (1969), 'Integrating personnel and training', *Personnel Management*, May, pp. 24–7.

SOFER, C. (1970), *Men in Mid-Career*, Cambridge University Press.

235

SOFER, C. (1972), *Organisations in Theory and Practice*, London: Heinemann.

SOFER, C. (1974), 'Introduction', to Williams, W. M. (ed.) (1974).

SOLOMON, D. N. (1968), 'Sociological perspectives on occupations', in Becker *et al.* (eds) (1968).

STAMMER, O. (ed.) (1971), *Max Weber and Sociology Today*, Oxford University Press.

STANWORTH, P. and GIDDENS, A. (1974), *Elites and Power in British Society*, Cambridge University Press.

STEWART, P. and CANTOR, M. (eds) (1974), *Varieties of Work Experience*, New York: Wiley.

STOKES, R. (1971), 'A company fit to live in', *Personnel Management*, August, pp. 33–6.

STOLZMAN, J. D. (1975), 'Objective and subjective concepts of interest in sociological analysis', *Sociological Analysis and Theory*, vol. 5, pp. 107–15.

STRAUSS, G. and SAYLES, L. R. (1968), *Personnel: The Human Problems of Management*, Englewood Cliffs: Prentice Hall.

STROTHER, G. B. (1959), 'Personnel management in theory and practice', *Personnel*, vol. 36, pp. 63–71.

SUPER, D. E. (1957), *The Psychology of Careers*, New York: Harper & Row.

SUTTON, F. X., HARRIS, S. E., KAYSEN, C. and TOBIN, J. (1956), *The American Business Creed*, Cambridge, Mass.: Harvard University Press.

SWANNACK, A. R. (1975), 'Laying a ghost to rest', *Personnel Management*, December, p. 3.

TAWNEY, R. H. (1961), *The Acquisitive Society*, London: Fontana.

TAYLOR, L. (1968), *Occupational Sociology*, New York: Oxford University Press.

TAYLOR, T. C. L., MACMILLAN, K. and WILD, R. (1976), 'Why investment is your business too', *Personnel Management*, February, p. 3.

THOMAS, C. (1976), 'Strategy for a sit-in', *Personnel Management*, January, pp. 33–5, 37.

THOMASON, G. (1975), *A Textbook of Personnel Management*, London: I.P.M.

THOMPSON, E. P. (1968), *The Making of the English Working Class*, Harmondsworth: Penguin.

THOMPSON, J. D. (1967), *Organisations in Action*, New York: McGraw-Hill.

TILLETT, A. D., KEMPNER, T. and WILLS, G. (eds) (1970), *Management Thinkers*, Harmondsworth: Penguin.

TIMPERLEY, S. R. (1972), *Survey of I.P.M. Merseyside Branch Membership*, Liverpool: I.P.M.

TIMPERLEY, S. R. (1974a), *Personnel Planning and Occupational Choice*, London: Allen & Unwin.

TIMPERLEY, S. R. (1974b), 'The process of organisational entry', *Personnel Review*, vol. 3, pp. 34–7.

TIMPERLEY, S. R. and OSBALDESTON, M. D. (1975), 'The professionalisation process: an aspiring occupational organisation', *Sociological Review*, Vol. 23, pp. 607–27.

TIRYAKIAN, E. A. (ed.) (1963), *Sociological Theory, Values and Socio-Culture Change*, New York: Free Press.

TOWERS, B., WHITTINGHAM, T. and GOTTSCHALK, A. (eds) (1972), *Bargaining For Change*, London: Macmillan.

TURNER, C. and HODGE, M. N. (1970), 'Occupations and professions', in Jackson, J. A. (ed.) (1970).

URRY, J. and WAKEFORD, J. (eds) (1973), *Power in Britain*, London: Heinemann.

VOLLMER, H. M. and MILLS, D. L. (eds) (1966), *Professionalisation*, Englewood Cliffs: Prentice Hall.

WATSON, T. J. (1972), *Some Sociological Aspects of Organisational Change*, M.Sc. thesis, Loughborough University of Technology.

WATSON, T. J. (1976a), 'Working theory: a reflexive account of research and theorising in an industrial setting', unpublished paper, Dept. of Sociology, University of Nottingham.

WATSON, T. J. (1976b), 'The professionalisation process: a critical note', *Sociological Review*, vol. 24, pp. 599–608.

WEBER, M. (1927), *General Economic History*, Chicago: Free Press.

WEBER, M. (1964), *The Theory of Social and Economic Organisation*, New York: Free Press.

WEBER, M. (1965), *The Protestant Ethic and the Spirit of Capitalism*, London: Allen & Unwin.

WEBER, M. (1968), *Economy and Society*, New York: Bedminster Press.

WEBER, M. (1970), 'Science as a vocation', in Gerth, H. H. and Mills, C. W., *From Max Weber*, London: Routledge & Kegan Paul.

WEDDERBURN, D. (1974), 'Perspective on Sweden', *Personnel Management*, May.

WEDDERBURN, D. and CROMPTON, R. (1972), *Workers' Attitudes and Technology*, Cambridge University Press.

WELFORD, A. T. (ed.) (1962), *Society: Problems and Methods of Study*, London: Routledge & Kegan Paul.

WERTHEIM, W. F. (1974), *Evolution and Revolution*, Harmondsworth: Penguin.

WESTERGAARD, J. and RESLER, H. (1975), *Class in a Capitalist Society: A Study of Contemporary Britain*, London: Heinemann.

WHYTE, W. H. (1960), *The Organisation Man*, Harmondsworth: Penguin.

WILENSKY, H. L. (1960), 'Work careers and social integration', *International Social Science Journal*, vol. 12, pp. 543–60.

WILENSKY, H. L. and LEBAUX, C. N. (1965), *Industrial Society and Social Welfare*, New York: Free Press.

WILLIAMS, W. M. (ed.) (1974), *Occupational Choice*, London: Allen & Unwin.

WILSON, B. (ed.) (1970), *Rationality*, Oxford: Blackwell.

WINKLER, J. T. (1974), 'The ghost at the bargaining table: directors and industrial relations', *British Journal Of Industrial Relations*, vol. 12, pp. 191–212.

WINSBURY, R. (1968), 'The emergent breed of personnel specialists', *Financial Times*, 30 September, p. 21.

WINTER, J. A. (1974), 'Elective affinities between religious beliefs and ideologies of management in two eras', *American Journal of Sociology*, vol. 79, pp. 1134–50.

WOOD, N. J. (1960), 'Industrial relations policies of American management, 1900–1933', *Business History Review*, Winter, pp. 403–20.

WOODWARD, J. (1958), *Management and Technology*, London: H.M.S.O.

WORSLEY, P. (1964), *The Distribution of Power in Industrial Society*, Sociological Review Monograph No. 8, Keele University, pp. 16–34.

WRONG, D. H. (1961), 'The oversocialised conception of man in modern sociology', *American Sociological Review*, vol. 26, pp. 183–93.

WRONG, D. (ed.) (1970), *Max Weber*, Englewood Cliffs: Prentice Hall.

ZALD, M. N. (ed.) (1970), *Power in Organisations*, Nashville: Vanderbilt University Press.

ZEITLIN, M. (1974), 'Corporate Ownership and Control: The Large Corporation and the Capitalist Class', *American Journal of Sociology*, vol. 79, pp. 1073–119.

ZIMMERMAN, D. H. (1971), 'The practicalities of rule use', in Douglas, J. D. (1971).

ZYTOWSKI, D. G. (1968), *Vocational Behaviour*, New York: Holt, Rinehart & Winston.

Index

Routledge Social Science Series

Routledge & Kegan Paul   London, Henley and Boston

39 Store Street, London WC1E 7DD
Broadway House, Newtown Road, Henley-on-Thames,
Oxon RG9 1EN
9 Park Street, Boston, Mass. 02108

Contents

Authors wishing to submit manuscripts for any series in
this catalogue should send them to the Social Science Editor,
Routledge & Kegan Paul Ltd, 39 Store Street,
London WC1E 7DD

● *Books so marked are available in paperback*
All books are in Metric Demy 8vo format (216 × 138mm approx.)

International Library of Sociology

General Editor John Rex

GENERAL SOCIOLOGY

Barnsley, J. H. The Social Reality of Ethics. *464 pp.*
Belshaw, Cyril. The Conditions of Social Performance. *An Exploratory Theory. 144 pp.*
Brown, Robert. Explanation in Social Science. *208 pp.*
● Rules and Laws in Sociology. *192 pp.*
Bruford, W. H. Chekhov and His Russia. *A Sociological Study. 244 pp.*
Cain, Maureen E. Society and the Policeman's Role. *326 pp.*
●**Fletcher, Colin.** Beneath the Surface. *An Account of Three Styles of Sociological Research. 221 pp.*
Gibson, Quentin. The Logic of Social Enquiry. *240 pp.*
Glucksmann, M. Structuralist Analysis in Contemporary Social Thought. *212 pp.*
Gurvitch, Georges. Sociology of Law. *Preface by Roscoe Pound. 264 pp.*
Hodge, H. A. Wilhelm Dilthey. *An Introduction. 184 pp.*
Homans, George C. Sentiments and Activities. *336 pp.*
Johnson, Harry M. Sociology: *a Systematic Introduction. Foreword by Robert K. Merton. 710 pp.*
●**Keat, Russell,** and **Urry, John.** Social Theory as Science. *278 pp.*
Mannheim, Karl. Essays on Sociology and Social Psychology. *Edited by Paul Kecskemeti. With Editorial Note by Adolph Lowe. 344 pp.*
Systematic Sociology: *An Introduction to the Study of Society. Edited by J. S. Erös and Professor W. A. C. Stewart. 220 pp.*
Martindale, Don. The Nature and Types of Sociological Theory. *292 pp.*
●**Maus, Heinz.** A Short History of Sociology. *234 pp.*
Mey, Harald. Field-Theory. *A Study of its Application in the Social Sciences. 352 pp.*
Myrdal, Gunnar. Value in Social Theory: *A Collection of Essays on Methodology. Edited by Paul Streeten. 332 pp.*
Ogburn, William F., and **Nimkoff, Meyer F.** A Handbook of Sociology. *Preface by Karl Mannheim. 656 pp. 46 figures. 35 tables.*
Parsons, Talcott, and **Smelser, Neil J.** Economy and Society: *A Study in the Integration of Economic and Social Theory. 362 pp.*
Podgórecki, Adam. Practical Social Sciences. *About 200 pp.*
●**Rex, John.** Key Problems of Sociological Theory. *220 pp.*
Sociology and the Demystification of the Modern World. *282 pp.*
●**Rex, John** (Ed.) Approaches to Sociology. *Contributions by Peter Abell, Frank Bechhofer, Basil Bernstein, Ronald Fletcher, David Frisby, Miriam Glucksmann, Peter Lassman, Herminio Martins, John Rex, Roland Robertson, John Westergaard and Jock Young. 302 pp.*
Rigby, A. Alternative Realities. *352 pp.*
Roche, M. Phenomenology, Language and the Social Sciences. *374 pp.*

Sahay, A. Sociological Analysis. *220 pp.*

Simirenko, Alex (Ed.) Soviet Sociology. *Historical Antecedents and Current Appraisals. Introduction by Alex Simirenko. 376 pp.*

Strasser, Hermann. The Normative Structure of Sociology. *Conservative and Emancipatory Themes in Social Thought. About 340 pp.*

Urry, John. Reference Groups and the Theory of Revolution. *244 pp.*

Weinberg, E. Development of Sociology in the Soviet Union. *173 pp.*

FOREIGN CLASSICS OF SOCIOLOGY

●**Durkheim, Emile.** Suicide. *A Study in Sociology. Edited and with an Introduction by George Simpson. 404 pp.*

●**Gerth, H. H.,** and **Mills, C. Wright.** From Max Weber: *Essays in Sociology. 502 pp.*

●**Tönnies, Ferdinand.** Community and Association. *(Gemeinschaft und Gesellschaft.) Translated and Supplemented by Charles P. Loomis. Foreword by Pitirim A. Sorokin. 334 pp.*

SOCIAL STRUCTURE

Andreski, Stanislav. Military Organization and Society. *Foreword by Professor A. R. Radcliffe-Brown. 226 pp. 1 folder.*

Carlton, Eric. Ideology and Social Order. *Preface by Professor Philip Abrahams. About 320 pp.*

Coontz, Sydney H. Population Theories and the Economic Interpretation. *202 pp.*

Coser, Lewis. The Functions of Social Conflict. *204 pp.*

Dickie-Clark, H. F. Marginal Situation: *A Sociological Study of a Coloured Group. 240 pp. 11 tables.*

Glaser, Barney, and **Strauss, Anselm L.** Status Passage. *A Formal Theory. 208 pp.*

Glass, D. V. (Ed.) Social Mobility in Britain. *Contributions by J. Berent, T. Bottomore, R. C. Chambers, J. Floud, D. V. Glass, J. R. Hall, H. T. Himmelweit, R. K. Kelsall, F. M. Martin, C. A. Moser, R. Mukherjee, and W. Ziegel. 420 pp.*

Johnstone, Frederick A. Class, Race and Gold. *A Study of Class Relations and Racial Discrimination in South Africa. 312 pp.*

Jones, Garth N. Planned Organizational Change: *An Exploratory Study Using an Empirical Approach. 268 pp.*

Kelsall, R. K. Higher Civil Servants in Britain: *From 1870 to the Present Day. 268 pp. 31 tables.*

König, René. The Community. *232 pp. Illustrated.*

●**Lawton, Denis.** Social Class, Language and Education. *192 pp.*

McLeish, John. The Theory of Social Change: *Four Views Considered. 128 pp.*

Marsh, David C. The Changing Social Structure of England and Waies, *1871-1961. 288 pp.*

Menzies, Ken. Talcott Parsons and the Social Image of Man. *About 208 pp.*

●**Mouzelis, Nicos.** Organization and Bureaucracy. *An Analysis of Modern Theories. 240 pp.*

Mulkay, M. J. Functionalism, Exchange and Theoretical Strategy. *272 pp.*

Ossowski, Stanislaw. Class Structure in the Social Consciousness. *210 pp.*

●**Podgórecki, Adam.** Law and Society. *302 pp.*

Renner, Karl. Institutions of Private Law and Their Social Functions. *Edited, with an Introduction and Notes, by O. Kahn-Freud. Translated by Agnes Schwarzschild. 316 pp.*

SOCIOLOGY AND POLITICS

Acton, T. A. Gypsy Politics and Social Change. *316 pp.*

Clegg, Stuart. Power, Rule and Domination. *A Critical and Empirical Understanding of Power in Sociological Theory and Organisational Life. About 300 pp.*

Hechter, Michael. Internal Colonialism. *The Celtic Fringe in British National Development, 1536–1966. 361 pp.*

Hertz, Frederick. Nationality in History and Politics: *A Psychology and Sociology of National Sentiment and Nationalism. 432 pp.*

Kornhauser, William. The Politics of Mass Society. *272 pp. 20 tables.*

●**Kroes, R.** Soldiers and Students. *A Study of Right- and Left-wing Students. 174 pp.*

Laidler, Harry W. History of Socialism. *Social-Economic Movements: An Historical and Comparative Survey of Socialism, Communism, Co-operation, Utopianism; and other Systems of Reform and Reconstruction. 992 pp.*

Lasswell, H. D. Analysis of Political Behaviour. *324 pp.*

Martin, David A. Pacifism: *an Historical and Sociological Study. 262 pp.*

Martin, Roderick. Sociology of Power. *About 272 pp.*

Myrdal, Gunnar. The Political Element in the Development of Economic Theory. *Translated from the German by Paul Streeten. 282 pp.*

Wilson, H. T. The American Ideology. *Science, Technology and Organization of Modes of Rationality. About 280 pp.*

Wootton, Graham. Workers, Unions and the State. *188 pp.*

CRIMINOLOGY

Ancel, Marc. Social Defence: *A Modern Approach to Criminal Problems. Foreword by Leon Radzinowicz. 240 pp.*

Cain, Maureen E. Society and the Policeman's Role. *326 pp.*

Cloward, Richard A., and **Ohlin, Lloyd E.** Delinquency and Opportunity: *A Theory of Delinquent Gangs. 248 pp.*

Downes, David M. The Delinquent Solution. *A Study in Subcultural Theory. 296 pp.*

Dunlop, A. B., and **McCabe, S.** Young Men in Detention Centres. *192 pp.*

Friedlander, Kate. The Psycho-Analytical Approach to Juvenile Delinquency: *Theory, Case Studies, Treatment. 320 pp.*

Glueck, Sheldon, and **Eleanor.** Family Environment and Delinquency. *With the statistical assistance of Rose W. Kneznek. 340 pp.*

Lopez-Rey, Manuel. Crime. *An Analytical Appraisal. 288 pp.*

Mannheim, Hermann. Comparative Criminology: *a Text Book. Two volumes. 442 pp. and 380 pp.*

Morris, Terence. The Criminal Area: *A Study in Social Ecology. Foreword by Hermann Mannheim. 232 pp. 25 tables. 4 maps.*

Rock, Paul. Making People Pay. *338 pp.*

●**Taylor, Ian, Walton, Paul,** and **Young, Jock.** The New Criminology. *For a Social Theory of Deviance. 325 pp.*

●**Taylor, Ian, Walton, Paul,** and **Young, Jock** (Eds). Critical Criminology. *268 pp.*

SOCIAL PSYCHOLOGY

Bagley, Christopher. The Social Psychology of the Epileptic Child. *320 pp.*

Barbu, Zevedei. Problems of Historical Psychology. *248 pp.*

Blackburn, Julian. Psychology and the Social Pattern. *184 pp.*

●**Brittan, Arthur.** Meanings and Situations. *224 pp.*

Carroll, J. Break-Out from the Crystal Palace. *200 pp.*

●**Fleming, C. M.** Adolescence: Its Social Psychology. *With an Introduction to recent findings from the fields of Anthropology, Physiology, Medicine, Psychometrics and Sociometry. 288 pp.*

● The Social Psychology of Education: *An Introduction and Guide to Its Study. 136 pp.*

●**Homans, George C.** The Human Group. *Foreword by Bernard DeVoto. Introduction by Robert K. Merton. 526 pp.*

● Social Behaviour: *its Elementary Forms. 416 pp.*

●**Klein, Josephine.** The Study of Groups. *226 pp. 31 figures. 5 tables.*

Linton, Ralph. The Cultural Background of Personality. *132 pp.*

●**Mayo, Elton.** The Social Problems of an Industrial Civilization. *With an appendix on the Political Problem. 180 pp.*

Ottaway, A. K. C. Learning Through Group Experience. *176 pp.*

Plummer, Ken. Sexual Stigma. *An Interactionist Account. 254 pp.* .

●**Rose, Arnold M.** (Ed.) Human Behaviour and Social Processes: *an Interactionist Approach. Contributions by Arnold M. Rose, Ralph H. Turner, Anselm Strauss, Everett C. Hughes, E. Franklin Frazier, Howard S. Becker, et al. 696 pp.*

Smelser, Neil J. Theory of Collective Behaviour. *448 pp.*

Stephenson, Geoffrey M. The Development of Conscience. *128 pp.*

Young, Kimball. Handbook of Social Psychology. *658 pp. 16 figures. 10 tables.*

SOCIOLOGY OF THE FAMILY

Banks, J. A. Prosperity and Parenthood: *A Study of Family Planning among The Victorian Middle Classes. 262 pp.*

Bell, Colin R. Middle Class Families: *Social and Geographical Mobility. 224 pp.*

Burton, Lindy. Vulnerable Children. *272 pp.*

Gavron, Hannah. The Captive Wife: *Conflicts of Household Mothers.* *190 pp.*

George, Victor, and **Wilding, Paul.** Motherless Families. *248 pp.*

Klein, Josephine. Samples from English Cultures.
1. Three Preliminary Studies and Aspects of Adult Life in England. *447 pp.*
2. Child-Rearing Practices and Index. *247 pp.*

Klein, Viola. The Feminine Character. *History of an Ideology. 244 pp.*

McWhinnie, Alexina M. Adopted Children. *How They Grow Up. 304 pp.*

● **Morgan, D. H. J.** Social Theory and the Family. *About 320 pp.*

● **Myrdal, Alva,** and **Klein, Viola.** Women's Two Roles: *Home and Work.* *238 pp. 27 tables.*

Parsons, Talcott, and **Bales, Robert F.** Family: Socialization and Inter-action Process. *In collaboration with James Olds, Morris Zelditch and Philip E. Slater. 456 pp. 50 figures and tables.*

SOCIAL SERVICES

Bastide, Roger. The Sociology of Mental Disorder. *Translated from the French by Jean McNeil. 260 pp.*

Carlebach, Julius. Caring For Children in Trouble. *266 pp.*

George, Victor. Foster Care. *Theory and Practice. 234 pp.*
Social Security: *Beveridge and After. 258 pp.*

George, V., and **Wilding, P.** Motherless Families. *248 pp.*

● **Goetschius, George W.** Working, with Community Groups. *256 pp.*

Goetschius, George W., and **Tash, Joan.** Working with Unattached Youth. *416 pp.*

Hall, M. P., and **Howes, I. V.** The Church in Social Work. *A Study of Moral Welfare Work undertaken by the Church of England. 320 pp.*

Heywood, Jean S. Children in Care: *the Development of the Service for the Deprived Child. 264 pp.*

Hoenig, J., and **Hamilton, Marian W.** The De-Segregation of the Mentally Ill. *284 pp.*

Jones, Kathleen. Mental Health and Social Policy, 1845-1959. *264 pp.*

King, Roy D., Raynes, Norma V., and **Tizard, Jack.** Patterns of Residential Care. *356 pp.*

Leigh, John. Young People and Leisure. *256 pp.*

● **Mays, John.** (Ed.) Penelope Hall's Social Services of England and Wales. *About 324 pp.*

Morris, Mary. Voluntary Work and the Welfare State. *300 pp.*

Nokes, P. L. The Professional Task in Welfare Practice. *152 pp.*

Timms, Noel. Psychiatric Social Work in Great Britain (1939-1962). *280 pp.*

● Social Casework: *Principles and Practice. 256 pp.*

Young, A. F. Social Services in British Industry. *272 pp.*

SOCIOLOGY OF EDUCATION

Banks, Olive. Parity and Prestige in English Secondary Education: a Study in Educational Sociology. *272 pp.*

Bentwich, Joseph. Education in Israel. *224 pp. 8 pp. plates.*

●**Blyth, W. A. L.** English Primary Education. *A Sociological Description.*
1. Schools. *232 pp.*
2. Background. *168 pp.*

Collier, K. G. The Social Purposes of Education: *Personal and Social Values in Education. 268 pp.*

Dale, R. R., and **Griffith, S.** Down Stream: *Failure in the Grammar School. 108 pp.*

Evans, K. M. Sociometry and Education. *158 pp.*

●**Ford, Julienne.** Social Class and the Comprehensive School. *192 pp.*

Foster, P. J. Education and Social Change in Ghana. *336 pp. 3 maps.*

Fraser, W. R. Education and Society in Modern France. *150 pp.*

Grace, Gerald R. Role Conflict and the Teacher. *150 pp.*

Hans, Nicholas. New Trends in Education in the Eighteenth Century. *278 pp. 19 tables.*

● Comparative Education: *A Study of Educational Factors and Traditions. 360 pp.*

●**Hargreaves, David.** Interpersonal Relations and Education. *432 pp.*

● Social Relations in a Secondary School. *240 pp.*

Holmes, Brian. Problems in Education. *A Comparative Approach. 336 pp.*

King, Ronald. Values and Involvement in a Grammar School. *164 pp.*

School Organization and Pupil Involvement. *A Study of Secondary Schools.*

●**Mannheim, Karl,** and **Stewart, W. A. C.** An Introduction to the Sociology of Education. *206 pp.*

Morris, Raymond N. The Sixth Form and College Entrance. *231 pp.*

●**Musgrove, F.** Youth and the Social Order. *176 pp.*

●**Ottaway, A. K. C.** Education and Society: An Introduction to the Sociology of Education. *With an Introduction by W. O. Lester Smith. 212 pp.*

Peers, Robert. Adult Education: *A Comparative Study. 398 pp.*

Pritchard, D. G. Education and the Handicapped: *1760 to 1960. 258 pp.*

Stratta, Erica. The Education of Borstal Boys. *A Study of their Educational Experiences prior to, and during, Borstal Training. 256 pp.*

Taylor, P. H., Reid, W. A., and **Holley, B. J.** The English Sixth Form. *A Case Study in Curriculum Research. 200 pp.*

SOCIOLOGY OF CULTURE

Eppel, E. M., and **M.** Adolescents and Morality: *A Study of some Moral Values and Dilemmas of Working Adolescents in the Context of a changing Climate of Opinion. Foreword by W. J. H. Sprott. 268 pp. 39 tables.*

●**Fromm, Erich.** The Fear of Freedom. *286 pp.*

● The Sane Society. *400 pp.*

Mannheim, Karl. Essays on the Sociology of Culture. *Edited by Ernst Mannheim in co-operation with Paul Kecskemeti. Editorial Note by Adolph Lowe. 280 pp.*

Weber, Alfred. Farewell to European History: *or The Conquest of Nihilism. Translated from the German by R. F. C. Hull. 224 pp.*

SOCIOLOGY OF RELIGION

Argyle, Michael and **Beit-Hallahmi, Benjamin.** The Social Psychology of Religion. *About 256 pp.*

Glasner, Peter E. The Sociology of Secularisation. *A Critique of a Concept. About 180 pp.*

Nelson, G. K. Spiritualism and Society. *313 pp.*

Stark, Werner. The Sociology of Religion. *A Study of Christendom.*
  Volume I. *Established Religion. 248 pp.*
  Volume II. *Sectarian Religion. 368 pp.*
  Volume III. *The Universal Church. 464 pp.*
  Volume IV. *Types of Religious Man. 352 pp.*
  Volume V. *Types of Religious Culture. 464 pp.*

Turner, B. S. Weber and Islam. *216 pp.*

Watt, W. Montgomery. Islam and the Integration of Society. *320 pp.*

SOCIOLOGY OF ART AND LITERATURE

Jarvie, Ian C. Towards a Sociology of the Cinema. *A Comparative Essay on the Structure and Functioning of a Major Entertainment Industry. 405 pp.*

Rust, Frances S. Dance in Society. *An Analysis of the Relationships between the Social Dance and Society in England from the Middle Ages to the Present Day. 256 pp. 8 pp. of plates.*

Schücking, L. L. The Sociology of Literary Taste. *112 pp.*

Wolff, Janet. Hermeneutic Philosophy and the Sociology of Art. *150 pp.*

SOCIOLOGY OF KNOWLEDGE

Diesing, P. Patterns of Discovery in the Social Sciences. *262 pp.*

●**Douglas, J. D.** (Ed.) Understanding Everyday Life. *370 pp.*

●**Hamilton, P.** Knowledge and Social Structure. *174 pp.*

Jarvie, I. C. Concepts and Society. *232 pp.*

Mannheim, Karl. Essays on the Sociology of Knowledge. *Edited by Paul Kecskemeti. Editorial Note by Adolph Lowe. 353 pp.*

Remmling, Gunter W. The Sociology cf Karl Mannheim. *With a Bibliographical Guide to the Sociology of Knowledge, Ideological Analysis, and Social Planning. 255 pp.*

9

Remmling, Gunter W. (Ed.) Towards the Sociology of Knowledge. *Origin and Development of a Sociological Thought Style. 463 pp.*

Stark, Werner. The Sociology of Knowledge: *An Essay in Aid of a Deeper Understanding of the History of Ideas. 384 pp.*

URBAN SOCIOLOGY

Ashworth, William. The Genesis of Modern British Town Planning: *A Study in Economic and Social History of the Nineteenth and Twentieth Centuries. 288 pp.*

Cullingworth, J. B. Housing Needs and Planning Policy: *A Restatement of the Problems of Housing Need and 'Overspill' in England and Wales. 232 pp. 44 tables. 8 maps.*

Dickinson, Robert E. City and Region: *A Geographical Interpretation 608 pp. 125 figures.*

The West European City: *A Geographical Interpretation. 600 pp. 129 maps. 29 plates.*

● The City Region in Western Europe. *320 pp. Maps.*

Humphreys, Alexander J. New Dubliners: *Urbanization and the Irish Family. Foreword by George C. Homans. 304 pp.*

Jackson, Brian. Working Class Community: *Some General Notions raised by a Series of Studies in Northern England. 192 pp.*

Jennings, Hilda. Societies in the Making: *a Study of Development and Re-development within a County Borough. Foreword by D. A. Clark. 286 pp.*

●**Mann, P. H.** An Approach to Urban Sociology. *240 pp.*

Morris, R. N., and **Mogey, J.** The Sociology of Housing. *Studies at Berinsfield. 232 pp. 4 pp. plates.*

Rosser, C., and **Harris, C.** The Family and Social Change. *A Study of Family and Kinship in a South Wales Town. 352 pp. 8 maps.*

●**Stacey, Margaret, Batsone, Eric, Bell, Colin,** and **Thurcott, Anne.** Power, Persistence and Change. *A Second Study of Banbury. 196 pp.*

RURAL SOCIOLOGY

Haswell, M. R. The Economics of Development in Village India. *120 pp.*

Littlejohn, James. Westrigg: *the Sociology of a Cheviot Parish. 172 pp. 5 figures.*

Mayer, Adrian C. Peasants in the Pacific. *A Study of Fiji Indian Rural Society. 248 pp. 20 plates.*

Williams, W. M. The Sociology of an English Village: *Gosforth. 272 pp. 12 figures. 13 tables.*

SOCIOLOGY OF INDUSTRY AND DISTRIBUTION

Anderson, Nels. Work and Leisure. *280 pp.*

● **Blau, Peter M.**, and **Scott, W. Richard.** Formal Organizations: *a Comparative approach. Introduction and Additional Bibliography by J. H. Smith. 326 pp.*

Dunkerley, David. The Foreman. *Aspects of Task and Structure. 192 pp.*

Eldridge, J. E. T. Industrial Disputes. *Essays in the Sociology of Industrial Relations. 288 pp.*

Hetzler, Stanley. Applied Measures for Promoting Technological Growth. *352 pp.*

Technological Growth and Social Change. *Achieving Modernization. 269 pp.*

Hollowell, Peter G. The Lorry Driver. *272 pp.*

● **Oxaal, I., Barnett, T.,** and **Booth, D.** (Eds). Beyond the Sociology of Development. *Economy and Society in Latin America and Africa. 295 pp.*

Smelser, Neil J. Social Change in the Industrial Revolution: *An Application of Theory to the Lancashire Cotton Industry, 1770–1840. 468 pp. 12 figures. 14 tables.*

ANTHROPOLOGY

Ammar, Hamed. Growing up in an Egyptian Village: *Silwa, Province of Aswan. 336 pp.*

Brandel-Syrier, Mia. Reeftown Elite. *A Study of Social Mobility in a Modern African Community on the Reef. 376 pp.*

Dickie-Clark, H. F. The Marginal Situation. *A Sociological Study of a Coloured Group. 236 pp.*

Dube, S. C. Indian Village. *Foreword by Morris Edward Opler. 276 pp. 4 plates.*

India's Changing Villages: *Human Factors in Community Development. 260 pp. 8 plates. 1 map.*

Firth, Raymond. Malay Fishermen. *Their Peasant Economy. 420 pp. 17 pp. plates.*

Gulliver, P. H. Social Control in an African Society: a Study of the Arusha, Agricultural Masai of Northern Tanganyika. *320 pp. 8 plates. 10 figures.*

Family Herds. *288 pp.*

Ishwaran, K. Tradition and Economy in Village India: *An Interactionist Approach.*
Foreword by Conrad Arensburg. 176 pp.

Jarvie, Ian C. The Revolution in Anthropology. *268 pp.*

Little, Kenneth L. Mende of Sierra Leone. *308 pp. and folder.*

Negroes in Britain. *With a New Introduction and Contemporary Study by Leonard Bloom. 320 pp.*

Lowie, Robert H. Social Organization. *494 pp.*

Mayer, A. C. Peasants in the Pacific. *A Study of Fiji Indian Rural Society. 248 pp.*

Meer, Fatima. Race and Suicide in South Africa. *325 pp.*

Smith, Raymond T. The Negro Family in British Guiana: *Family Structure and Social Status in the Villages. With a Foreword by Meyer Fortes. 314 pp. 8 plates. 1 figure. 4 maps.*

Smooha, Sammy. Israel: Pluralism and Conflict. *About 320 pp.*

SOCIOLOGY AND PHILOSOPHY

Barnsley, John H. The Social Reality of Ethics. *A Comparative Analysis of Moral Codes. 448 pp.*

Diesing, Paul. Patterns of Discovery in the Social Sciences. *362 pp.*

●**Douglas, Jack D.** (Ed.) Understanding Everyday Life. *Toward the Reconstruction of Sociological Knowledge. Contributions by Alan F. Blum. Aaron W. Cicourel, Norman K. Denzin, Jack D. Douglas, John Heeren, Peter McHugh, Peter K. Manning, Melvin Power, Matthew Speier, Roy Turner, D. Lawrence Wieder, Thomas P. Wilson and Don H. Zimmerman. 370 pp.*

Gorman, Robert A. The Dual Vision. *Alfred Schutz and the Myth of Phenomenological Social Science. About 300 pp.*

Jarvie, Ian C. Concepts and Society. *216 pp.*

●**Pelz, Werner.** The Scope of Understanding in Sociology. *Towards a more radical reorientation in the social humanistic sciences. 283 pp.*

Roche, Maurice. Phenomenology, Language and the Social Sciences.*371 pp.*

Sahay, Arun. Sociological Analysis. *212 pp.*

Sklair, Leslie. The Sociology of Progress. *320 pp.*

Slater, P. Origin and Significance of the Frankfurt School. *A Marxist Perspective. About 192 pp.*

Smart, Barry. Sociology, Phenomenology and Marxian Analysis. *A Critical Discussion of the Theory and Practice of a Science of Society. 220 pp.*

International Library of Anthropology

General Editor Adam Kuper

Ahmed, A. S. Millenium and Charisma Among Pathans. *A Critical Essay in Social Anthropology. 192 pp.*

Brown, Paula. The Chimbu. *A Study of Change in the New Guinea Highlands. 151 pp.*

Gudeman, Stephen. Relationships, Residence and the Individual. *A Rural Panamanian Community. 288 pp. 11 Plates, 5 Figures, 2 Maps, 10 Tables.*

Hamnett, Ian. Chieftainship and Legitimacy. *An Anthropological Study of Executive Law in Lesotho. 163 pp.*

Hanson, F. Allan. Meaning in Culture. *127 pp.*

Lloyd, P. C. Power and Independence. *Urban Africans' Perception of Social Inequality. 264 pp.*

Pettigrew, Joyce. Robber Noblemen. *A Study of the Political System of the Sikh Jats. 284 pp.*

Street, Brian V. The Savage in Literature. *Representations of 'Primitive' Society in English Fiction, 1858–1920. 207 pp.*

Van Den Berghe, Pierre L. Power and Privilege at an African University. *278 pp.*

International Library of Social Policy

General Editor Kathleen Jones

Bayley, M. Mental Handicap and Community Care. *426 pp.*

Bottoms, A. E., and **McClean, J. D.** Defendants in the Criminal Process. *284 pp.*

Butler, J. R. Family Doctors and Public Policy. *208 pp.*

Davies, Martin. Prisoners of Society. *Attitudes and Aftercare. 204 pp.*

Gittus, Elizabeth. Flats, Families and the Under-Fives. *285 pp.*

Holman, Robert. Trading in Children. *A Study of Private Fostering. 355 pp.*

Jones, Howard, and **Cornes, Paul.** Open Prisons. *About 248 pp.*

Jones, Kathleen. History of the Mental Health Service. *428 pp.*

Jones, Kathleen, with **Brown, John, Cunningham, W. J., Roberts, Julian,** and **Williams, Peter.** Opening the Door. *A Study of New Policies for the Mentally Handicapped. 278 pp.*

Karn, Valerie. Retiring to the Seaside. *About 280 pp. 2 maps. Numerous tables.*

Thomas, J. E. The English Prison Officer since 1850: *A Study in Conflict. 258 pp.*

Walton, R. G. Women in Social Work. *303 pp.*

Woodward, J. To Do the Sick No Harm. *A Study of the British Voluntary Hospital System to 1875. 221 pp.*

International Library of Welfare and Philosophy

General Editors Noel Timms and David Watson

● **Plant, Raymond.** Community and Ideology. *104 pp.*

● **McDermott, F. E.** (Ed.) Self-Determination in Social Work. *A Collection of Essays on Self-determination and Related Concepts by Philosophers and Social Work Theorists. Contributors: F. P. Biestek, S. Bernstein, A. Keith-Lucas, D. Sayer, H. H. Perelman, C. Whittington, R. F. Stalley, F. E. McDermott, I. Berlin, H. J. McCloskey, H. L. A. Hart, J. Wilson, A. I. Melden, S. I. Benn. 254 pp.*

Ragg, Nicholas M. People Not Cases. *A Philosophical Approach to Social Work. About 250 pp.*

13

● **Timms, Noel,** and **Watson, David** (Eds). Talking About Welfare. *Readings in Philosophy and Social Policy. Contributors: T. H. Marshall, R. B. Brandt, G. H. von Wright, K. Nielsen, M. Cranston, R. M. Titmuss, R. S. Downie, E. Telfer, D. Donnison, J. Benson, P. Leonard, A. Keith-Lucas, D. Walsh, I. T. Ramsey. 320 pp.*

Primary Socialization, Language and Education

General Editor Basil Bernstein

Adlam, Diana S., *with the assistance of Geoffrey Turner and Lesley Lineker.* Code in Context. *About 272 pp.*

Bernstein, Basil. Class, Codes and Control. *3 volumes.*
    1. *Theoretical Studies Towards a Sociology of Language. 254 pp.*
    2. *Applied Studies Towards a Sociology of Language. 377 pp.*
●   3. *Towards a Theory of Educatiomal Transmission. 167 pp.*

Brandis, W., and **Bernstein, B.** Selection and Control. *176 pp.*

Brandis, Walter, and **Henderson, Dorothy.** Social Class, Language and Communication. *288 pp.*

Cook-Gumperz, Jenny. Social Control and Socialization. *A Study of Class Differences in the Language of Maternal Control. 290 pp.*

● **Gahagan, D. M.,** and **G. A.** Talk Reform. *Exploration in Language for Infant School Children. 160 pp.*

Hawkins, P. R. Social Class, the Nominal Group and Verbal Strategies. *About 220 pp.*

Robinson, W. P., and **Rackstraw, Susan D. A.** A Question of Answers. *2 volumes. 192 pp. and 180 pp.*

Turner, Geoffrey J., and **Mohan, Bernard A.** A Linguistic Description and Computer Programme for Children's Speech. *208 pp.*

Reports of the Institute of Community Studies

● **Cartwright, Ann.** Parents and Family Planning Services. *306 pp.*
    Patients and their Doctors. *A Study of General Practice. 304 pp.*

Dench, Geoff. Maltese in London. *A Case-study in the Erosion of Ethnic Consciousness. 302 pp.*

● **Jackson, Brian.** Streaming: *an Education System in Miniature. 168 pp.*

Jackson, Brian, and **Marsden, Dennis.** Education and the Working Class: *Some General Themes raised by a Study of 88 Working-class Children in a Northern Industrial City. 268 pp. 2 folders.*

Marris, Peter. The Experience of Higher Education. *232 pp. 27 tables.*
    Loss and Change. *192 pp.*

Marris, Peter, and **Rein, Martin.** Dilemmas of Social Reform. *Poverty and Community Action in the United States. 256 pp.*

Marris, Peter, and Somerset, Anthony. African Businessmen. *A Study of Entrepreneurship and Development in Kenya. 256 pp.*

Mills, Richard. Young Outsiders: *a Study in Alternative Communities. 216 pp.*

Runciman, W. G. Relative Deprivation and Social Justice. *A Study of Attitudes to Social Inequality in Twentieth-Century England. 352 pp.*

Willmott, Peter. Adolescent Boys in East London. *230 pp.*

Willmott, Peter, and Young, Michael. Family and Class in a London Suburb. *202 pp. 47 tables.*

Young, Michael. Innovation and Research in Education. *192 pp.*

●Young, Michael, and McGeeney, Patrick. Learning Begins at Home. *A Study of a Junior School and its Parents. 128 pp.*

Young, Michael, and Willmott, Peter. Family and Kinship in East London. *Foreword by Richard M. Titmuss. 252 pp. 39 tables.*
The Symmetrical Family. *410 pp.*

Reports of the Institute for Social Studies in Medical Care

Cartwright, Ann, Hockey, Lisbeth, and Anderson, John L. Life Before Death. *310 pp.*

Dunnell, Karen, and Cartwright, Ann. Medicine Takers, Prescribers and Hoarders. *190 pp.*

Medicine, Illness and Society

General Editor W. M. Williams

Robinson, David. The Process of Becoming Ill. *142 pp.*

Stacey, Margaret, *et al.* Hospitals, Children and Their Families. *The Report of a Pilot Study. 202 pp.*

Stimson, G. V., and Webb, B. Going to See the Doctor. *The Consultation Process in General Practice. 155 pp.*

Monographs in Social Theory

General Editor Arthur Brittan

●Barnes, B. Scientific Knowledge and Sociological Theory. *192 pp.*

Bauman, Zygmunt. Culture as Praxis. *204 pp.*

●Dixon, Keith. Sociological Theory. *Pretence and Possibility. 142 pp.*

Meltzer, B. N., Petras, J. W., and Reynolds, L. T. Symbolic Interactionism. *Genesis, Varieties and Criticisms. 144 pp.*

●Smith, Anthony D. The Concept of Social Change. *A Critique of the Functionalist Theory of Social Change. 208 pp.*

Routledge Social Science Journals

The British Journal of Sociology. *Editor – Angus Stewart; Associate Editor – Leslie Sklair. Vol. 1, No. 1 – March 1950 and Quarterly. Roy. 8vo. All back issues available. An international journal publishing original papers in the field of sociology and related areas.*

Community Work. *Edited by David Jones and Marjorie Mayo. 1973. Published annually.*

Economy and Society. *Vol. 1, No. 1. February 1972 and Quarterly. Metric Roy. 8vo. A journal for all social scientists covering sociology, philosophy, anthropology, economics and history. All back numbers available.*

Religion. Journal of Religion and Religions. *Chairman of Editorial Board, Ninian Smart. Vol. 1, No. 1, Spring 1971. A journal with an inter-disciplinary approach to the study of the phenomena of religion. All back numbers available.*

Year Book of Social Policy in Britain, The. *Edited by Kathleen Jones. 1971. Published annually.*

Social and Psychological Aspects of Medical Practice

Editor Trevor Silverstone

Lader, Malcolm. Psychophysiology of Mental Illness. *280 pp.*

● **Silverstone, Trevor,** and **Turner, Paul.** Drug Treatment in Psychiatry. *232 pp.*

Printed in Great Britain by Unwin Brothers Limited
The Gresham Press Old Woking Surrey
A member of the Staples Printing Group

Personal
|
Professional   } Interests / Orientations / Ambiguities.
|
Institutional.

                           Division within mgᵗ
                            Trust

Moral — Technical

Theory — Practice   — Experience — Qualification

Man & Organisation.   Function
                        Dimensions

Subjective — Objective. (Self-concept)

Direct & indirect contours to variety of wayˢ functions.
                                        org-   ᵃ

Derivation of legitimacy
          of competence — experience, qualification

What sort of knowledge/understanding is most practical
relevant for the p/s.
Why are they particularly useful?

P.M. as management educator re contᵗ of human resources
Familiarity with theories / theorists

The effective use of human resources is dependent upon
                                        (rank order)

                    (i) human rels
                    (ii) correct